GACE
011

Middle Grades
Language Arts
Teacher Certification Exam

By: Sharon Wynne, M.S.
Southern Connecticut State University

"And, while there's no reason yet to panic, I think it's only prudent that we make preparations to panic."

XAMonline, INC.

Boston

XAMonline, Inc.
21 Orient Ave.
Melrose, MA 02176
Toll Free 1-800-509-4128
Email: info@xamonline.com
Web www.xamonline.com
Fax: 1-781-662-9268

Library of Congress Cataloging-in-Publication Data

Wynne, Sharon A.
　　Middle Grades Language Arts: Teacher Certification / Sharon A. Wynne. -2nd ed.
　　ISBN 978-1-58197-598-7
　　1. Middle Grades Language Arts.　　2. Study Guides.　　3. GACE
　　4. Teachers' Certification & Licensure.　　5. Careers

Disclaimer:
The opinions expressed in this publication are the sole works of XAMonline and were created independently from the National Education Association, Educational Testing Service, or any State Department of Education, National Evaluation Systems or other testing affiliates.

Between the time of publication and printing, state specific standards as well as testing formats and website information may change that is not included in part or in whole within this product. Sample test questions are developed by XAMonline and reflect similar content as on real tests; however, they are not former tests. XAMonline assembles content that aligns with state standards but makes no claims nor guarantees teacher candidates a passing score. Numerical scores are determined by testing companies such as NES or ETS and then are compared with individual state standards. A passing score varies from state to state.

Printed in the United States of America　　　　　　　　　　　œ-1

GACE: Middle Grades Language Arts
ISBN: 978-1-58197-598-7

Table of Contents

SUBAREA IV.   LISTENING, SPEAKING, AND VIEWING

Great Study and Testing Tips!

What to study in order to prepare for the subject assessments is the focus of this study guide but equally important is *how* you study.

You can increase your chances of truly mastering the information by taking some simple, but effective steps.

Study Tips:

1. <u>**Some foods aid the learning process.**</u> Foods such as milk, nuts, seeds, rice, and oats help your study efforts by releasing natural memory enhancers called CCKs (*cholecystokinin*) composed of *tryptopha*n, *choline*, and *phenylalanine*. All of these chemicals enhance the neurotransmitters associated with memory. Before studying, try a light, protein-rich meal of eggs, turkey, and fish. All of these foods release the memory enhancing chemicals. The better the connections, the more you comprehend.

Likewise, before you take a test, stick to a light snack of energy boosting and relaxing foods. A glass of milk, a piece of fruit, or some peanuts all release various memory-boosting chemicals and help you to relax and focus on the subject at hand.

2. <u>**Learn to take great notes.**</u> A by-product of our modern culture is that we have grown accustomed to getting our information in short doses (i.e. TV news sound bites or USA Today style newspaper articles.)

Consequently, we've subconsciously trained ourselves to assimilate information better in <u>neat little packages</u>. If your notes are scrawled all over the paper, it fragments the flow of the information. Strive for clarity. Newspapers use a standard format to achieve clarity. Your notes can be much clearer through use of proper formatting. A very effective format is called the <u>*"Cornell Method."*</u>

Take a sheet of loose-leaf lined notebook paper and draw a line all the way down the paper about 1-2" from the left-hand edge.

Draw another line across the width of the paper about 1-2" up from the bottom. Repeat this process on the reverse side of the page.

Look at the highly effective result. You have ample room for notes, a left hand margin for special emphasis items or inserting supplementary data from the textbook, a large area at the bottom for a brief summary, and a little rectangular space for just about anything you want.

3. Get the concept then the details. Too often we focus on the details and don't gather an understanding of the concept. However, if you simply memorize only dates, places, or names, you may well miss the whole point of the subject.

A key way to understand things is to put them in your own words. If you are working from a textbook, automatically summarize each paragraph in your mind. If you are outlining text, don't simply copy the author's words.

Rephrase them in your own words. You remember your own thoughts and words much better than someone else's, and subconsciously tend to associate the important details to the core concepts.

4. Ask Why? Pull apart written material paragraph by paragraph and don't forget the captions under the illustrations.

Example: If the heading is "Stream Erosion", flip it around to read "Why do streams erode?" Then answer the questions.

If you train your mind to think in a series of questions and answers, not only will you learn more, but it also helps to lessen the test anxiety because you are used to answering questions.

5. Read for reinforcement and future needs. Even if you only have 10 minutes, put your notes or a book in your hand. Your mind is similar to a computer; you have to input data in order to have it processed. *By reading, you are creating the neural connections for future retrieval.* The more times you read something, the more you reinforce the learning of ideas.

Even if you don't fully understand something on the first pass, *your mind stores much of the material for later recall.*

6. Relax to learn so go into exile. Our bodies respond to an inner clock called biorhythms. Burning the midnight oil works well for some people, but not everyone.

If possible, set aside a particular place to study that is free of distractions. Shut off the television, cell phone, pager and exile your friends and family during your study period.

If you really are bothered by silence, try background music. Light classical music at a low volume has been shown to aid in concentration over other types. Music that evokes pleasant emotions without lyrics are highly suggested. Try just about anything by Mozart. It relaxes you.

7. Use arrows not highlighters. At best, it's difficult to read a page full of yellow, pink, blue, and green streaks. Try staring at a neon sign for a while and you'll soon see that the horde of colors obscure the message.

A quick note, a brief dash of color, an underline, and an arrow pointing to a particular passage is much clearer than a horde of highlighted words.

8. Budget your study time. Although you shouldn't ignore any of the material, *allocate your available study time in the same ratio that topics may appear on the test.*

Testing Tips:

1. <u>Get smart, play dumb</u>. **Don't read anything into the question.** Don't make an assumption that the test writer is looking for something else than what is asked. Stick to the question as written and don't read extra things into it.

2. <u>Read the question and all the choices *twice* before answering the question.</u> You may miss something by not carefully reading, and then re-reading both the question and the answers.

If you really don't have a clue as to the right answer, leave it blank on the first time through. Go on to the other questions, as they may provide a clue as to how to answer the skipped questions.

If later on, you still can't answer the skipped ones . . . *Guess.* The only penalty for guessing is that you *might* get it wrong. Only one thing is certain; if you don't put anything down, you will get it wrong!

3. <u>Turn the question into a statement</u>. Look at the way the questions are worded. The syntax of the question usually provides a clue. Does it seem more familiar as a statement rather than as a question? Does it sound strange?

By turning a question into a statement, you may be able to spot if an answer sounds right, and it may also trigger memories of material you have read.

4. <u>Look for hidden clues</u>. It's actually very difficult to compose multiple-foil (choice) questions without giving away part of the answer in the options presented.

In most multiple-choice questions you can often readily eliminate one or two of the potential answers. This leaves you with only two real possibilities and automatically your odds go to Fifty-Fifty for very little work.

5. <u>Trust your instincts</u>. For every fact that you have read, you subconsciously retain something of that knowledge. On questions that you aren't really certain about, go with your basic instincts. **Your first impression on how to answer a question is usually correct.**

6. <u>Mark your answers directly on the test booklet</u>. Don't bother trying to fill in the optical scan sheet on the first pass through the test.

Be careful not to miss-mark your answers when you transcribe them to the scan sheet.

7. <u>Watch the clock</u>! You have a set amount of time to answer the questions. Don't get bogged down trying to answer a single question at the expense of 10 questions you can more readily answer.

COMPETENCY 1.0   UNDERSTAND THE CHARACTERISTICS OF VARIOUS LITERARY GENRES AND FORMS OF INFORMATIONAL TEXTS AND THEIR CULTURAL AND HISTORICAL ASPECTS

Skill 1.0   Distinguish various literary genres (e.g., prose [short story, novel, essay, editorial, biography], poetry, drama)

Prose

A Narrative can be defined as an interpretive story that is historically and/or culturally based. Narratives are stories, and when orally presented, they often take on a unique flavor and characteristic of the content. For example, slave narratives are often told in the voice and persona of nineteenth-century slaves. Organizationally, narratives are chronological, but various disruptions in time-sequence can occur—sometimes quite suddenly. Occasionally, narratives get side-tracked based on the specific content.

Essay: Typically a limited length prose work focusing on a topic and propounding a definite point of view and authoritative tone. Great essayists include Carlyle, Lamb, DeQuincy, Emerson and Montaigne, who is credited with defining this genre.

Novel: The longest form of fictional prose containing a variety of characterizations, settings, local color and regionalism. Most have complex plots, expanded description, and attention to detail. Some of the great novelists include Austin, the Brontes, Twain, Tolstoy, Hugo, Hardy, Dickens, Hawthorne, Forster, and Flaubert.

Short Story: Typically a terse narrative, with less developmental background about characters. May include description, author's point of view, and tone. Poe emphasized that a successful short story should create one focused impact. Some great short story writers are Hemingway, Faulkner, Twain, Joyce, Shirley Jackson, Flannery O'Connor, de Maupasssant, Saki, Edgar Allen Poe, and Pushkin.

Poetry
People read poetry for many reasons, often the very same reasons poets would give for writing it. Just the feel and sounds of the words that are turned by the artistic hands and mind of a poet into a satisfying and sometimes delightful experience is a good reason to read a poem. Good poetry constantly surprises.

However, the major purpose a writer of poetry has for creating his works of art is the sharing of an experience, a feeling, an emotion, and that is also the reason a reader turns to poetry rather than prose in his search for variety, joy, and satisfaction.

There is another important reason that poets create and that readers are drawn to their poems: they are interpreters of life. Poets feel deeply the things that others feel or even things that may be overlooked by others, and they have the skill and inspiration to recreate those feelings and interpret them in such a way that understanding and insight may come from the experience. They often bring understanding to life's big (or even not-so-big) questions.

Children can respond to poetry at very early stages. Elementary students are still at the stage where the sounds of unusual words intrigue them and entertain them. They are also very open to emotional meanings of passages. Teaching poetry to fifth-graders can be an important introduction to seeking for meaning in literature. If a fifth-grader enjoys reading poetry both silently and aloud, a habit may be formed that will last a lifetime.

When we speak of *structure* with regard to poetry, we usually mean one of three things:

A. The pattern of the sound and rhythm
It helps to know the history of this peculiarity of poetry. History was passed down in oral form almost exclusively until the invention of the printing press and was often set to music. A rhymed story is much easier to commit to memory. Adding a tune makes it even easier to remember, so it's not a surprise that much of the earliest literature—epics, odes, etc., are rhymed and were probably sung. When we speak of the pattern of sound and rhythm, we are referring to two things: verse form and stanza form.

The verse form is the rhythmic pattern of a single verse. An example would be any meter: blank verse, for instance, is iambic pentameter. A stanza is a group of a certain number of verses (lines), having a rhyme scheme. If the poem is written, there is usually white space between the verses, although a short poem may be only one stanza. If the poem is spoken, there will be a pause between stanzas.

B. The visible shape it takes
In the seventeenth century, some poets shaped their poems to reflect the theme. A good example is George Herbert's "Easter Wings." Since that time, poets have occasionally played with this device; it is, however, generally viewed as nothing more than a demonstration of ingenuity. The rhythm, effect, and meaning are often sacrificed to the forcing of the shape.

C. Rhyme and free verse

Poets also use devices to establish form that will underscore the meaning of their poems. A very common one is alliteration. When the poem is read (as poetry is usually intended to be), the repetition of a sound may not only underscore the meaning, it may also add pleasure to the reading. Following a strict rhyming pattern can add intensity to the meaning of the poem in the hands of a skilled and creative poet. On the other hand, the meaning can be drowned out by the steady beat-beat-beat of it. Shakespeare very skillfully used the regularity of rhyme in his poetry, breaking the rhythm at certain points to very effectively underscore a point. For example, in Sonnet #130, "My mistress' eyes are nothing like the sun," the rhythm is primarily iambic pentameter. It lulls the reader (or listener) to accept that this poet is following the standard conventions for love poetry, which in that day reliably used rhyme and more often than not iambic pentameter to express feelings of romantic love along conventional lines. However, in Sonnet #130, the last two lines sharply break from the monotonous pattern, forcing the reader or speaker to pause:

> And yet, by heaven, I think my love as rare
> As any she belied with false compare

Shakespeare's purpose is clear: he is not writing a conventional love poem; the object of his love is not the red-and-white conventional woman written about in other poems of the period. This is a good example where a poet uses form to underscore meaning.

Poets eventually began to feel constricted by the rhyming conventions and began to break away and make new rules for poetry. When poetry was written in rhyme only, it was easy to define it. When free verse, or poetry written in a flexible form, came upon the scene in France in the 1880s, it quickly began to influence English-language poets such as T. S. Eliot, whose memorable poem, *The Wasteland*, had an alarming but desolate message for the modern world. It's impossible to imagine that it could have been written in the soothing, lulling rhymed verse of previous periods. Those who first began writing in free verse in English were responding to the influence of the French *vers libre*. However, it should be noted that it could be loosely applied to the poetry of Walt Whitman, writing in the mid-nineteenth century, as can be seen in the first stanza of *Song of Myself*:

> I celebrate myself, and sing myself,
> And what I assume you shall assume,
> For every atom belonging to me as good belongs to you.

When poetry was no longer defined as a piece of writing arranged in verses that had a rhyme-scheme of some sort, distinguishing poetry from prose became a point of discussion. Merriam Webster's *Encyclopedia of Literature* defines poetry as follows: "Writing that formulates a concentrated imaginative awareness of experience in language chosen and arranged to create a specific emotional response through its meaning, sound and rhythm."

A poet chooses the form of his poetry deliberately, based upon the emotional response he hopes to evoke and the meaning he wishes to convey. Robert Frost, a twentieth-century poet who chose to use conventional rhyming verse to make his point, is a memorable and often-quoted modern poet. Who can forget his closing lines in "Stopping by Woods"?

> And miles to go before I sleep,
> And miles to go before I sleep.

Would they be as memorable if the poem had been written in free verse?

Slant Rhyme: Occurs when the final consonant sounds are the same, but the vowels are different. Occurs frequently in Irish, Welsh, and Icelandic verse. Examples include: green and gone, that and hit, ill and shell.

Alliteration: Alliteration occurs when the initial sounds of a word, beginning either with a consonant or a vowel, are repeated in close succession. Examples include: Athena and Apollo, Nate never knows, People who pen poetry.

Note that the words only have to be close to one another: Alliteration that repeats and attempts to connect a number of words is little more than a tongue-twister.

The function of alliteration, like rhyme, might be to accentuate the beauty of language in a given context, or to unite words or concepts through a kind of repetition. Alliteration, like rhyme, can follow specific patterns. Sometimes the consonants aren't always the initial ones, but they are generally the stressed syllables. Alliteration is less common than rhyme, but because it is less common, it can call our attention to a word or line in a poem that might not have the same emphasis otherwise.

Assonance: If alliteration occurs at the beginning of a word and rhyme at the end, assonance takes the middle territory. Assonance occurs when the vowel sound within a word matches the same sound in a nearby word, but the surrounding consonant sounds are different. "Tune" and "June" are rhymes; "tune" and "food" are assonant. The function of assonance is frequently the same as end rhyme or alliteration; all serve to give a sense of continuity or fluidity to the verse. Assonance might be especially effective when rhyme is absent: It gives the poet more flexibility, and it is not typically used as part of a predetermined pattern. Like alliteration, it does not so much determine the structure or form of a poem; rather, it is more ornamental.

Onomatopoeia: Word used to evoke the sound in its meaning. The early Batman series used *pow, zap, whop, zonk* and *eek* in an onomatopoetic way.

Rhythm in poetry refers to the recurrence of stresses at equal intervals. A stress (accent) is a greater amount of force given to one syllable in speaking than is given to another. For example, we put the stress on the first syllable of such words as father, mother, daughter, children. The unstressed or unaccented syllable is sometimes called a slack syllable. All English words carry at least one stress except articles and some prepositions such as by, from, at, etc. Indicating where stresses occur is to scan; the process is called scansion. Very little is gained in understanding a poem or making a statement about it by merely scanning it. The pattern of the rhythm—the meter—should be analyzed in terms of its overall relationship to the message and impression of the poem.

Slack syllables, when they recur in pairs, cause rhythmic trippings and bouncings; on the other hand, recurrent pairs of stresses will create a heavier rocking effect. The rhythm is dependent on words to convey meaning. Alone, they communicate nothing. When examining the rhythm and meaning of a poem, a good question to ask is whether the rhythm is appropriate to the theme. A bouncing rhythm, for example, might be dissonant in a solemn elegy.

Stops are those places in a poem where the punctuation requires a pause. An end-stopped line is one that *ends* in a pause, whereas one that has no punctuation at its end and is therefore read with only a slight pause is said to be run-on; the running on of its thought into the next line is called enjambment. These are used by a poet to underscore, intensify or communicate meaning.

Rhythm, then, is a *pattern of recurrence* and in poetry is made up of stressed and relatively unstressed syllables. The poet can manipulate the rhythm by making the intervals between his stresses regular or varied, by making his lines short or long, by end-stopping his lines or running them over, by choosing words that are easier or less easy to say, by choosing polysyllabic words or monosyllables. The most important thing to remember about rhythm is that it conveys meaning.

Drama

Drama: In its most general sense, a drama is any work that is designed to be performed by actors onstage. It can also refer to the broad literary genre that includes comedy and tragedy. Contemporary usage, however, denotes drama as a work that treats serious subjects and themes but does not aim for the same grandeur as tragedy.

Drama usually deals with characters of a less stately nature than tragedy. A classical example is Sophocles' tragedy *Oedipus Rex,* while Eugene O'Neill's *The Iceman Cometh* represents modern drama.

Comedy: The comedic form of dramatic literature is meant to amuse, and often ends happily. It uses techniques such as satire or parody and can take many forms, from farce to burlesque. Examples include Dante Alighieri's *The Divine Comedy,* Noel Coward's *Private Lives,* and some of Geoffrey Chaucer's *Canterbury Tales* and William Shakespeare's plays.

Tragedy: Tragedy is comedy's other half. It is defined as a work of drama written in either prose or poetry, telling the story of a brave, noble hero who, because of some tragic character flaw, brings ruin upon himself. It is characterized by serious, poetic language that evokes pity and fear. In modern times, dramatists have tried to update its image by drawing its main characters from the middle class and showing their nobility through their nature instead of their standing. The classic example of tragedy is Sophocles' *Oedipus Rex,* while Henrik Ibsen and Arthur Miller epitomize modern tragedy.

Dramatic Monologue: A dramatic monologue is a speech given by an actor, usually intended as reflection, but with the intended audience in mind. It reveals key aspects of the character's psyche and sheds insight on the situation at hand. The audience takes the part of the silent listener, passing judgment and giving sympathy at the same time. This form was invented and used predominantly by Victorian poet Robert Browning.

Skill 1.2 **Distinguish various forms of informational texts (e.g., journal, letter, biography, newspaper and magazine articles)**

Essays: Usually, essays take an opinion (whether it is about a concept, a work of literature, a person, or an event) and describe how the opinion was arrived at or why the opinion is a good one.

Letters: When letters are read and analyzed in the classroom, students generally are studying the writer's style or the writer's true, deep-down opinions and feelings about certain events. Often, students will find letters of a famous individual in history reprinted in textbooks.

Journals: Similar to letters, journals present very personal ideas. They give students, when available (as many people do not want their journals published), an opportunity to see peoples' thought processes about various events or issues.

Biography: A form of nonfiction prose, the subject of which is the life of an individual. The earliest biographical writings were probably funeral speeches and inscriptions, usually praising the life and example of the deceased. Early biographies evolved from this and were almost invariably uncritical, even distorted, and always laudatory. Beginning in the eighteenth century, this form of literature saw major development; an eminent example is James Boswell's *Life of Johnson*, which is very detailed and even records conversations. Eventually, the antithesis of the grossly exaggerated tomes praising an individual, usually a person of circumstance, developed. This form is denunciatory, debunking, and often inflammatory. A famous modern example is Lytton Strachey's *Eminent Victorians* (1918).

Autobiography: A form of biography, but it is written by the subject himself or herself. Autobiographies can range from the very formal to intimate writings made during one's life that were not intended for publication. These include letters, diaries, journals, memoirs, and reminiscences. Autobiography, generally speaking, began in the fifteenth century; one of the first examples was written in England by Margery Kempe. There are four kinds of autobiography: thematic, religious, intellectual, and fictionalized. Some "novels" may be thinly disguised autobiography, such as the novels of Thomas Wolfe.

Informational books and articles: Make up much of the reading of modern Americans. Magazines began to be popular in the nineteenth century in this country, and while many of the contributors to those publications intended to influence the political/social/religious convictions of their readers, many also simply intended to pass on information. A book or article whose purpose is simply to be informative, that is, not to persuade, is called exposition (adjectival form: expository). An example of an expository book is the *MLA Style Manual*. The writers do not intend to persuade their readers to use the recommended stylistic features in their writing; they are simply making the information available in case a reader needs such a guide. Articles in magazines such as *Time* may be persuasive in purpose, such as Joe Klein's regular column, but for the most part they are expository, giving information that television coverage of a news story might not have time to include.

Newspaper accounts of events: Expository in nature, of course, a reporting of a happening. That happening might be a school board meeting, an automobile accident that sent several people to a hospital and accounted for the death of a passenger, or the election of the mayor. They are not intended to be persuasive although the bias of a reporter or of an editor must be factored in. A newspaper's editorial stance is often openly declared and it may be reflected in such things as news reports. Reporters are expected to be unbiased in their coverage and most of them will defend their disinterest fiercely, but what a writer *sees* in an event is inevitably shaped to some extent by the writer's beliefs and experiences.

Skill 1.3   Interpret literary works and informational texts according to their cultural and historical contexts

American Literature is defined by a number of clearly identifiable periods.

The Colonial Period

William Bradford's excerpts from *The Mayflower Compact* relate vividly the hardships of crossing the Atlantic in such a tiny vessel, the misery and suffering of the first winter, the approaches of the American Indians, the decimation of their ranks, and the establishment of the Bay Colony of Massachusetts.

Anne Bradstreet's poetry relates much concerning colonial New England life. From her journals, modern readers learn of the everyday life of the early settlers, the hardships of travel, and the responsibilities of different groups and individuals in the community, Early American literature also reveals the commercial and political adventures of the Cavaliers who came to the New World with King George's blessing.

William Byrd's journal, *A History of the Dividing Line,* concerning his trek into the Dismal Swamp separating the Carolinian territories from Virginia and Maryland makes quite lively reading. A privileged insider to the English Royal Court, Byrd, like other Southern Cavaliers, was given grants to pursue business ventures.

The Revolutionary Period

There were great orations such as Patrick Henry's *Speech to the Virginia House of Burgesses* -- the "Give me liberty or give me death" speech -- and George Washington's *Farewell to the Army of the Potomac.* Less memorable are Washington's inaugural addresses, which modern readers consider to be somewhat rambling.

The *Declaration of Independence*, the brainchild predominantly of Thomas Jefferson, with some prudent editing by Ben Franklin, is a prime example of neoclassical writing -- balanced, well crafted, and focused.

Epistles include the exquisitely written, moving correspondence between John Adams and Abigail Adams. The poignancy of their separation - she in Boston, he in Philadelphia - is palpable and real.

The Romantic Period

Early American folktales, and the emergence of a distinctly American writing, not just a stepchild to English forms, constitute the next period.
Washington Irving's characters, Icabod Crane and Rip Van Winkle, create a uniquely American folklore devoid of English influences. The characters are indelibly marked by their environment and the superstitions of the New Englander. The early American writings of James Fenimore Cooper and his Leatherstocking Tales with their stirring accounts of drums along the Mohawk and the French and Indian Wars, the futile British defense of Fort William Henry and the brutalities of this era allow readers a window into their uniquely American world. Natty Bumppo, Chingachgook, Uncas, and Magua are unforgettable characters that reflect the American spirit in thought and action.

The poetry of the Fireside Poets - James Russell Lowell, Oliver Wendell Holmes, Henry Wadsworth Longfellow, and John Greenleaf Whittier - was recited by American families and read in the long New England winters. In "The Courtin'," Lowell used Yankee dialect to tell a narrative. Spellbinding epics by Longfellow such as *Hiawatha, The Courtship of Miles Standish*, and *Evangeline* told of adversity, sorrow, and ultimate happiness in a uniquely American warp. "Snowbound" by Whittier relates the story of a captive family isolated by a blizzard, stressing family closeness. Holmes' "The Chambered Nautilus" and his famous line, "Fired the shot heard round the world," put American poetry on a firm footing with other world writers.

Nathaniel Hawthorne and Herman Melville are the preeminent early American novelists, writing on subjects definitely regional, specific and American, yet sharing insights about human foibles, fears, loves, doubts, and triumphs. Hawthorne's writings range from children's stories, like the Cricket on the Hearth series, to adult fare of dark, brooding short stories such as "Dr. Heidegger's Experiment," "The Devil and Tom Walker," and "Rapuccini's Daughter." His masterpiece, *The Scarlet Letter*, takes on the society of hypocritical Puritan New Englanders, who ostensibly left England to establish religious freedom, but who have been entrenched in judgmental finger wagging. They ostracize Hester Prynne and condemn her child, Pearl, as a child of Satan. Great love, sacrifice, loyalty, suffering, and related epiphanies add universality to this tale. *The House of the Seven Gables* also deals with kept secrets, loneliness, societal pariahs, and love ultimately triumphing over horrible wrong. Herman Melville's great opus, *Moby Dick*, follows a crazed Captain Ahab on his Homeric odyssey to conquer the great white whale that has outwitted him and his whaling crews time and again. The whale has even taken Ahab's leg and, according to Ahab, wants all of him. Melville recreates in painstaking detail and an insider's knowledge the harsh life of a whaler out of New Bedford, by way of Nantucket.

For those who don't want to learn about every guy rope or all parts of the whaler's rigging, Melville offers up in *Billy Budd* the succinct tale of Billy Budd and his Christ-like sacrifice to the black and white maritime laws on the high seas. An accident results in the death of one of the ship's officers, a slug of a fellow, who had taken a dislike to the young, affable, shy Billy. Captain Vere must hang Billy for the death of Claggert, but knows that this is not right. However, an example must be given to the rest of the crew so that discipline can be maintained.

Edgar Allan Poe creates a distinctly American version of romanticism with his 16-syllable line in "The Raven," the classical "To Helen," and his Gothic "Annabelle Lee." The horror short story can be said to originate from Poe's pen. "The Tell - Tale Heart," "The Cask of Amontillado," "The Fall of the House of Usher," and "The Masque of the Red Death" are exemplary short stories. The new genre of detective story also emerges with Poe's "Murders in the Rue Morgue."

American Romanticism has its own offshoot in the Transcendentalism of Ralph Waldo Emerson and Henry David Thoreau. One wrote about transcending the complexities of life; the other, who wanted to get to the marrow of life, pitted himself against nature at Walden Pond and wrote an inspiring autobiographical account of his sojourn, aptly titled *On Walden Pond*. He also wrote passionately on his objections to the interference of government on the individual in "On the Duty of Civil Disobedience." Emerson's elegantly crafted essays and war poetry still give validation to several important universal truths. Probably most remembered for his address to Thoreau's Harvard graduating class, "The American Scholar," he defined the qualities of hard work and intellectual spirit required of Americans in their growing nation.

The Transition between Romanticism and Realism

The Civil War period ushers in the poignant poetry of Walt Whitman and his homages to all who suffer from the ripple effects of war and presidential assassination. His "Come up from the Fields, Father" about a Civil War soldier's death and his family's reaction and "When Lilacs Last in the Courtyard Bloom'd" about the effects of Abraham Lincoln's death on the poet and the nation should be required readings in any American literature course. Further, his *Leaves of Grass* gave America its first poetry truly unique in form, structure, and subject matter.

Emily Dickinson, like Walt Whitman, leaves her literary fingerprints on a vast array of poems, all but three of which were never published in her lifetime. Her themes of introspection and attention to nature's details and wonders are, by any measurement, world-class works. Her posthumous recognition reveals the timeliness of her work. American writing had most certainly arrived!

During this period such legendary figures as Paul Bunyan and Pecos Bill rose from the oral tradition. Anonymous storytellers around campfires told tales of a huge lumberman and his giant blue ox, Babe, whose adventures were explanations of natural phenomena like those of footprints filled with rainwater becoming the Great Lakes. Or the whirling-dervish speed of Pecos Bill explained the tornadoes of the Southwest. Like ancient peoples, finding reasons for the happenings in their lives, these American pioneer storytellers created a mythology appropriate to the vast reaches of the unsettled frontier.

Mark Twain also left giant footprints with his unique blend of tall tale and fable. "The Celebrated Jumping Frog of Calaveras County" and "The Man who Stole Hadleyburg" are epitomes of short story writing. Move to novel creation, and Twain again rises head and shoulders above others by his bold, still disputed, oft-banned *The Adventures of Huckleberry Finn*, which examines such taboo subjects as a white person's love of a slave, the issue of leaving children with abusive parents, and the outcomes of family feuds. Written partly in dialect and southern vernacular, *The Adventures of Huckleberry Finn* is touted by some as the greatest American novel.

The Realistic Period

The late nineteenth century saw a reaction against the tendency of romantic writers to look at the world through rose-colored glasses. Writers like Frank Norris (*The Pit*) and Upton Sinclair (*The Jungle*) used their novels to decry conditions for workers in slaughterhouses and wheat mills. In *The Red Badge of Courage*, Stephen Crane wrote of the daily sufferings of the common soldier in the Civil War. Realistic writers wrote of common, ordinary people and events using detail that would reveal the harsh realities of life. They broached taboos by creating protagonists whose environments often destroyed them. Romantic writers would have only protagonists whose indomitable wills helped them rise above adversity. Crane's *Maggie: A Girl of the Streets* deals with a young woman forced into prostitution to survive. In "The Occurrence at Owl Creek Bridge," Ambrose Bierce relates the unfortunate hanging of a Confederate soldier.

Upton Sinclair

Short stories, like Bret Harte's "The Outcasts of Poker Flat" and Jack London's "To Build a Fire," deal with unfortunate people whose luck in life has run out. Many writers, sub-classified as naturalists, believed that man was subject to a fate over which he had no control.

British Literature

Anglo-Saxon

The Anglo-Saxon period spans six centuries but produced only a smattering of literature. The first British epic is *Beowulf,* anonymously written by Christian monks many years after the events in the narrative supposedly occurred. This Teutonic saga relates the triumph three times over monsters by the hero, Beowulf. "The Seafarer," a shorter poem, some history, and some riddles are the rest of the Anglo-Saxon canon.

Medieval

The Medieval period introduces Geoffrey Chaucer, the father of English literature, whose *Canterbury Tales* are written in the vernacular, or street language, of England, not in Latin. Thus, the tales are said to be the first work of British literature. Next, Thomas Malory's *Le Morte d'Arthur* calls together the extant tales from Europe as well as England concerning the legendary King Arthur, Merlin, Guinevere, and the Knights of the Round Table. This work is the generative work that gave rise to the many Arthurian legends that stir the chivalric imagination.

Renaissance and Elizabethan

The Renaissance, the most important period since it is synonymous with William Shakespeare, begins with importing the idea of the Petrarchan or Italian sonnet into England. Sir Thomas Wyatt and Sir Philip Sydney wrote English versions. Next, Sir Edmund Spenser invented a variation on this Italian sonnet form, aptly called the Spenserian sonnet. His masterpiece is the epic *The Fairie Queene*, honoring Queen Elizabeth I's reign. He also wrote books on the Red Cross Knight, St. George and the Dragon, and a series of Arthurian adventures. Spencer was dubbed the Poet's Poet. He created a nine-line stanza, eight lines of iambic pentameter and an extra-footed ninth line, an alexandrine. Thus, he invented the Spenserian stanza as well.

William Shakespeare, the Bard of Avon, wrote 154 sonnets, 39 plays, and two long narrative poems. The sonnets are justifiably called the greatest sonnet sequence in all literature. Shakespeare dispensed with the octave/sestet format of the Italian sonnet and invented his three quatrains, one heroic couplet format. His plays are divided into comedies, history plays, and tragedies. Great lines from these plays are more often quoted than from any other author. The Big Four tragedies, *Hamlet*, *Macbeth*, *Othello*, and *King Lear,* are acknowledged to be the most brilliant examples of this genre.

Seventeenth century

John Milton's devout Puritanism was the wellspring of his creative genius that closes the remarkable productivity of the English Renaissance. His social commentary in such works as *Aereopagitica*, *Samson Agonistes*, and his elegant sonnets would be enough to solidify his stature as a great writer. It is his masterpiece based in part on the Book of Genesis that places Milton very near the top of the rung of a handful of the most renowned of all writers. *Paradise Lost*, written in balanced, elegant Neoclassic form, truly does justify the ways of God to man. The greatest allegory about man's journey to the Celestial City (Heaven) was written at the end of the English Renaissance, as was John Bunyan's *The Pilgrim's Progress*, which describes virtues and vices personified.

This work is, or was for a long time, second only to the *Bible* in numbers of copies printed and sold.

The Jacobean Age gave us the marvelously witty and cleverly constructed conceits of John Donne's metaphysical sonnets, as well as his insightful meditations, and his version of sermons or homilies. "Ask not for whom the bell tolls", and "No man is an island unto himself" are famous epigrams from Donne's *Meditations*. His most famous conceit is that which compares lovers to a footed compass, traveling seemingly separate, but always leaning towards one another and conjoined in "A Valediction Forbidding Mourning."

Eighteenth century

Ben Johnson, author of the wickedly droll play, *Volpone,* and the Cavalier *carpe diem* poets Robert Herrick, Sir John Suckling, and Richard Lovelace also wrote during King James I's reign.

The Restoration and Enlightenment reflect the political turmoil of the regicide of Charles I, the Interregnum Puritan government of Oliver Cromwell, and the restoring of the monarchy to England by the coronation of Charles II, who had been given refuge by the French King Louis. Neoclassicism became the preferred writing style, especially for Alexander Pope. New genres, such as *The Diary of Samuel Pepys*, the novels of Daniel Defoe, the periodical essays and editorials of Joseph Addison and Richard Steele, and Alexander Pope's mock epic, *The Rape of the Lock*, demonstrate the diversity of expression during this time.

Writers who followed were contemporaries of Dr. Samuel Johnson, the lexicographer of *The Dictionary of the English Language*. Fittingly, this Age of Johnson, which encompasses James Boswell's biography of Dr. Johnson, Robert Burns' Scottish dialect and regionalism in his evocative poetry and the mystical pre-Romantic poetry of William Blake, ushers in the Romantic Age and its revolution against Neoclassicism.

Romantic period

The Romantic Age encompasses what is known as the First Generation Romantics, William Wordsworth and Samuel Taylor Coleridge, who collaborated on *Lyrical Ballads,* which defines and exemplifies the tenets of this style of writing. The Second Generation includes George Gordon, Lord Byron, Percy Bysshe Shelley, and John Keats. These poets wrote sonnets, odes, epics, and narrative poems, most dealing with homage to nature. Wordsworth's most famous other works are "Intimations on Immortality" and "The Prelude." Byron's satirical epic, *Don Juan,* and his autobiographical *Childe Harold's Pilgrimage* are irreverent, witty, self-deprecating and, in part, cuttingly critical of other writers and critics. Shelley's odes and sonnets are remarkable for sensory imagery. Keats' sonnets, odes, and longer narrative poem, *The Eve of St. Agnes,* are remarkable for their introspection and the tender age of the poet, who died when he was only twenty-five. In fact, all of the Second Generation died before their times. Wordsworth, who lived to be eighty, outlived them all, as well as his friend and collaborator, Coleridge. Others who wrote during the Romantic Age are the essayist Charles Lamb, and the novelist Jane Austin. The Bronte sisters, Charlotte and Emily, wrote one novel each, which are noted as two of the finest ever written, *Jane Eyre* and *Wuthering Heights.* Marianne Evans, also known as George Eliot, wrote several important novels (including her masterpiece *Middlemarch*): *Silas Marner, Adam Bede,* and *Mill on the Floss.*

Nineteenth century

The Victorian Period is remarkable for the diversity and proliferation of work in three major areas. Poets who are typified as Victorians include Alfred, Lord Tennyson, who wrote *Idylls of the King*, twelve narrative poems about the Arthurian legend, and Robert Browning, who wrote chilling, dramatic monologues such as "My Last Duchess," as well as long poetic narratives such as *The Pied Piper of Hamlin*. His wife Elizabeth wrote two major works, the epic feminist poem, *Aurora Leigh*, and her deeply moving and provocative *Sonnets from the Portuguese,* in which she details her deep love for Robert and her startling awareness that he reciprocated that love. A. E. Housman, Matthew Arnold, and the Pre-Raphaelites, especially the brother and sister duo Dante Gabriel Rosetti and Christina Rosetti, contributed much to round out the Victorian Era poetic scene. The Pre-Raphaelites, a group of 19th-century English painters, poets, and critics, reacted against Victorian materialism and the neoclassical conventions of academic art by producing earnest, quasi-religious works. Medieval and early Renaissance painters up to the time of the Italian painter Raphael inspired the group. Robert Louis Stevenson, the great Scottish novelist, wrote his adventure/history lessons for young adults. Victorian prose ranges from the incomparable, keenly woven plot structures of Charles Dickens to the deeply moving Dorset/Wessex novels of Thomas Hardy, in which women are repressed and life is more struggle than euphoria. Rudyard Kipling wrote about Colonialism in India in works like *Kim* and *The Jungle Book,* which create exotic locales and a distinct main point concerning the Raj, the British Colonial government during Queen Victoria's reign. Victorian drama is a product mainly of Oscar Wilde, whose satirical masterpiece *The Importance of Being Earnest* farcically details and lampoons Victorian social mores.

Twentieth century

The early twentieth century is represented mainly by the towering achievement of George Bernard Shaw's dramas *St. Joan, Man and Superman, Major Barbara,* and *Arms and the Man,* to name a few. Novelists are too numerous to list, but Joseph Conrad, E. M. Forster, Virginia Woolf, James Joyce, Nadine Gordimer, Graham Greene, George Orwell, and D. H. Lawrence comprise some of the century's very best.

Twentieth-century poets of renown and merit include W. H. Auden, Robert Graves, T. S. Eliot, Edith Sitwell, Stephen Spender, Dylan Thomas, Philip Larkin, Ted Hughes, Sylvia Plath, and Hugh MacDarmid. This list is by no means complete.

Skill 1.4   **Identify similarities and differences (e.g., regarding plot, character, or theme) among literary works and informational texts from various cultures and historical periods**

Civil Rights

Many abolitionists were also early crusaders for civil rights. However, the 1960s movement focused attention on the plight of the people who had been "freed" by the Civil War in ways that brought about long overdue changes in the opportunities and rights of African Americans. David Halberstam, who had been a reporter in Nashville at the time of the sit-ins by eight young black college students that initiated the revolution, wrote *The Children*, published in 1998 by Random House, for the purpose of reminding Americans of their courage, suffering, and achievements. Congressman John Lewis (Fifth District, Georgia) was one of those eight young men who has gone on to a life of public service. Halberstam records that when older black ministers tried to persuade these young people not to pursue their protest, John Lewis responded: "If not us, then who? If not now, then when?"

The following are some examples of protest literature:

- James Baldwin, *Blues for Mister Charlie*
- Martin Luther King, *Where Do We Go from Here?*
- Langston Hughes, *Fight for Freedom: The Story of the NAACP*
- Eldridge Cleaver, *Soul on Ice*
- Malcolm X, *The Autobiography of Malcolm X*
- Stokely Carmichael and Charles V. Hamilton, *Black Power*
- Leroi Jones, *Home*

Vietnam

An America that was already divided over the civil rights movement faced even greater divisions over the war in Vietnam. Those who were in favor of the war and who opposed withdrawal saw it as the major front in the war against communism. Those who opposed the war and who favored withdrawal of the troops believed that it would not serve to defeat communism and was a quagmire.

Catch-22 by Joseph Heller was a popular antiwar novel that became a successful movie of the time. *Authors Take Sides on Vietnam*, edited by Cecil Woolf and John Bagguley, is a collection of essays by 168 well-known authors throughout the world. *Where is Vietnam?* edited by Walter Lowenfels consists of 92 poems about the war.

Many writers were publishing works for and against the war, but the genre that had the most impact was rock music. Bob Dylan was an example of the musicians of the time. His music represented the hippie aesthetic and brilliant, swirling colors and hallucinogenic imagery and created a style that came to be called psychedelic. Some other bands that originated during this time and became well-known for their psychedelic music, primarily about the Vietnam War in the early years, are the Grateful Dead, Jefferson Airplane, Big Brother, and Sly and the Family Stone. In England, the movement attracted the Beatles and the Rolling Stones.

Immigration

John Steinbeck's *Cannery Row* and *Tortilla Flats* glorify the lives of Mexican migrants in California. Amy Tan's *The Joy Luck Club* deals with the problems faced by Chinese immigrants.

Leon Uris' *Exodus* deals with the social history that led to the founding of the modern state of Israel. It was published in 1958, only a short time after the Holocaust. It also deals with attempts of concentration camp survivors to get to the land that had become the new Israel. In many ways, it is the quintessential work on immigration—its causes and effects.

Feminist / gender concern literature written by women in the United States

Edith Wharton's *Ethan Frome* is a heartbreaking tale of lack of communication, lack of funds, the unrelenting cold of the Massachusetts winter, and a toboggan ride which gnarls Ethan and Mattie just like the old tree which they smash into. The *Age of Innocence*, in contrast to *Ethan Frome*, is set in the upper echelons of fin-de-siècle New York and explores marriage without stifling social protocols.

Willa Cather's work moves the reader to the prairies of Nebraska and the harsh eking out of existence by the immigrant families who chose to stay there and farm. Her most acclaimed works include *My Antonia* and *Death Comes for the Archbishop*.

Kate Chopin's regionalism and local color takes her readers to the upper-crust Creole society of New Orleans and resort isles off the Louisiana coast. "The Story of an Hour" is lauded as one of the greatest of all short stories. Her feminist liberation novel, *The Awakening*, is still hotly debated.

Eudora Welty's regionalism and dialect shine in her short stories of rural Mississippi, especially in "The Worn Path."

Modern black female writers who explore the world of feminist/gender issues as well as class prohibitions are Alice Walker (*The Color Purple*), Zora Neale Hurston (*Their Eyes Were Watching God*), and Toni Morrison (*Beloved, Jazz,* and *Song of Solomon*).

British Literature

There are four major time periods of literature. They are neoclassicism, romanticism, realism, and naturalism. Certain authors, among these Chaucer, Shakespeare, and Donne, though writing during a particular literary period, are considered to have a style all their own.

Neoclassicism: Patterned after the greatest writings of classical Greece and Rome, this type of writing is characterized by a balanced, graceful, well-crafted, refined, elevated style. Major proponents of this style are poet laureates John Dryden and Alexander Pope. The eras in which they wrote are called the Ages of Dryden and Pope. The self is not exalted and the focus is on the group, not the individual, in neoclassic writing.

Romanticism: Writings emphasize the individual and validate emotion and feeling. Nature acts as an inspiration for creativity; it is a balm of the spirit. Romantics harken back to medieval, chivalric themes and ambiance. They also emphasize supernatural, Gothic themes and settings, which are characterized by gloom and darkness. Imagination is stressed. New types of writings include detective and horror stories and autobiographical introspection (Wordsworth). There are two generations in British Literature: First Generation includes William Wordsworth and Samuel Taylor Coleridge whose collaboration, *Lyrical Ballads*, defines romanticism and its exponents. Wordsworth maintained that the scenes and events of everyday life and the speech of ordinary people were the raw material of which poetry could and should be made. Romanticism spread to the United States, where Ralph Waldo Emerson and Henry David Thoreau adopted it in their transcendental romanticism, emphasizing reasoning. Further extensions of this style are found in Edgar Allan Poe's Gothic writings. Second Generation romantics include the ill-fated Englishmen Lord Byron, John Keats, and Percy Bysshe Shelley. Byron and Shelley, who for some most epitomize the romantic poet (in their personal lives as well as in their work), wrote resoundingly in protest against social and political wrongs and in defense of the struggles for liberty in Italy and Greece. The Second Generation romantics stressed personal introspection and the love of beauty and nature as requisites of inspiration.

Realism: Unlike classical and neoclassical writing, which often deal with aristocracies and nobility or the gods, realistic writers deal with the common man and his socioeconomic problems in a non-sentimental way. Muckraking, social injustice, domestic abuse, and inner city conflicts are some issues that are dealt with by writers of realism. Realistic writers include Thomas Hardy, George Bernard Shaw, and Henrik Ibsen.

Naturalism: This is realism pushed to the maximum, writing which exposes the underbelly of society, usually the lower class struggles. This is the world of penury, injustice, abuse, ghetto survival, hungry children, single parenting, and substance abuse. Émile Zola was inspired by his readings in history and medicine and attempted to apply methods of scientific observation to the depiction of pathological human character, notably in his series of novels devoted to several generations of one French family.

North American Literature

North American literature is divided between the United States, Canada, and Mexico. The American writers have been amply discussed in 1.0. Canadian writers of note include feminist Margaret Atwood, (*The Hand Maid's Tale*); Alice Munro, a remarkable short story writer; and W. P. Kinsella, another short story writer whose two major subjects are North American Indians and baseball. Mexican writers include 1990 Nobel Prize winning poet, Octavio Paz, (*The Labyrinth of Solitude*) and feminist Rosarian Castillanos (*The Nine Guardians*).

Central American/Caribbean Literature

The Caribbean and Central America encompass a vast area and cultures that reflect oppression and colonialism by England, Spain, Portugal, France, and The Netherlands. The Caribbean writers include Samuel Selvon from Trinidad and Armado Valladres of Cuba. Central American authors include dramatist Carlos Solorzano, from Guatemala, whose plays include *Dona Beatriz, The Hapless, The Magician,* and *The Hands of God.*

South American Literature

Chilean Gabriela Mistral was the first Latin American writer to win the Nobel Prize for literature. She is best known for her collections of poetry, *Desolation and Feeling*. Chile was also home to Pablo Neruda, who in 1971 also won the Nobel Prize for literature for his poetry. His 29 volumes of poetry have been translated into more than 60 languages, attesting to his universal appeal. *Twenty Love Poems* and *Song of Despair* are justly famous. Isabel Allende is carrying on the Chilean literary standards with her acclaimed novel, *House of Spirits.* Argentine Jorge Luis Borges is considered by many literary critics to be the most important writer of his century from South America. His collections of short stories, *Ficciones*, brought him universal recognition. Also from Argentina, Silvina Ocampo, a collaborator with Borges on a collection of poetry, is famed for her poetry and short story collections, which include *The Fury* and *The Days of the Night*.

Noncontinental European Literature

Horacio Quiroga represents Uruguay and Brazil has Joao Guimaraes Rosa, whose novel *The Devil to Pay* is considered first-rank world literature.

Continental European Literature

This category excludes British Literature, since the entire section 1.1 deals with writings from Scotland, Ireland, Wales and England.

Germany

German poet and playwright Friedrich von Schiller is best known for his history plays, *William Tell* and *The Maid of Orleans*. He is a leading literary figure in Germany's Golden Age of Literature. Also from Germany, Rainer Maria Rilke, the great lyric poet, is one of the poets of the unconscious, or stream of consciousness. Germany also has given the world Herman Hesse, (*Siddartha*), Gunter Grass (*The Tin Drum*), and the greatest of all German writers, Goethe.

Scandinavia

Scandinavia has encouraged the work of Hans Christian Andersen in Denmark, who advanced the fairy tale genre with such wistful tales as "The Little Mermaid" and "Thumbelina." The social commentary of Henrik Ibsen in Norway startled the world of drama with such issues as feminism (*The Doll's House* and *Hedda Gabler*) and the effects of sexually transmitted diseases (*The Wild Duck* and *Ghosts*). Sweden's Selma Lagerlof is the first woman to ever win the Nobel Prize for literature. Her novels include *Gosta Berling's Saga* and the world-renowned *The Wonderful Adventures of Nils*, a children's work.

Slavic nations

Austrian writer Franz Kafka (*The Metamorphosis, The Trial,* and *The Castle*) is considered by many to be the literary voice of the first-half of the twentieth century. Representing the Czech Republic is the poet Vaclav Havel. Slovakia has dramatist Karel Capek (*R.U.R.*) Romania is represented by Elie Weisel (*Night*), a Nobel Prize winner.

Spain

Spain's great writers include Miguel de Cervantes (*Don Quixote*) and Juan Ramon Jimenez. The anonymous national epic *El Cid* has been translated into many languages.

Russia

Russian literature is vast and monumental. Who has not heard of Fyodor Dostoyevsky's *Crime and Punishment* or *The Brothers Karamazov* or Count Leo Tolstoy's *War and Peace*? These are examples of psychological realism. Dostoyevsky's influence on modern writers cannot be over-stressed. Tolstoy's *War and Peace* is the sweeping account of the invasion of Russia and Napoleon's taking of Moscow, abandoned by the Russians. This novel is called the national novel of Russia. Further advancing Tolstoy's greatness is his ability to create believable, unforgettable female characters, especially Natasha in *War and Peace* and the heroine of *Anna Karenina*. Pushkin is famous for great short stories; Anton Chekhov for drama, (*Uncle Vanya*, *The Three Sisters*, *The Cherry Orchard*); Yevteshenko for poetry (*Babi Yar*). Boris Pasternak won the Nobel Prize (*Dr. Zhivago*). Aleksandr Solzhenitsyn (*The Gulag Archipelago*) is only recently back in Russia after years of expatriation in Vermont. Ilya Varshavsky, who creates fictional societies that are dystopias, the opposite of utopias, represents the genre of science fiction.

France

France has a multifaceted canon of great literature that is universal in scope, almost always championing some social cause: the poignant short stories of Guy de Maupassant; the fantastic poetry of Charles Baudelaire (*Fleurs du Mal*); the groundbreaking lyrical poetry of Rimbaud and Verlaine; and the existentialism of Jean-Paul Sartre (*No Exit*, *The Flies*, *Nausea*), Andre Malraux, (*The Fall*), and Albert Camus (*The Stranger*, *The Plague*), the recipient of the 1957 Nobel Prize for literature. Drama in France is best represented by Rostand's *Cyrano de Bergerac*, and the neo-classical dramas of Racine and Corneille (*El Cid*). Feminist writings include those of Sidonie-Gabrielle Colette, known for her short stories and novels, as well as Simone de Beauvoir. The great French novelists include Andre Gide, Honore de Balzac (*Cousin Bette*), Stendhal (*The Red and the Black*), the father/son duo of Alexandre Dumas (*The Three Musketeers* and *The Man in the Iron Mask*. Victor Hugo is the Charles Dickens of French literature, having penned the masterpieces *The Hunchback of Notre Dame* and the French national novel *Les Miserables*. The stream of consciousness of Proust's *Remembrance of Things Past*, and the Absurdist theatre of Samuel Beckett and Eugene Ionesco (*The Rhinoceros*) attest to the groundbreaking genius of the French writers.

Italy

Italy's greatest writers include Virgil, who wrote the great epic *The Aeneid*; Giovanni Boccaccio (*The Decameron*); Dante Alighieri (*The Divine Comedy*); and Alberto Moravia.

Ancient Greece

Greece will always be foremost in literary assessments due to Homer's epics *The Iliad* and *The Odyssey*. No one, except Shakespeare, is more often cited. Add to these the works of Plato and Aristotle for philosophy; the dramatists Aeschylus, Euripides, and Sophocles for tragedy, and Aristophanes for comedy. Greece is the cradle not only of democracy, but of literature as well.

Africa

African literary greats include South Africans Nadine Gordimer (Nobel Prize for literature) and Peter Abrahams (*Tell Freedom: Memories of Africa*), an auto-biography of life in Johannesburg. Chinua Achebe (*Things Fall Apart*) and the poet Wole Soyinka hail from Nigeria. Mark Mathabane wrote an autobiography, *Kaffir Boy*, about growing up in South Africa. Egyptian writer Naguib Mahfouz, and Doris Lessing from Rhodesia, now Zimbabwe, write about race relations in their respective countries. Because of her radical politics, Lessing was banned from her homeland and The Union of South Africa, as was Alan Paton, whose seemingly simple story *Cry, the Beloved Country* brought the plight of blacks and the whites' fear of blacks under apartheid to the rest of the world.

Far East

Asia has many modern writers who are being translated for the western reading public. India's Krishan Chandar has authored more than 300 stories. Rabindranath Tagore won the Nobel Prize for literature in 1913 (*Song Offerings*). Narayan, India's most famous writer (*The Guide*), is highly interested in the mythology and legends of India. Santha Rama Rau's work *Gifts of Passage* is her true story of life in a British school where she tries to preserve her Indian culture and traditional home.

Revered as Japan's most famous female author, Fumiko Hayashi (*Drifting Clouds*) had written more than 270 literary works by the time of her death. The classical age of Japanese literary achievement includes the father Kiyotsugu Kan ami and the son Motokkiyo Zeami who developed the theatrical experience known as Noh drama to its highest aesthetic degree. The son is said to have authored over 200 plays, of which 100 still exist.

In 1968 the Nobel Prize for literature was awarded to Yasunari Kawabata, whose *The Sound of the Mountain* and *The Snow Country* are considered to be his masterpieces. His Palm-of-the-Hand Stories take the essentials of Haiku poetry and transform them into the short story genre.

Katai Tayama (*The Quilt*) is touted as the father of the genre known as the Japanese confessional novel. He also wrote in the "ism" of naturalism. His works are definitely not for the squeamish.

The "slice of life" psychological writings of Ryunosuke Akutagawa gained him acclaim in the western world. His short stories, especially "Rashamon" and "In a Grove," are greatly praised for style as well as content.

China too has given to the literary world. Li Po, the T'ang dynasty poet from the Chinese Golden Age, revealed his interest in folklore by preserving the folk songs and mythology of China. Po further allows his reader to enter into the Chinese philosophy of Taoism and to know this feeling against expansionism during the T'ang dynastic rule. During the T'ang dynasty, which was one of great diversity in the arts, the Chinese version of a short story was created with the help of Jiang Fang. His themes often express love between a man and a woman. Modern feminist and political concerns are written eloquently by Ting Ling, who used the pseudonym Chiang Ping-Chih. Her stories reflect her concerns about social injustice and her commitment to the women's movement.

Skill 1.5 Analyze the roles of authors and works in influencing public opinion and changing attitudes about social issues

In looking at any piece of writing, regardless of genre, it's important to think about what was going on in the writer's world at the time the piece was being written. This includes the political milieu, societal mores, the social level of the writer, and cultural influences. "A writer can only write what he knows" is a statement often heard in discussions about literature. However, Tom Wolfe, a contemporary writer (*Bonfire of the Vanities*), disputes that. He insists that a writer can use exploration and research to write effectively and successfully about topics that he hasn't experienced first-hand. Even so, it's important to think about the way in which current events influence a writer's work.

A good example is John Steinbeck and his popular novel *The Grapes of Wrath*. It would certainly be possible to read this book and be moved by it, even to understand the point Steinbeck intended to make without knowing that it was written during America's Great Depression of the 1930s, but it is much better understood when viewed through that context.

This writer didn't suffer the tribulations that many did during the Depression; his own family was little affected by it. Once he decided that he wanted to write about the people who were being displaced by the political, cultural, and social crisis, he went to Oklahoma and lived with a family that had lost its farm not only because of the economic disaster but also because of the dust bowl effect in that part of the country. In other words, he obtained the information and experience he needed in order to be sure that he wrote "what he knew" via exploration and research. The result is a family that Steinbeck named the Joads, who illustrate and demonstrate in clear, moving, and understandable terms what the Great Depression meant in human lives.

He doesn't just stop there, however. He also interposes chapters that fill in the cultural, political, and social situation that make certain his readers understand clearly where the life of the Joads fits in those environments. He tells what is going on in the churches, where the common approach was to pretend either that the suffering was the fault of the victims themselves or that the drastic effects were not happening at all. The social situation that most accounted for a lack of concern for these suffering fellow-Americans was that the economic well-being of the wealthy landowners in California was dependent on these migrants, and the landowners were more often than not deacons and elders in the churches. They had a vested interest in the status quo. Politically, President Hoover, who had devoted his life to providing food for hungry people all over the world, found himself in a dilemma: he couldn't meet the needs of his own people. Congress opposed his efforts to make organizational changes to avoid such things as the crisis of the migrants that Steinbeck wrote about. Hoover got much of the blame for the situation, although there were many forces beyond his control that accounted for it.

Another important aspect of a piece of writing that is directly related to political, cultural, and social influences is the writer's *purpose* for writing it in the first place. In Steinbeck's case, his purpose was to bring about change. His book is considered a novel of protest, a social document.

It's important to note that *Grapes of Wrath* is an extreme example of a novel that was strongly influenced by the political, cultural, and social background of the times in which it was written. Even so, most works, whether written or presented via some other medium, reflect the times and the cultural, social, and political atmosphere of the time in which they are written.

COMPETENCY 2.0 UNDERSTAND THE STRUCTURES AND ELEMENTS OF LITERARY WORKS

Skill 2.1 **Use significant details in a literary work to analyze the traits, emotions, and motivations of various characters in the work**

Character is portrayed in many ways: description of physical characteristics, dialogue, interior monologue, the thoughts of the character, the attitudes of other characters toward this one, etc. Descriptive language depends on the ability to recreate a sensory experience for the reader. If the description of the character's appearance is a visual one, then the reader must be able to *see* the character. What's the shape of the nose? What color are the eyes? How tall or how short is this character? Thin or chubby? How does the character move? How does the character walk? Terms must be chosen that will create a picture for the reader. It's not enough to say the eyes are blue, for example. What blue? Often the color of eyes is compared to something else to enhance the readers' ability to visualize the character. A good test of characterization is the level of emotional involvement of the reader in the character. If the reader is to become involved, the description must provide an actual experience—seeing, smelling, hearing, tasting, or feeling.

Dialogue will reflect characteristics. Is it clipped? Is it highly dialectal? Does a character use a lot of colloquialisms? The ability to portray the speech of a character can make or break a story. The kind of person the character is in the mind of the reader is dependent on impressions created by description and dialogue. How do other characters feel about this one as revealed by their treatment of him/her, their discussions of him/her with each other, or their overt descriptions of the character? For example, "John, of course, can't be trusted with another person's possessions." In analyzing a story, it's useful to discuss the devices used to produce character.

Skill 2.2 **Demonstrate knowledge of types of plot (e.g., climactic, episodic)**

Written and spoken discourse can be categorized as follows: a) persuasive; b) informative; c) descriptive; d) narrative. A single document may contain examples of all of the above, or the purpose of a piece of writing is often identified by one of these classifiers. An essay whose purpose is to persuade will probably use an informative opening to fill in the background, for example.

Literature is typically narrative—that is, it tells a story. At the same time, the other types of discourse are an inevitable part of a good story. A writer may even stop the narrative and lapse into a persuasive section to bring the reader around to a particular point of view, or one character may attempt to persuade another one. Description and explanation are also used in many ways and in many places in a good story.

A story is a piece of writing that is arranged chronologically. In other words, it is about a series of events that happen one after the other—this happens, and this happens, then this happens. For that reason, a writer's control over and handling of the chronology in a story is very important. If the sequence of events is clouded or confusing to the reader, the story is not effective. On the other hand, successful writers handle the chronology of their stories creatively and effectively.

In media res. One device that has remained popular since the time of Homer is called *in media res*. This tool makes it possible for a writer to open the story somewhere in the middle for the purpose of grabbing and holding the attention of the reader. The writer will, of course, go back and fill in the necessary details so the reader can eventually fit the introductory episode into the overall narrative and chronology. In the *Iliad*, Homer begins his story with the quarrel between Achilles and Agamemnon. As we continue to read, we fit this quarrel into the context of the rest of the "this happened, and this happened, and this happened" chronology of the entire story.

Epistolary. A writer may use a series of letters or correspondences between two characters to tell the story. This technique is called epistolary. The letters are, of course, arranged according to the date on each one. *In media res* can be used in this arrangement where a story in the middle of the series is presented first to pique the reader's curiosity and keep him/her reading to find out how it came out.

Flashback. Another tool a writer may use to manipulate the chronology in a story is the flashback. The story moves along in a normal chronology—this happens, and this happens, then this happens. However, inserted from time to time will be an episode from an earlier time. These are usually used to fill in background information in an interesting way.

Frame Narrative. This is a story where there is an overall underlying story within which one or more tales are related. A main story is composed, at least in part, for the purpose of organizing a set of shorter stories, each of which is a story within a story or for surrounding a single story within a story. An early example of a frame narrative is Chaucer's *Canterbury Tales*. In this series of stories, the pilgrimage is the frame story that brings together all the tellers.

Skill 2.3   Recognize the structural elements of plot (e.g., exposition, internal and external conflict, climax, resolution, subplot, parallel plot)

Dramatic Arc

Good drama is built on conflict of some kind — an opposition of forces or desires that must be resolved by the end of the story. The conflict can be internal, involving emotional and psychological pressures, or it can be external, drawing the characters into tumultuous events. These themes are presented to the audience in a narrative arc that looks roughly like this:

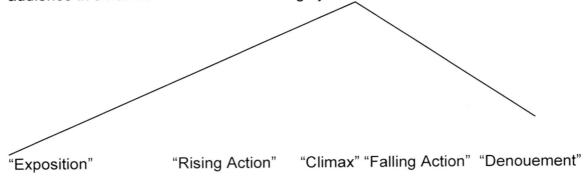

"Exposition"   "Rising Action"   "Climax" "Falling Action" "Denouement"

Following the Arc

Exposition is where characters and their situations are introduced. *Rising action* is the point at which conflict starts to occur. *Climax* is the highest point of conflict, often a turning point. *Falling action* is the result of the climax. *Denouement* is the final resolution of the plot.

Although any piece of literature may have a series of rising and falling levels of intensity, in general the opening should set in motion the events which will generate an emotional high toward the middle or end of the story. Then, regardless of whether the ending is happy, sad, bittersweet, or despairing, the resolution eases the reader down from those heights and establishes some sense of closure. Reaching the climax too soon undermines the dramatic impact of the remaining portion of the work, whereas reaching it too late rushes the ending and creates a jarringly abrupt end to events.

Skill 2.4   Evaluate the development of plot in a literary work, including the ways in which conflicts are or are not addressed and resolved

See Skill 2.3.

Skill 2.5   Analyze the use of theme and thematic elements in a literary work

See COMPETENCY 1.0.

Skill 2.6   **Recognize recurrent themes across a variety of literary works**

See Skills 1.3 and 1.4.

Skill 2.7   **Analyze the effects of an author's choice of words on creating tone and mood in a literary work**

A piece of writing is an integrated whole. It's not enough to just look at the various parts; the total entity must be examined. It should be considered in two ways: As an emotional expression of the author and as an artistic embodiment of a meaning or set of meanings.

This is what is sometimes called **tone** in literary criticism.

It's important to remember that the writer is a human being with his/her own individual bents, prejudices, and emotions. A writer is telling the readers about the world as he/she sees it and will give voice to certain phases of his/her own personality. By reading a writer's works, we can know the personal qualities and emotions of the writer embodied in the work itself. However, it's important to remember that not all the writer's characteristics will be revealed in a single work. People change and may have very different attitudes at different times in their lives. Sometimes, a writer will be influenced by a desire to have a piece of work accepted or to appear to be current or by the interests and desires of the readers he/she hopes to attract. It can destroy a work or make it less than it might be. Sometimes the best works are not commercial successes in the generation when they were written but are discovered at a later time and by another generation.

There are three places to look for tone:
- Choice of form: tragedy or comedy; melodrama or farce; parody or sober lyric.
- Choice of materials: characters that have human qualities that are attractive; others that are repugnant. What an author shows in a setting will often indicate what his/her interests are.
- The writer's interpretation: it may be explicit—telling us how he/she feels.
- The writer's implicit interpretations: the author's feelings for a character come through in the description. For example, the use of "smirked" instead of "laughed"; "minced," "stalked," "marched," instead of walked.

The reader is asked to join the writer in the feelings expressed about the world and the things that happen in it. The tone of a piece of writing is important in a critical review of it.

Style, in literature, means a distinctive manner of expression and applies to all levels of language, beginning at the phonemic level—word choices, alliteration, assonance, etc.; the syntactic level—length of sentences, choice of structure and phraseology, patterns, etc.; and extends even beyond the sentence to paragraphs and chapters. What is distinctive about this writer's use of these elements?

In Steinbeck's *Grapes of Wrath*, for instance, the style is quite simple in the narrative sections and the dialogue is dialectal. Because the emphasis is on the story—the narrative—his style is straightforward, for the most part. He just tells the story. However, there are chapters where he varies his style. He uses symbols and combines them with description that is realistic. He sometimes shifts to a crisp, repetitive pattern to underscore the beeping and speeding of cars. By contrast, some of those inter chapters are lyrical, almost poetic. These shifts in style reflect the attitude of the author toward the subject matter. He intends to make a statement, and he uses a variety of styles to strengthen the point.

In both fiction and non-fiction, authors portray ideas in very subtle ways through their skillful use of language. Style, tone, and point of view are the most basic of ways in which authors do this.

Style is the artful adaptation of language to meet various purposes. For example, authors can modify their word choice, sentence structure, and organization in order to convey certain ideas. For example, an author may write on a topic (say, the environment) in many different styles. In an academic style, the author would use long, complex sentences, advanced vocabulary, and very structured paragraphing. However, in an informal explanation in a popular magazine, the author may use a conversational tone where simple words and simple sentence structures are utilized.

Tone is the attitude an author takes toward his or her subject. That tone is exemplified in the language of the text. For example, consider the environment once again. One author may dismiss the idea of global warming; his tone may be one of derision against environmentalists. A reader might notice this through the style (word choice, for example), the details the author decides to present, and the order in which details are presented. Another author may be angry about global warming and therefore might use harsh words and other tones that indicate anger. Finally, yet another author may not care one bit about the issue of the environment, either way. Let's say this author is a comedian who likes to poke fun at political activists. Her tone is humorous, so she will adjust her language accordingly, as well. All types of tones are about the same subject— they simply reveal, through language, different opinions and attitudes about the subject.

Finally, point of view is perspective. While most of us think of point of view in terms of first or third person (or even the points of view of various characters in stories), point of view also helps explain a lot of language and presentation of ideas in non-fiction and fiction texts. The above environmentalism example proves this. Three points of view are represented and each creates a different style of language.

Skill 2.8   **Analyze the effects of an author's use of sound (e.g., alliteration, onomatopoeia, rhyme, meter) and figurative language (e.g., personification, metaphor, simile, hyperbole, metonymy) on conveying meaning in a literary work**

Imagery can be described as a word or sequence of words that refers to any sensory experience—that is, anything that can be seen, tasted, smelled, heard, or felt on the skin or fingers. While writers of prose may also use these devices, it is most distinctive of poetry. The poet intends to make an experience available to the reader. In order to do that, he/she must appeal to one of the senses. The most often used one, of course, is the visual sense. The poet will deliberately paint a scene in such a way that the reader can see it. However, the purpose is not simply to stir the visceral feeling but also to stir the emotions. A good example is *The Piercing Chill* by Taniguchi Buson (1715-1783):

>   The piercing chill I feel:
>   My dead wife's comb, in our bedroom,
>   Under my heel . . .

In only a few short words, the reader can feel many things: the shock that might come from touching the corpse, a literal sense of death, the contrast between her death and the memories he has of her when she was alive. Imagery might be defined as speaking of the abstract in concrete terms, a powerful device in the hands of a skillful poet.

A **symbol** is an object or action that can be observed with the senses in addition to its suggesting many other things. The lion is a symbol of courage; the cross a symbol of Christianity. These can almost be defined as metaphors because society pretty much agrees on the one-to-one meaning of them. Symbols used in literature are usually of a different sort. They tend to be private and personal; their significance is only evident in the context of the work where they are used. A good example is the huge pair of spectacles on a sign board in F. Scott Fitzgerald's *The Great Gatsby*. They are interesting as a part of the landscape, but they also symbolize divine myopia. A symbol can certainly have more than one meaning, and the meaning may be as personal as the memories and experiences of the particular reader. In analyzing a poem or a story, it's important to identify the symbols and their possible meanings.

Looking for symbols is often challenging, especially for novice poetry readers. However, these suggestions may be useful: First, pick out all the references to concrete objects such as a newspaper, black cats, etc. Note any that the poet emphasizes by describing in detail, by repeating, or by placing at the very beginning or ending of a poem. Ask: what is the poem about? What does it add up to? Paraphrase the poem and determine whether or not the meaning depends upon certain concrete objects. Then ponder what the concrete object symbolizes in this particular poem. Look for a character with the name of a prophet who does little but utter prophecy or a trio of women who resemble the Three Fates. A symbol may be a part of a person's body such as the eye of the murder victim in Poe's story *The Tell-Tale Heart* or a look, a voice, or a mannerism.

Some things a symbol is not: an abstraction such as truth, death, and love; in narrative, a well-developed character who is not at all mysterious; the second term in a metaphor. In Emily Dickinson's *The Lightning Is a Yellow Fork*, the symbol is the lightning, not the fork.

An **allusion** is very like a symbol and the two sometimes tend to run together. An allusion is defined by Merriam Webster's *Encyclopedia of Literature* as "an implied reference to a person, event, thing, or a part of another text." Allusions are based on the assumption that there is a common body of knowledge shared by poet and reader and that a reference to that body of knowledge will be immediately understood. Allusions to the Bible and classical mythology are common in western literature on the assumption that they will be immediately understood. This is not always the case, of course. T. S. Eliot's *The Wasteland* requires research and annotation for understanding. He assumed more background on the part of the average reader than actually exists. However, when Michael Moore on his web page headlines an article on the war in Iraq "Déjà Fallouja: Ramadi surrounded, thousands of families trapped, no electricity or water, onslaught impending," we understand immediately that he is referring first of all to a repeat of the human disaster in New Orleans, although the "onslaught" is not a storm but an invasion by American and Iraqi troops.

Tempo

Interpretation of dialogue must be connected to motivation and detail. During this time, the director is also concerned with pace and seeks a variation of tempo. If the overall pace is too slow, then the action becomes dull and dragging. If the overall pace is too fast, then the audience will not be able to understand what is going on, for they are being hit with too much information to process.

Figurative language is also called figures of speech. If all figures of speech that have ever been identified were listed, it would be a very long list. However, for purposes of analyzing poetry, a few are sufficient.

1. Simile: Direct comparison between two things. "My love is like a red-red rose."
2. Metaphor: Indirect comparison between two things. The use of a word or phrase denoting one kind of object or action in place of another to suggest a comparison between them. While poets use them extensively, they are also integral to everyday speech. For example, chairs are said to have "legs" and "arms" although we know that it's humans and other animals that have these appendages.
3. Parallelism: The arrangement of ideas in phrases, sentences, and paragraphs that balance one element with another of equal importance and similar wording. An example from Francis Bacon's *Of Studies:* "Reading maketh a full man, conference a ready man, and writing an exact man."
4. Personification: Human characteristics are attributed to an inanimate object, an abstract quality, or animal. Examples: John Bunyan wrote characters named Death, Knowledge, Giant Despair, Sloth, and Piety in his *Pilgrim's Progress.* The metaphor of an arm of a chair is a form of personification.
5. Euphemism: The substitution of an agreeable or inoffensive term for one that might offend or suggest something unpleasant. Many euphemisms are used to refer to death to avoid using the real word such as "passed away," "crossed over," or nowadays "passed."
5. Hyperbole: Deliberate exaggeration for effect or comic effect. An example from Shakespeare's *The Merchant of Venice*:
    > Why, if two gods should play some heavenly match
    > And on the wager lay two earthly women,
    > And Portia one, there must be something else
    > Pawned with the other, for the poor rude world
    > Hath not her fellow.
6. Climax: A number of phrases or sentences are arranged in ascending order of rhetorical forcefulness. Example from Melville's *Moby Dick*:
    > All that most maddens and torments; all that stirs up the lees of things; all truth with malice in it; all that cracks the sinews and cakes the brain; all the subtle demonisms of life and thought; all evil, to crazy Ahab, were visibly personified and made practically assailable in Moby Dick.
7. Bathos: A ludicrous attempt to portray pathos—that is, to evoke pity, sympathy, or sorrow. It may result from inappropriately dignifying the commonplace, elevated language to describe something trivial, or greatly exaggerated pathos.
8. Oxymoron: A contradiction in terms deliberately employed for effect. It is usually seen in a qualifying adjective whose meaning is contrary to that of the noun it modifies such as wise folly.

9. Irony: Expressing something other than and particularly opposite the literal meaning such as words of praise when blame is intended. In poetry, it is often used as a sophisticated or resigned awareness of contrast between what is and what ought to be and expresses a controlled pathos without sentimentality. It is a form of indirection that avoids overt praise or censure. An early example: the Greek comic character Eiron, a clever underdog who by his wit repeatedly triumphs over the boastful character Alazon.

10. Alliteration: The repetition of consonant sounds in two or more neighboring words or syllables. In its simplest form, it reinforces one or two consonant sounds. Example: Shakespeare's Sonnet #12:

   When I do count the clock that tells the time.

   Some poets have used more complex patterns of alliteration by creating consonants both at the beginning of words and at the beginning of stressed syllables within words. Example: from Shelley's "Stanzas Written in Dejection Near Naples":

   The City's voice itself is soft like Solitude's

11. Onomatopoeia: The naming of a thing or action by a vocal imitation of the sound associated with it such as buzz or hiss or the use of words whose sound suggests the sense. A good example: from "The Brook" by Tennyson:

   I chatter over stony ways,
   In little sharps and trebles,
   I bubble into eddying bays,
   I babble on the pebbles.

12. Malapropism: A verbal blunder in which one word is replaced by another similar in sound but different in meaning. Comes from Sheridan's Mrs. Malaprop in *The Rivals* (1775). Thinking of the geography of contiguous countries, she spoke of the "geometry" of "contagious countries."

COMPETENCY 3.0 UNDERSTAND THE STRUCTURES AND ELEMENTS OF INFORMATIONAL TEXTS

Skill 3.1 **Identify the author's main idea or purpose in an informational text**

A written work is an extended discussion of a writer's point of view about a particular topic. This point of view may be supported by using such writing modes as examples, argument and persuasion, analysis or comparison/contrast. In any case, a good essay is clear, coherent, well-organized and fully developed.

When an author sets out to write a passage, he/she usually has a purpose for doing so. That purpose may be to simply give information that might be interesting or useful to some reader or other; it may be to persuade the reader to a point of view or to move the reader to act in a particular way; it may be to tell a story; or it may be to describe something in such a way that an experience becomes available to the reader through one of the five senses. Following are the primary devices for expressing a particular purpose in a piece of writing:

- **Basic expository writing** simply gives information not previously known about a topic or is used to explain or define one. Facts, examples, statistics, cause and effect, direct tone, objective rather than subjective delivery, and non-emotional information is presented in a formal manner.

- **Descriptive writing** centers on person, place, or object, using concrete and sensory words to create a mood or impression and arranging details in a chronological or spatial sequence.

- **Narrative writing** is developed using an incident or anecdote or related series of events. Chronology, the 5 W's, topic sentence, and conclusion are essential ingredients.

- **Persuasive writing** implies the writer's ability to select vocabulary and arrange facts and opinions in such a way as to direct the actions of the listener/reader. Persuasive writing may incorporate exposition and narration as they illustrate the main idea.

- **Journalistic writing** is theoretically free of author bias. It is essential when relaying information about an event, person, or thing that it be factual and objective. Provide students with an opportunity to examine newspapers and create their own. Many newspapers have educational programs that are offered free to schools.

Skill 3.2   **Recognize the method used by the author to develop an argument or express a point of view that supports the main idea or purpose of an informational text**

In a well-organized informational text, the main idea or purpose will appear at the beginning of each chapter or subsection in a clear **thesis statement**. Headings and chapter titles also provide good clues to the major points that are going to be enumerated in each section of the text.

A clear, well-written thesis statement makes a point, claim or assertion. This argument is then followed by several paragraphs with supporting points and concrete facts, to validate the assertion. This provides the evidence needed to justify the claim or prove the assertion.

Sound arguments will rely upon **empirical evidence**, such as facts and statistics, to prove a point or justify a claim. Empirical evidence is scientifically gathered and objective, not mere opinions. In keeping with the study of **rhetoric**, the art or technique of persuasion through language, a solid argument must also follow certain rules of logical and rational thinking.

The art of rhetoric involves what the ancient Greeks like **Aristotle** and **Plato** called "logos"—the use of reasoning, either inductive or deductive, to construct an argument or prove a point. Indeed, most of our modern ideas about what constitutes a sound debate or argument descend from the ideas of the ancient Greeks.

Making a credible argument involves following basic elements of logic. By following established logical methods and justifying points with the use of appropriate information (evidence), we are able to arrive at reasonable conclusions. Two basic methods of logic are **inductive** and **deductive** reasoning.

Inductive reasoning involves first stating specific facts or premises and then using these to draw a conclusion or make a generalization. Thus, inductive reasoning moves from the specific to the general. When we use inductive reasoning, we examine whether the evidence clearly supports the conclusions. Inductive reasoning uses examples (historical, mythical, or hypothetical) to draw conclusions. It is interesting to note that inductive reasoning is the logical basis on which scientific experimentation rests.

Example of inductive reasoning:
Enrollment data show us that fewer students are signing up for courses in classical music, so we have to assume that this musical style is not popular with students.

Deductive reasoning moves in the other direction, from the general (or generalization) to the specific (facts). We make a general statement, and then justify it with facts and supporting evidence.

Example of deductive reasoning:
Students generally prefer modern, recent art forms to older art forms. As an example, consider that the numbers of students currently enrolling in classical music classes has been declining every year, while the number enrolling in classes on rap and hip hop are increasing.

Deductive reasoning uses facts to support assertions. A specific form of deductive reasoning is called the **syllogism**. This is a type of logical argument in which a proposition, or conclusion, is inferred from two prior bits of information, already accepted as true. A syllogism involves a major premise, a minor premise, and a conclusion.

Example of a syllogism:
All men are mortal (major premise)
Socrates is a man (minor premise)
Therefore, Socrates is mortal (conclusion)

Other methods an author may use to present an argument include organizing ideas logically and presented them in a format that is easy to understand and follow. Appropriate ways to organize ideas for maximum comprehension include grouping similar ideas together or presenting ideas chronologically.

Finally, in a textbook, information should be presented in a fair and unbiased fashion, letting the evidence make the case. Opinions should not override facts.

Skill 3.3   Evaluate the structural elements of informational text (e.g., paragraphs, topic sentences, introduction, supporting details, conclusion, footnotes, summary/abstract, bibliography, index)

Language is hierarchal. The lowest level in the hierarchy is sounds (spoken) and letters (written). This is the phonemic stage in the hierarchy. The second stage is words, which are made out of sounds (letters). This is the morphological level. Words are used to make sentences (the syntactic level). However, in English, sentences include *classes* of words (sometimes called parts of speech) that are strictly arranged according to order. English is one of the few languages that depend on word order for parts-function. For example, Spanish depends on case and inflection in word endings to signal subjects and predicates. Just as the subject of a sentence announces what the topic is, so the verb says something about that subject. The dog (subject) barks (verb).

Paragraphs echo the sentence in that they will include a topic sentence that states the subject and supporting sentences, usually examples, that say something about the topic sentence. The same is true in longer discourses. In an essay, the thesis states the subject of the document. Paragraphs will develop that thesis—i.e. they will say something about the thesis.

It's useful to keep in mind as a teacher that this hierarchical nature of language is innate and is embedded in the minds of speakers of the language, including students. It's useful to tap into this innate characteristic in helping students understand the importance of the topic sentence and thesis statement and to help them in their own composition. It's also extremely useful in helping them learn to analyze written text, be it persuasive, expository, technical, etc. If they understand how language works (including their own) in stating a subject and saying something about it, they can more easily understand how another writer has done that very thing. What was this writer's subject, and what did he/she say about it?

The very notion of table of contents is based on this characteristic of language. It will be a map to the arrangement of the document by topic, sub-topics, and sometimes sub-sub topics. If this is understood, then creating a table of contents for a written piece comes naturally.

It's extremely frustrating to have headlines for newspaper articles that do not provide clues to what the article is about. The same is true of chapter heads. This is not a good time to be creative. Effective chapter heads function as guides to the reader with the express function of mapping out what is to come.

If the student comes to see written and spoken language in the terms delineated above, then summarizing a piece becomes much easier. The summarizer simply looks for the "bones" of the piece being summarized and bypasses details that are only supporters of the significant structure parts. This is easy to oversimplify, and students need much practice with these functions. Practice may not make perfect, but it does lead to deeper understanding of how language works.

Skill 3.4 **Analyze various methods (e.g., chronological order, cause and effect, comparison and contrast) for organizing informational text**

The **organization** of a written work includes two factors: the order in which the writer has chosen to present the different parts of the discussion or argument, and the relationships he or she constructs between these parts. Written ideas need to be presented in a **logical order** so that a reader can follow the information easily and quickly. There are many different ways in which to order a series of ideas but they all share one thing in common: to lead the reader along a desired path in order to give a clear, strong presentation of the writer's main idea. *Some* of the ways in which a text may be organized are listed here.

- **Sequence of events** – In this type of organization the details are presented in the order in which they have occurred. Paragraphs that describe a process or procedure, give directions or outline a given period of time (such as a day or a month) are often arranged chronologically.

- **Statement support** – In this type of organization the main idea is stated and the rest of the paragraph explains or proves it. This is also referred to as relative or order of importance. There are four ways in which this type of order is organized: most to least, least to most, most-least-most, and least-most-least.

- **Comparison-Contrast** – In this type of organization the compare-contrast pattern is used when a paragraph describes the differences or similarities of two or more ideas, actions, events, or things. Usually the topic sentence describes the basic relationship between the ideas or items and the rest of the paragraph explains this relationship.

- **Classification** – in this type of organization, the paragraph presents grouped information about a topic. The topic sentence usually states the general category and the rest of the sentences show how various elements of the category have a common base and also how they differ from the common base.

- **Cause and Effect** – This pattern describes how two or more events are connected. The main sentence usually states the primary cause(s) and the primary effect(s) and how they are basically connected. The rest of the sentences explain the connection – how one event caused the next.

- **Spatial/Place** – In this type of organization, certain descriptions are organized according to the location of items in relation to each other and to a larger context. The orderly arrangement guides the reader's eye as he or she mentally envisions the scene or place being described.

- **Example, Clarification and Definition** – These types of organizations show, explain or elaborate on the main idea. This can be done by showing specific cases, examining meaning multiple times or extensive description of one term

Skill 3.5   Demonstrate the ability to follow multistep directions in technical or informational texts

In their adult lives, students will often be expected to make use of and follow written directions from a variety of sources. Following written directions can be a frustrating experience, especially if they are not clearly written.

Classroom teachers can devise a number of possible activities in which students can first develop and then demonstrate their ability to follow directions. Teachers should stay alert for examples of directions or instruction manuals that would be adaptable to classroom use. Good examples will be clearly written and be highly motivating to the students (i.e., pertain to a subject that would be of some personal interest to them).

Examples from daily life help students to apprehend the relationship of their coursework in school to tasks they will encounter in their lives. It would be advisable for teachers to locate actual or simulated manuals that require students to accomplish something they might be called upon to do in a real-life situation.

The more "real" and personally relevant the material students are called upon to utilize, the higher their motivation to complete the task should be. Instructors should be on the lookout for engaging manuals with multi-step directions that would be appropriate. This could include things like changing a tire, programming a new cell phone, putting together the components of a new computer, or filling out a government form.

There are many opportunities for hands-on learning with this skill, but this may require the teacher to engage in ample preparation. For example, students could be given an unassembled product with assembly directions and be asked to follow the instructions to create the finished product, correctly. Such a task would provide an opportunity for an **authentic assessment**, which is when students are asked to perform real-world tasks that demonstrate meaningful application of essential knowledge and skills.

Before beginning this task, it is advisable for teachers to discuss various strategies for following written directions. The teacher may also want to share some frustrating experiences with directions of his/her own (e.g., trying to assemble something for a birthday) and to elicit such stories from students.

Some helpful strategies for following multistep directions would be to read through all of the instructions before beginning and to look up any unfamiliar vocabulary to be sure that comprehension is complete. Many times, directions will include a list of required materials. Advise students to gather these before beginning.

The only way for students to demonstrate this ability is for teachers to construct a task or assessment that requires students to follow instructions to accomplish a specific task or to create a predetermined final product.

An English teacher may find it useful to collaborate with teachers in other courses, for example, to locate directions pertaining to a real task students may be expected to accomplish in other coursework. In this way, students learn to apply the skills acquired in English class to other disciplines. A good example might be following lab directions in the construction of a scientific experiment.

When students fail to follow the multi-step directions correctly, teachers will want to ascertain what went wrong. For example, was the problem in reading, decoding the information, understanding the instructions themselves, or in carrying out the instructions?

The content chosen for this demonstration should not matter as long as the required skills are the same: the ability to interpret and follow clearly written instructions. If students have difficulty interpreting some of the vocabulary in the instructions, this is an embedded learning opportunity to point out the importance of knowing how to find information (in this case, definitions) independently. Instructions that are difficult to interpret should be avoided; often these are the case with foreign-manufactured goods whose directions have been translated. Particularly bad translations, however, could serve as negative examples of why clear writing is so important.

Skill 3.6 Demonstrate knowledge of techniques for using information from a variety of consumer, professional, and public documents to solve problems

The only way for students to demonstrate something is by doing. The best way to prepare for this demonstration is to offer simulated experiences or assessments that require students to do what is being expected of them. Teachers will therefore need to gather examples of appropriate documents to facilitate demonstration of this competency.

Consumer documents include written material a person encounters when in a store or retail environment. Some of these documents contain information that a consumer would be wise to review before making an informed purchase. The information may tell the details about a product, which can be compared to the features of another product before making a buying decision.

<u>Sample exercise</u>: Students could gain excellent practice in this competency by comparing retail literature about two different products that would be appealing to them or their families. A good example might be a cell phone. The students could be asked to compare literature detailing the features of two different cell phones and then to present their purchase recommendation, which must be justified based on the information gleaned from the consumer literature.

Professional documents might include professionally prepared documents, such as legal documents or contracts. They might also include materials that a professional would be expected to handle and use in the course of a workday, or something like a business letter or memo. This could include email communication, which has become an acceptable means for conducting business correspondence.

<u>Sample exercise</u>: Students could demonstrate their ability to use professional information by executing an appropriate reply to an emailed inquiry or expectation. If the email asked the student to include specified information or documentation, this would be part of the expected response to satisfy the requirements of this competency.

Public documents generally present information that could be available to the general public including statistics, demographics, and other information that would be relevant to people seeking to make decisions using public information. Many public documents will come from government offices.

<u>Sample exercise</u>: Most cities and towns have a chamber of commerce, which provides detailed information about the characteristics of the people residing in the particular town and the businesses that operate there. Students could be given chamber materials from two towns with which they are familiar and then asked to make a decision as to which town they would recommend to a hypothetical new family just moving to the area. The recommendation would have to be based on the information in the documents.

Skill 3.7   Use knowledge of common graphic features (e.g., graphic organizers, diagrams, captions, illustrations) of informational texts to draw conclusions and make judgments

Tables that simply store descriptive information in a form available for general use are called repository tables. They usually contain primary data, which simply summarize raw data. They are not intended to analyze the data, so any analysis is left to the reader or user of the table. A good example of a repository table would be a report of birth statistics by the federal Health and Human Services Department. An analytical table, on the other hand, is constructed from some sort of analysis of primary or secondary data, possibly from a repository table or from the raw data itself. An example of an analytical table would be one that compares birth statistics in 1980 to birth statistics in 2005 for the country at large. It might also break the data down into comparisons by state.

Graphs also present data in visual form. Whereas tables are useful for showing large numbers of specific, related facts or statistics in a brief space, trends, movements, distributions and cycles are more readily apparent in a graph.

Bar graphs are used to display data in a similar way to line graphs. However, rather than using a point on a plane to define a value, a bar graph uses a horizontal or vertical rectangular bar that levels off at the appropriate level. Bar graphs clearly show trends in data, meaning that they show how one variable is affected as the other rises or falls. These graphs make comparisons between different variables very easy to see.

Example: A class had the following grades:
4 A's, 9 B's, 8 C's, 1 D, 3 F's.
Graph these on a bar graph

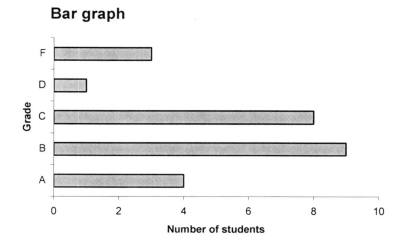

Bar graph

Line graphs compare two variables. Each variable is plotted along an **axis**. A line graph has a vertical axis and a horizontal axis. So, for example, if you wanted to graph the height of a ball after you have thrown it, you could put time along the horizontal, or x-axis, and height along the vertical, or y-axis. Line graphs are good at showing specific values of data, meaning that given one variable the other can easily be determined. They also show trends in data clearly, meaning that they visibly show how one variable is affected by the other as it increases or decreases. In addition, line graphs enable the viewer to make predictions about the results of data not yet recorded.

Example: Graph the following information using a line graph.

The number of National Merit finalists/school year

	90-91	91-92	92-93	93-94	94-95	95-96
Central	3	5	1	4	6	8
Wilson	4	2	3	2	3	2

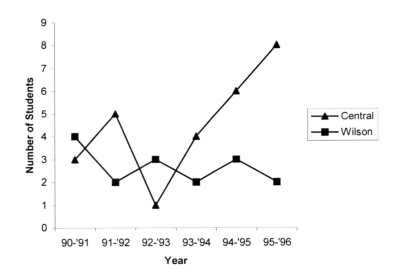

A **pie chart/graph** is used to compare parts of a whole with each other or the fraction of the whole each part takes up.

Example: Graph this information on a circle graph:

Monthly expenses:

Rent, $400
Food, $150
Utilities, $75
Clothes, $75
Church, $100
Misc., $200

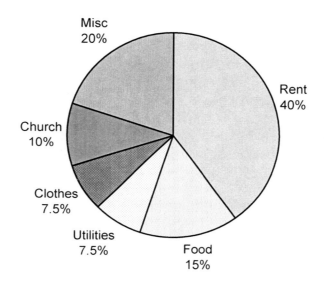

A wide range of **illustrations** may be used to illuminate the text in a document. They may also be a part of a graphic layout designed to make the page more attractive.

Questions to ask regarding an illustration: Why is it in this document? What was the writer's purpose in putting it in the document and why at this particular place? Does it make a point clearer? What implications are inherent in a table that shows birth statistics in all states or even in some selected states? What does that have to do with the point and purpose of this piece of writing? Is there adequate preparation in the text for the inclusion of the illustration? Does the illustration underscore or clarify any of the points made in the text? Is there a clear connection between the illustration and the subject matter of the text?

COMPETENCY 4.0 UNDERSTAND WORD IDENTIFICATION STRATEGIES AND METHODS FOR PROMOTING VOCABULARY DEVELOPMENT

Skill 4.1 **Identify instructional strategies and activities that help students to apply word identification strategies in addition to phonics (e.g., structural analysis, context clues)**

Phonological Awareness

Phonological awareness means the ability of the reader to recognize the sound of spoken language. This recognition includes how these sounds can be blended together, segmented (divided up), and manipulated (switched around). This awareness then leads to phonics, a method for teaching students to read. It helps them sound out words. Instructional methods to teach phonological awareness may include any or all of the following: Auditory games and drills during which students recognize and manipulate the sounds of words, separate or segment the sounds of words, take out sounds, blend sounds, add in new sounds, or take apart sound to recombine them in new formations are good way to foster phonological awareness.

Context clues help readers determine the meaning of words they are not familiar with. The context of a word is the sentence or sentences that surround the word.

Read the following sentences and attempt to determine the meanings of the words in bold print.

> The **luminosity** of the room was so incredible that there was no need for lights.

>> If there was no need for lights then one must assume that the word luminosity has something to do with giving off light. The definition of luminosity is the emission of light.

> Jamie could not understand Joe's feelings. His mood swings made Joe somewhat of an **enigma.**

>> The fact that he could not be understood made him somewhat of a puzzle. The definition of enigma is a mystery or puzzle.

Familiarity with word roots (the basic elements of words) and with prefixes can also help one determine the meanings of unknown words.

Root words: A root word is a word from which another word is developed. The second word can be said to have its "root" in the first. This structural component nicely lends itself to a tree with roots illustration which can concretize the meaning for students. Students may also want to literally construct root words using cardboard trees and/or actual roots from plants to create word family models. This is a lovely way to help students own their root words.

Base words: A stand-alone linguistic unit which can not be deconstructed or broken down into smaller words. For example, in the word "re-tell," the base word is "tell."

Contractions: These are shortened forms of two words in which a letter or letters have been deleted. These deleted letters have been replaced by an apostrophe.

Prefixes: These are beginning units of meaning which can be added (the vocabulary word for this type of structural adding is "affixed") to a base word or root word. They can not stand alone. They are also sometimes known as "bound morphemes," meaning that they cannot stand alone as a base word.

Suffixes: These are ending units of meaning which can be affixed or added on to the ends of root or base words. Suffixes transform the original meanings of base and root words. Like prefixes, they are also known as "bound morphemes," because they can not stand alone as words. **Inflectional endings** are types are suffixes that impart a new meaning to the base or root word. These endings in particular change the gender, number, tense, or form of the base or root words. Just like other suffixes, these are also termed "bound morphemes."

Compound words: These occur when two or more base words are connected to form a new word. The meaning of the new word is in some way connected with that of the base word.

Following is a partial list of roots and prefixes. It might be useful to review these.

Root	Meaning	Example
aqua	water	aqualung
astro	stars	astrology
bio	life	biology
carn	meat	carnivorous
circum	around	circumnavigate
geo	earth	geology
herb	plant	herbivorous
mal	bad	malicious
neo	new	neonatal
tele	distant	telescope

Prefix	Meaning	Example
un-	not	unnamed
re-	again	reenter
il-	not	illegible
pre-	before	preset
mis-	incorrectly	misstate
in-	not	informal
anti-	against	antiwar
de-	opposite	derail
post-	after	postwar
ir-	not	irresponsible

Word forms

Sometimes a very familiar word can appear as a different part of speech.

You may have heard that *fraud* involves a criminal misrepresentation, so when it appears as the adjective form *fraudulent* ("he was suspected of fraudulent activities") you can make an educated guess. You probably know that something out of date is *obsolete;* therefore, when you read about "built-in *obsolescence,"* you can detect the meaning of the unfamiliar word.

Practice questions: Read the following sentences and attempt to determine the meanings of the underlined words.

1. Farmer John got a two-horse plow and went to work. Straight <u>furrows</u> stretched out behind him.

   The word <u>furrows</u> means

   (A) long cuts made by plow
   (B) vast, open fields
   (C) rows of corn
   (D) pairs of hitched horses

2. The survivors struggled ahead, <u>shambling</u> through the terrible cold, doing their best not to fall.

   The word <u>shambling</u> means

   (A) frozen in place
   (B) running
   (C) shivering uncontrollably
   (D) walking awkwardly

Answers:

1. (A) is the correct answer. The words "straight" and the expression "stretched out behind him" are your clues.

2. (D) is the correct answer. The words "ahead" and "through" are your clues.

The context for a word is the written passage that surrounds it. Sometimes the writer offers synonyms—words that have nearly the same meaning. Context clues can appear within the sentence itself, within the preceding and/or following sentence(s), or in the passage as a whole.

Sentence clues

Often, a writer will actually **define** a difficult or particularly important word for you the first time it appears in a passage. Phrases like *that is, such as, which is,* or *is called* might announce the writer's intention to give just the definition you need. Occasionally, a writer will simply use a synonym (a word that means the same thing) or near-synonym joined by the word *or*. Look at the following examples:

> The <u>credibility,</u> *that is to say the believability, of the witness was called into question by evidence of previous perjury.*
> *Nothing would <u>assuage</u> or lessen the child's grief.*

Punctuation at the sentence level is often a clue to the meaning of a word. Commas, parentheses, quotation marks and dashes tell the reader that a definition is being offered by the writer.

> *A tendency toward <u>hyperbole,</u> extravagant exaggeration, is a common flaw among persuasive writers.*

> *Political <u>apathy</u> - lack of interest - can lead to the death of the state.*

A writer might simply give an **explanation** in other words that you can understand in the same sentence:

> *The <u>xenophobic</u> townspeople were suspicious of every foreigner.*

Writers also explain a word in terms of its opposite at the sentence level:

> *His <u>incarceration</u> had ended and he was elated to be out of jail.*

Adjacent sentence clues

The context for a word goes beyond the sentence in which it appears. At times, the writer uses adjacent (adjoining) sentences to present an explanation or definition:

> *The 200 dollars for the car repair would have to come out of the <u>contingency</u> fund. Fortunately, Angela's father had taught her to keep some money set aside for just such emergencies.*

Analysis: The second sentence offers a clue to the definition of *contingency* as used in this sentence: "emergencies." Therefore, a fund for contingencies would be money tucked away for unforeseen and/or urgent events.

Entire passage clues

On occasion, you must look at an entire paragraph or passage to figure out the definition of a word or term. In the following paragraph, notice how the word *nostalgia* undergoes a form of extended definition throughout the selection rather than in just one sentence.

> *The word <u>nostalgia</u> links Greek words for "away from home" and "pain." If you're feeling <u>nostalgic,</u> then you are probably in some physical distress or discomfort, suffering from a feeling of alienation and separation from love ones or loved places. <u>Nostalgia</u> is that awful feeling you remember the first time you went away to camp or spent the weekend with a friend's family—homesickness or some condition even more painful than that. But in common use, <u>nostalgia</u> has come to have more sentimental associations. A few years back, for example, a <u>nostalgia</u> craze had to do with the 1950s. We resurrected poodle skirts and saddle shoes, built new restaurants to look like old ones, and tried to make chicken a la king just as mother probably never made it. In TV situation comedies, we recreated a pleasant world that probably never existed and relished our <u>nostalgia,</u> longing for a homey, comfortable lost time.*

Skill 4.2   **Demonstrate knowledge of the ways in which word identification strategies (e.g., applying knowledge of roots, affixes, and cognates) may be used to improve comprehension by analyzing the denotative and connotative meanings of words**

To effectively teach language, it is necessary to understand that as human beings acquire language they realize that words have <u>denotative</u> and <u>connotative</u> meanings. Generally, denotative words point to things and connotative words deal with mental suggestions that the words convey. The word *skunk* has a denotative meaning if the speaker can point to the actual animal as he speaks the word and intends the word to identify the animal. *Skunk* has connotative meaning depending upon the tone of delivery, the socially acceptable attitudes about the animal, and the speaker's personal feelings about the animal.

Informative connotations are definitions agreed upon by the society in which the learner operates. A *skunk* is "a black and white mammal of the weasel family with a pair of perineal glands which secrete a pungent odor." The *Merriam Webster Collegiate Dictionary* adds "...and offensive" odor. Identification of the color, species, and glandular characteristics are informative. The interpretation of the odor as *offensive* is affective.

Affective connotations are the personal feelings a word arouses. A child who has no personal experience with a skunk and its odor or has had a pet skunk will feel differently about the word *skunk* than a child who has smelled the spray or been conditioned vicariously to associate offensiveness with the animal denoted *skunk*. The very fact that our society views a skunk as an animal to be avoided will affect the child's interpretation of the word.

In fact, it is not necessary for one to have actually seen a skunk (that is, have a denotative understanding) to use the word in either connotative expression. For example, one child might call another child a skunk, connoting an unpleasant reaction (affective use) or, seeing another small black and white animal, call it a skunk based on the definition (informative use).

Using connotations

In everyday language, we attach affective meanings to words unconsciously; we exercise more conscious control of informative connotations. In the process of language development, the leaner must come not only to grasp the definitions of words but also to become more conscious of the affective connotations and how his listeners process these connotations. Gaining this conscious control over language makes it possible to use language appropriately in various situations and to evaluate its uses in literature and other forms of communication.

The manipulation of language for a variety of purposes is the goal of language instruction. Advertisers and satirists are especially conscious of the effect word choice has on their audiences. By evoking the proper responses from readers/listeners, we can prompt them to take action.

Choice of the medium through which the message is delivered to the receiver is a significant factor in controlling language. Spoken language relies as much on the gestures, facial expression, and tone of voice of the speaker as on the words he speaks. Slapstick comics can evoke laughter without speaking a word. Young children use body language overtly and older children more subtly to convey messages. This refining of body language is paralleled by an ability to recognize and apply the nuances of spoken language. To work strictly with the written work, the writer must use words to imply the body language.

Skill 4.3   Demonstrate knowledge of instructional strategies and activities that promote vocabulary development (e.g., reading and listening to a wide variety of texts, word classification, semantic mapping)

Students hear and understand many words that they do not use themselves, an indication that there are two sets of words in their vocabularies. The *productive vocabulary* is the set of words they know the meanings of when they speak or read orally. *Recognition vocabulary* is the set that a student can assign meanings to when listening or reading. The latter is typically much larger than the former. The *recognition vocabulary* is developed through reading and listening and over time many words from that set will move into the *productive vocabulary*. The goal of the teacher, then, should be to help students to enlarge both of these vocabularies as they move through the middle school years.

There is a clear correspondence between the size of one's vocabulary and comprehension. Middle school students will be asked, probably for the first time, to read and comprehend text-book assignments. There are skills associated with developing comprehension that can be taught, but none is more important than the development of the two kinds of vocabulary. From the cradle to the grave, our vocabularies constantly grow because of our involvement with the world around us. All of us have expanded our own vocabularies enormously with the advent of computers and our use of them. A mouse is no longer just a mouse. We all know the difference between storing information and sending it or even deleting it, for that matter. These and the hundreds of other words that have entered our vocabularies in the past few years are essential to our functioning in the world as it is at the present moment.

What happens with middle-schoolers is very much like that. They are ready to learn many new concepts, explore worlds they never knew existed, and move toward citizenship in a country they need to be able to navigate. What this means is that during the middle school years, their vocabularies must be growing at a very rapid rate—not only the *recognition* but also *the productive vocabulary.*

The National Reading Panel has put forth the following conclusions about vocabulary instruction.

1. There is a need for direct instruction of vocabulary items required for a specific text.
2. Repetition and multiple exposure to vocabulary items are important. Students should be given items that will be likely to appear in many contexts.
3. Learning in rich contexts is valuable for vocabulary learning. Vocabulary words should be those that the learner will find useful in many contexts. When vocabulary items are derived from content learning materials, the learner will be better equipped to deal with specific reading matter in content areas.
4. Vocabulary tasks should be restructured as necessary. It is important to be certain that students fully understand what is asked of them in the context of reading rather than focusing only on the words to be learned.
5. Vocabulary learning is effective when it entails active engagement in learning tasks.
6. Computer technology can be used effectively to help teach vocabulary.
7. Vocabulary can be acquired through incidental learning. Much of a student's vocabulary will have to be learned in the course of doing things other than explicit vocabulary learning. Repetition, richness of context, and motivation may also add to the efficacy of incidental learning of vocabulary.
8. Dependence on a single vocabulary instruction method will not result in optimal learning. A variety of methods was used effectively with emphasis on multimedia aspects of learning, richness of context in which words are to be learned, and the number of exposures to words that learners receive.

The Panel found that a critical feature of effective classrooms is the instruction of specific words that includes lessons and activities where students apply their vocabulary knowledge and strategies to reading and writing. Included in the activities were discussions in which teachers and students talked about words, their features, and strategies for understanding unfamiliar words.

There are many methods for directly and explicitly teaching words. In fact, the Panel found twenty-one methods that have been found effective in research projects. Many emphasize the underlying concept of a word and its connections to other words such as semantic mapping and diagrams that use graphics. The keyword method uses words and illustrations that highlight salient features of meaning. Visualizing or drawing a picture either by the student or by the teacher was found to be effective. Many words cannot be learned in this way, of course, so it should be used as only one method among others. Effective classrooms provide multiple ways for students to learn and interact with words. The Panel also found that computer-assisted activities can have a very positive role in the development of vocabulary.

Word identification skills help individuals recognize unknown words accurately and rapidly. These skills include phonetic analysis, structural analysis, and contextual analysis. In content-area classes, students are required to read large amounts of text that often contain multisyllabic words the students may not know. Students need word identification skills to tackle these unknown words. In addition, the ability to decode unknown words rapidly and accurately is necessary for effective and efficient comprehension. When students do not recognize words automatically, they spend time on decoding that could be devoted to comprehending text. The goal of word identification instruction for secondary students is to help students develop and apply strategies for tackling unfamiliar or difficult words accurately, effortlessly, and rapidly.

Some instructional guidelines for teaching word identification skills

- Explicit, systematic instruction is an effective procedure for teaching students word identification skills and strategies.
- Words should be taken from the content-area materials that students have difficulty reading in the context of their classes.
- Students should possess basic word identification skills, including the following:
  1. sound-symbol correspondence,
  2. recognition of phonetically regular consonant-vowel-consonant words,
  3. recognition of some sight or high frequency words.
- Word identification skills include phonetic analysis, structural analysis, and contextual analysis to read multisyllabic words.

Some interventions for teaching word identification skills

Word Identification Strategy: Students learn how to break words into parts to facilitate decoding. It is helpful if students know prefixes and suffixes and have some knowledge of phonics.

Overt Word Parts Strategy: Student circle word parts at the beginning and end of the word and underline letters representing the vowel sounds in the remaining part of the word. Students pronounce the parts fast to say the word.

Making Words: long words. Students use their knowledge of sound-letter correspondences, orthographic patterns, structural analysis, and content-specific vocabulary to form words.

Skill 4.4   Recognize criteria for selecting relevant vocabulary words for study (e.g., words that are related to one another, words needed to comprehend a reading selection)

Vocabulary words selected for study must be relevant to the reading and writing that the student is doing. In a text the students have been assigned, the teacher will select two or three concept words. The teacher will also select passages in the text that provide strong context clues for each word. The teacher presents the word and the context aloud; the students follow along. Then the students will re-read the material silently. This will be followed by a child-centered discussion that will include questions designed to activate the children's prior knowledge and to use the contextual clues to figure out the correct meaning of the key concept word. It's important that the *children* make the definition of the concept word.

Next, the meaning of the word will be expanded by a search for synonyms, antonyms, and other contexts or other kinds of stories/texts where the word might appear. A thesaurus and dictionary should be used by the children in their search. The key to this strategy is that it allows the teacher to draw the child out and to grasp through the child's responses the individual child's contextual clue process. The more talk from the child, the better.

Skill 4.5 **Demonstrate knowledge of how the history of the English language is manifested in modern vocabulary, word structures, spelling, and pronunciation**

Perhaps the most basic principle about language in understanding its changes and variations is a simple one: language inevitably changes over time. If a community that speaks a homogeneous language and dialect are for some reason separated with no contact between the two resulting communities, over a few generations, they will be speaking different dialects and eventually will have difficulty understanding each other.

Language changes in all its manifestations: At the phonetic level, the sounds of a language will change as will its orthography. The vocabulary level will probably manifest the greatest changes. Changes in syntax are slower and less likely to occur. For example, English has changed in response to the influences of many other languages and cultures as well as internal cultural changes such as the development of the railroad and the computer; however, its syntax still relies on word order—it has not shifted to an inflected system even though many of the cultures that have impacted it have an inflected language, such as Spanish.

The most significant influence on a language is the blending of cultures. The Norman Conquest that brought the English speakers in the British Isles under the rule of French speakers impacted the language, but it's significant that English speakers did not adopt the language of the ruling class—they did not become speakers of French. Even so, many vocabulary items entered the language in that period. The Great Vowel Shift that occurred between the fourteenth and sixteenth centuries is somewhat of a mystery although it's generally attributed to the migration to Southeast England following the plague of the black death. The Great Vowel Shift largely accounts for the discrepancy between orthography and speech—the difficult spelling system in modern English.

Colonization of other countries has also brought new vocabulary items into the language. Indian English not only has its own easily recognizable attributes as does Australian and North American, those cultural interactions have added to items in the usages of each other and in the language at large. The fact that English is the most widely spoken and understood language all over the world in the twenty-first century implies that it is constantly being changed by the globalized world.

Other influences, of course, impact language. The introduction of television and its domination by the United States has had great influence on the English that is spoken and understood all over the world. The same is true of the computerizing of the world (Tom Friedman called it "flattening" in his *The World is Flat: A Brief History of the Twenty-first Century*). New terms have been added, old terms have changed meaning ("mouse," for instance), and nouns have been verbalized.

COMPETENCY 5.0 UNDERSTAND READING STRATEGIES USED TO CONSTRUCT MEANING, AID COMPREHENSION, AND INCREASE FLUENCY

Skill 5.1 **Demonstrate knowledge of strategies to use before, during, and after reading to enhance comprehension (e.g., recalling prior knowledge, making predictions, previewing, self-monitoring, self-correcting, rereading, outlining, summarizing, self-questioning, think-alouds)**

Content areas such as science, mathematics, history and social studies rely on textbooks and other printed materials that use primarily expository text to introduce, explain, and illustrate new subject matter. From a reading perspective, students face several challenges when approaching these texts, such as deciphering unfamiliar vocabulary, and adapting to new structures of content organization, that directly impact their ability to understand, synthesize, and apply the information contained therein.

Students lacking a solid foundation of reading strategies will likely experience difficulties in developing the competencies needed to master a subject area's academic requirements. At the secondary level, reading and understanding is only the beginning. Students are expected to absorb, evaluate, and form opinions and theories about topics within the subject matter, and then discuss, write about, and apply what they've learned on high level.

Meta-cognitive reading development strategies can help students engage effectively with their reading materials across the curriculum. The sample strategies below can be employed through structured activities that occur before reading, during reading, and after reading.

Before reading

- Incorporate prior knowledge: Draw a connection between students' previous experiences – both personal and educational – and the topic at hand. A student who has helped out in the family garden, for example, will have a visual and basic vocabulary starting point for the study of plant physiology.
- Make predictions about what will be learned: Encourage students to identify what they think they will learn from the text, based on cues in the material (e.g., book titles, chapter headings, pictures, etc.).
- Prepare questions: Write specific questions to be answered during reading.

During reading:

- Use context cues: Utilize other words and concepts in the same sentence or paragraph to determine the meaning of an unfamiliar word.
- Reread challenging text: Practice rereading a selection of text to check for understanding.
- Use visualizing techniques: Mental pictures formed during the reading of text can aid in comprehension and retention of information. Read-alouds, followed by a discussion of how these mental pictures factually reflect the text, provide opportunity for practicing and reinforcing this technique at all grade levels.
- Make inferences: Much of human communication relies on our ability to read between the lines of explicit statements and make logical guesses that fill in the blanks of information not provided. Similarly, for textbooks, making inferences means making connections to information extending beyond the text and subject matter at hand. For example, a geography book making the simple declaration that Brazil has a tropical climate can allow the student to deduce a wealth of information not stated in the text (e.g., tropical climates have warm year-round temperatures and high precipitation levels, so certain crops will grow quite successfully and can positively impact the local economy, etc.).
- Check the predictions made before reading: Use the text to confirm earlier predictions about content and answer the questions posed prior to reading.

After reading

- Summarize information: Students who understand the information they have read should be able to restate what they have learned in an organized manner. This activity can be practiced in both written and oral forms.
- Make critical evaluations: Encourage students to respond to the text with the ideas and opinions they've formed during reading. Facilitate discussions by devising questions that lead students to make qualitative and evaluative judgments about the content they've read.

Sample Activity: Summarizing and Outlining a Passage

Chili peppers may turn out to be the wonder drug of the decade. The fiery fruit comes in many sizes, shapes and colors, all of which grow on plants that are genetic descendants of the tepin plant, originally native to the Americas. Connoisseurs of the regional cuisines of the Southwest and Louisiana are already well aware that food flavored with chilies can cause a good sweat, but medical researchers are learning more every day about the medical power of capsaicin, the ingredient in the peppers that produces the heat.

Capsaicin as a pain medication has been a part of fold medicine for centuries. It is, in fact, the active ingredient in several currently available over-the-counter liniments for sore muscles. Recent research has been examining the value of the compound for the treatment of other painful conditions. Capsaicin shows some promise in the treatment of phantom limb syndrome, as well as shingles, and some types of headaches. Additional research focuses upon the use of capsaicin to relieve pain in post-surgical patients. Scientists speculate that application of the compound to the skin causes the body to release endorphins – natural pain relievers manufactured by the body itself. An alternative theory holds that capsaicin somehow interferes with transmission of signals along the nerve fibers, thus reducing the sensation of pain.

In addition to its well-documented history as a painkiller, capsaicin has recently received attention as a phytochemical, one of the naturally occurring compounds from foods that show cancer-fighting qualities. Like the phytochemical sulfoaphane found in broccoli, capsaicin might turn out to be an agent capable of short-circuiting the actions of carcinogens at the cell level before they can cause cancer.

Summary: Chili peppers contain a chemical called capsaicin which has proved useful for treating a variety of ailments. Recent research reveals that capsaicin is a phytochemical, a natural compound that may help fight cancer.

Outline: -Chili peppers could be the wonder drug of the decade
-Chili peppers contains capsaicin
-Capsaicin can be used as a pain medication
-Capsaicin is a phytochemical
-Phytochemicals show cancer-fighting qualities
-Capsaicin might be able to short-circuit the effects of carcinogens

Skill 5.2 **Demonstrate knowledge of literal comprehension skills (e.g., identifying the sequence of events in a text, identifying explicitly stated main ideas and supporting details in a text)**

Reading Comprehension. Many of the same things can be said for reading comprehension. Some children have reading difficulties, and there are tests that can determine what the exact nature of the difficulty is. There are several kinds of reading disabilities, some of which are linked to neurological dysfunction. If the teacher suspects that a student falls into one of these categories, testing and specialized instruction is in order. The student with such a deficit will have difficulty succeeding in a regular classroom and will either need to be in a special program or have professional supplemental out-of-class assistance.
Some special research studies have demonstrated that the student with a reading disability scores lower on comprehension tests than the student with ADHD; they are clearly two different things and that difference needs to be taken into account.

Assuming that the students in your classroom do not have reading disabilities, reading comprehension skills can be taught. This works particularly well if it goes hand-in-hand with teaching writing skills. Students need to practice looking for the *point* of a written discourse just as they need to learn to focus their writing. What was the writer's aim or purpose? Can the writing be said to be persuasive in nature, for instance, or is it simply conveying useful (or not useful) information? Is it purely expressive with the intention of opening up an experience for the reader? These skills will be taught in the writing classroom and can be reinforced in the reading classroom. If the student understands what the possible structures are in a piece of writing, he/she will be more skilled at comprehending what is being said.

Questioning is a powerful tool for developing reading comprehension skills. Asking questions before, during and after reading gives a goal to the reading process, helps students recognize what they do and do not know and engages the mind in higher-order thinking about a topic.

Further, different types of questions lead to different points of focus. Questions seeking factual information guide the student to read the text with an eye towards plucking certain facts out of the content. Generalized questions seeking inferential connections encourage students to seek broader meaning from the text than simply what is read.

Other question types include questions that elicit remembering, check for understanding, encourage application of information, and evaluate the quality of text.

The **main idea** of a passage or paragraph is the basic message, idea, point concept, or meaning that the author wants to convey to you, the reader. Understanding the main idea of a passage or paragraph is the key to understanding the more subtle components of the author's message. The main idea is what is being said about a topic or subject. Once you have identified the basic message, you will have an easier time answering other questions that test critical skills.

Main ideas are either *stated* or *implied*. A *stated main idea* is explicit: it is directly expressed in a sentence or two in the paragraph or passage. An *implied main idea* is suggested by the overall reading selection. In the first case, you need not pull information from various points in the paragraph or passage in order to form the main idea because it is already stated by the author. If a main idea is implied, however, you must formulate, in your own words, a main idea statement by condensing the overall message contained in the material itself.

Sample Activity: Read the following passage and select an answer

Sometimes too much of a good thing can become a very bad thing indeed. In an earnest attempt to consume a healthy diet, dietary supplement enthusiasts have been known to overdose. Vitamin C, for example, long thought to help people ward off cold viruses, is currently being studied for its possible role in warding off cancer and other disease that causes tissue degeneration. Unfortunately, an overdose of vitamin C – more than 10,000 mg – on a daily basis can cause nausea and diarrhea. Calcium supplements, commonly taken by women, are helpful in warding off osteoporosis. More than just a few grams a day, however, can lead to stomach upset and even kidney and bladder stones. Niacin, proven useful in reducing cholesterol levels, can be dangerous in large doses to those who suffer from heart problems, asthma or ulcers.

The main idea expressed in this paragraph is:

    A.   supplements taken in excess can be a bad thing indeed
    B.   dietary supplement enthusiasts have been known to overdose
    C.   vitamins can cause nausea, diarrhea, and kidney or bladder stones.
    D.   people who take supplements are preoccupied with their health.

Answer: Answer A is a paraphrase of the first sentence and provides a general framework for the rest of the paragraph: excess supplement intake is bad. The rest of the paragraph discusses the consequences of taking too many vitamins. Options B and C refer to major details, and Option D introduces the idea of preoccupation, which is not included in this paragraph.

Supporting details are examples, facts, ideas, illustrations, cases and anecdotes used by a writer to explain, expand on, and develop the more general main idea. A writer's choice of supporting materials is determined by the nature of the topic being covered. Supporting details are specifics that relate directly to the main idea. Writers select and shape material according to their purposes. An advertisement writer seeking to persuade the reader to buy a particular running shoe, for instance, will emphasize only the positive characteristics of the shoe for advertisement copy. A columnist for a running magazine, on the other hand, might list the good and bad points about the same shoe in an article recommending appropriate shoes for different kinds of runners. Both major details (those that directly support the main idea), and minor details (those that provide interesting, but not always essential, information) help create a well-written and fluid passage.

In the following paragraph, the sentences in **bold print** provide a skeleton of a paragraph on the benefits of recycling. The sentences in bold are generalizations that by themselves do not explain the need to recycle. The sentences in *italics* add details to SHOW the general points in bold. Notice how the supporting details help you understand the necessity for recycling.

While one day recycling may become mandatory in all states, right now it is voluntary in many communities. *Those of us who participate in recycling are amazed by how much material is recycled.* **For many communities, the blue-box recycling program has had an immediate effect.** *By just recycling glass, aluminum cans, and plastic bottles, we have reduced the volume of disposable trash by one third, thus extending the useful life of local landfills by over a decade. Imagine the difference if those dramatic results were achieved nationwide.* **The amount of reusable items we thoughtlessly dispose of is staggering.** *For example, Americans dispose of enough steel every day to supply Detroit car manufacturers for three months. Additionally, we dispose of enough aluminum annually to rebuild the nation's air fleet. These statistics, available from the Environmental Protection Agency (EPA), should encourage all of us to watch what we throw away.* **Clearly, recycling in our homes and in our communities directly improves the environment.**

Notice how the author's supporting examples enhance the message of the paragraph and relate to the author's thesis noted above. If you only read the bold-face sentences, you have a glimpse at the topic. This paragraph of illustration, however, is developed through numerous details creating specific images: *reduced the volume of disposable trash by one-third; extended the useful life of local landfills by over a decade; enough steel every day to supply Detroit car manufacturers for three months; enough aluminum to rebuild the nation's air fleet.* If the writer had merely written a few general sentences, as those shown in bold face, you would not fully understand the vast amount of trash involved in recycling or the positive results of current recycling efforts.

Skill 5.3 **Demonstrate knowledge of inferential comprehension skills (e.g., ability to draw conclusions or make generalizations from a text and to infer ideas and relationships that are not explicitly stated in a text)**

An **inference** is sometimes called an "educated guess" because it requires that you go beyond the strictly obvious to create additional meaning by taking the text one logical step further. Inferences and conclusions are based on the content of the passage – that is, on what the passage says or how the writer says it – and are derived by reasoning.

Inference is an essential and automatic component of most reading. For example, in making educated guesses about the meaning of unknown words, the author's main idea or whether he or she is writing with a bias. Such is the essence of inference: you use your own ability to reason in order to figure out what the writer implies. As a reader, then, you must often logically extend meaning that is only implied.

Consider the following example. Assume you are an employer, and you are reading over the letters of reference submitted by a prospective employee for the position of clerk/typist in your real estate office. The position requires the applicant to be neat, careful, trustworthy, and punctual. You come across this letter of reference submitted by an applicant:

To whom it may concern,

   Todd Finley has asked me to write a letter of reference for him. I am well qualified to do so because he worked for me for three months last year. His duties included answering the phone, greeting the public, and producing some simple memos and notices on the computer. Although Todd initially had few computer skills and little knowledge of telephone etiquette, he did acquire some during his stay with us. Todd's manner of speaking, both on the telephone and with the clients who came to my establishment, could be described as casual. He was particularly effective when communicating with peers. Please contact me by telephone if you wish to have further information about my experience.

Here the writer implies, rather than openly states, the main idea. This letter calls attention to itself because there's a problem with its tone. A truly positive letter would say something like "I have distinct honor to recommend Todd Finley." Here, however, the letter simply verifies that Todd worked in the office. Second, the praise is obviously lukewarm. For example, the writer says that Todd "was particularly effective when communicating with peers." An educated guess translates that statement into a nice way of saying Todd was not serious about his communication with clients.

In order to draw **inferences** and make **conclusions**, a reader must use prior knowledge and apply it to the current situation. A conclusion or inference is never stated. You must rely on your common sense.

Practice Activity: Read the following passages and select an answer

1.   The Smith family waited patiently at carousel number 7 for their luggage to arrive. They were exhausted after their five-hour trip and were anxious to get to their hotel. After about an hour, they realized that they no longer recognized any of the other passengers' faces. Mrs. Smith asked the person who appeared to be in charge if they were at the right carousel. The man replied, "Yes, this is it, but we finished unloading that baggage almost half an hour ago."

     From the man's response we can infer that:
     (A) The Smiths were ready to go to their hotel.
     (B) The Smith's luggage was lost.
     (C) The man had their luggage.
     (D) They were at the wrong carousel.

2.   Tim Sullivan had just turned 15. As a birthday present, his parents had given him a guitar and a certificate for 10 guitar lessons. He had always shown a love of music and a desire to learn an instrument. Tim began his lessons and before long, he was making up his own songs. At the music studio, Tim met Josh, who played the piano, and Roger, whose instrument was the saxophone. They all shared the same dream—to start a band— and each was praised by his teacher for having real talent.

     From this passage one can infer that
     (A) Tim, Roger & Josh are going to start their own band.
     (B) Tim is going to give up his guitar lessons.
     (C) Tim, Josh & Roger will no longer be friends.
     (D) Josh & Roger are going to start their own band.

Answers:

1. Since the Smiths were still waiting for their luggage, we know that they were not yet ready to go to their hotel. From the man's response, we know that they were not at the wrong carousel and that he did not have their luggage. Therefore, though not directly stated, it appears that their luggage was lost. Choice (B) is the correct answer.

2. (A) is the correct choice. Given the facts that Tim wanted to be a musician and start his own band, after meeting others who shared the same dreams, we can infer that they joined together in an attempt to make their dreams become a reality.

Skill 5.4 **Demonstrate knowledge of how to read a text with rhythm, meter, intonation, and overall fluency that is characteristic of everyday speech and appropriate to meaning**

Written language is meant to signify spoken language, and punctuation is what tells readers when to pause, what to emphasize, and how to express the various points. Like musical notation, punctuation signals the reader when to slow down, when to stop momentarily, and when to attach more emotional emphasis to the spoken expression of written statements.

It may be helpful for teachers to give explicit instructions to students on how to read expressively. For example, the teacher could suggest to students that they should pause for one beat or second with each comma, and for two beats or seconds with each semicolon, colon, or period.

Question marks and exclamation points call for special **inflection**, which is when the voice rises in either volume or pitch. In spoken language, a voice naturally rises at the end of a sentence that is a question; this is what should happen when a student reads a written question, as well. An exclamation point, as its name suggests, is used when someone wants to exclaim something. Hence, a reader's voice should become louder and more emphatic when reading a sentence that ends with an exclamation point.

Good readers will not speak in a **monotone**, which is when all of the words are spoken with the same level of pitch and intensity. This is boring, loses the listener's interest, and is not reflective of the intended content of most written works. (An exception could be informational texts, which are merely meant to inform rather than to persuade or evoke emotions. Even then, varied speech patterns will more appropriately express meaning.)

Intonation is the variation of tone used when speaking. Generally speaking, intonation should naturally rise and fall in normal conversation, with a rhythm that is even and balanced. Vocal variety involves using the voice to create interest and emotional involvement. This is accomplished by varying pitch, volume, and timing.

By changing inflection and intonation, you change meaning. For example, consider the following sentence and how its meaning can change by using inflection (raised pitch and volume) on certain words:

I was captain of the tennis team. (Me, not someone else)
I **was** captain of the tennis team. (I used to be captain, but then something happened.)
I was captain of the **tennis** team. (Not the golf or swim team)

When students read from a written work, their voices should convey the natural rhythm of speech, which has an up-down quality that engages and holds a listener's attention. Pitch refers to the highness or lowness in the sound of a voice. The best **pitch** is in the middle, with a range that heads higher or lower at certain points for special emphasis. When reading aloud, many students will also have to be reminded to speak clearly and at an audible level, above a whisper.

Pace is important. Many students will become nervous when reading aloud and will need to be reminded to speak at a normal speaking speed (between 120-160 words a minute.) This means reading quickly enough to maintain interest and slowly enough to be understandable, neither racing nor trudging.

Another important part of proper reading is clear **articulation**. This means that students will clearly include all of the sounds in each word, so that they may be properly heard and understood. Rushing and skipping sounds will make words sound slurred, thereby confusing meaning and limiting comprehension.

COMPETENCY 6.0   UNDERSTAND STRATEGIES FOR PROMOTING STUDENTS' INDEPENDENT READING IN MULTIPLE SUBJECT AREAS

Skill 6.1   Demonstrate knowledge of strategies for expanding students' experiences with diverse texts (e.g., historical, mathematical, scientific, journalistic, literary) and encouraging students to be lifelong learners

Tips to Encourage Independent Reading for Pleasure

Remember that books won't work by themselves. As a teacher, you have to make sure books are read by setting aside time regularly for reading. For example:

Have a DEAR period - Drop Everything and Read:
Everyone can participate in a DEAR period and read for 15 minutes. This often works well right at the beginning of the school day, every day.

SSR period: Sustained silent reading:
Have everyone choose a book and read without interruption for 20 to 30 minutes. Ideally this should take place daily but even twice a week will show results.

Independent reading sessions:
Set aside one day a week for learners to select new books, read independently or in pairs, and have time to respond to the books they have read. This should take place weekly. Break time, after school and free periods are good opportunities to read.

Read with children:
Taking books home is a very good option as learners can read to and with other family members. Even if children can read alone, they will still benefit from being read to.

Encourage reading of any suitable and relevant written material if books are not accessible. Try newspaper or magazine articles; street signs; food packaging labels; posters, etc. Anything can be used, provided it is at the correct level.

Encourage readers to make their own material and/or bring additional material to school for to read. Having books in a classroom is one of the easiest and most effective ways of increasing reading, linguistic and cognitive development. No other single variable can be shown to carry the same significance.

Once regular reading habits have been established, independent reading should be encouraged. Reading independently:

- Allows a learner to read, re-read and engage with a text at their own pace
- Allows learners to choose what they want to read about and so motivates them to read
- Impacts on language development in the areas of vocabulary and syntax
- Impacts on knowledge of sight words and phonics
- Is important for second language learners as it provides a wealth of real language input

Reading for pleasure should be encouraged synonymously with teaching reading and basic literacy. Reading for pleasure is therapeutic and enlightening, and paves the way for developing a culture of reading and of life-long learning.

Ideas for Interdisciplinary Classroom Activities:

- Have students produce a newspaper that incorporates many different subject areas (sports, weather, crossword puzzles, books reviews, pictures, poetry, advertisements, etc.).
- Connect each student with an "adoptive grandparent" at a nearby nursing home. Have students write their "grandparent" letters and stories, make timelines of their lives, and learn about life during the time period they grew up in.
- Have students create a Power Point presentation on a career they are interested in pursuing. Research pros and cons, salary information, skills necessary for the job, etc.
- Using a book the class as a whole is reading, have students pick out any words they are unfamiliar with. Research the origin of those words, their definitions, and then have them write a creative story using each word.

Skill 6.2   Identify appropriate methods for determining students' reading interests and helping students develop selection criteria for independent learning

Materials and activities that correspond to high levels of student interest will motivate students to immerse themselves in the lesson, thus opening the door for the application and reception of effective teaching strategies. Likewise, connecting a lesson to a student's knowledge base, life experience and cultural history provides a foundation of familiarity that allow the student to explore higher order concepts without feeling alienated from the material.

Technology is, of course, a key factor in modern society – especially adolescent culture – and must be incorporated into students' learning experiences. Email and internet-based activities (such as keyword searches for information) provide students with a variety of communication experiences by connecting them with peers, conveying and interpreting messages, obtaining, evaluating, and processing information from experts, preparing documents, and managing and using information responsibly.

The multimedia nature of technological tools, such as Microsoft Word and Power Point, allows for creative and practical dissemination of information that not only sparks student interest, but also covers the spectrum of individual learning styles by smoothly incorporating reading comprehension best practices, such as visual cues and graphic organizers, with the core text. The flexible nature of digital media allows the teacher to customize and share the same lesson material from class to class to reflect different needs of the students.

Recognize the roles of motivation and interest in reading.

George G. Spache; H. Alan Robinson; Edward B. Fry; Richard T. Vacca; Strang, McCullough, and Traxlor; and Delores Durkin are a select group of authors who provide the classroom teacher with concrete examples of how to provide insight into a student's reading style, skill development, interest, and other pertinent information regarding the individual student's needs. All this information will serve the classroom teacher in providing a challenging reading program for all.

These texts will assist the teacher with the following:

- Provide appropriate material to meet the need of the student for instruction, enrichment, or remediation
- Provide student-directed or teacher-directed activities in reading literature and content area curriculum texts.
- Provide resources and lessons that can provide a challenging opportunity for students to seek information from a wide variety of sources, such as television and computers.
- Provide suggestions and make recommendations that will foster a lifetime habit of seeking pleasure and knowledge from the printed word into the student.
- Provide the teacher an avenue of referral for students who are experiencing reading/learning disabilities and cannot have their needs met in the regular classroom setting.
- The inclusion of guidance counselors, speech pathologists, and school psychologists in a team approach are available in almost every school.

Recognizing the relationships of reading to writing, listening, and speaking

The last twenty years have seen great change in instruction in the English classroom. Gone are the days when literature is taught on Monday, Wednesday is grammar day and Friday you assign writing. Integrating reading, writing, speaking, listening and viewing allow students to make connections between each aspect of language development during each class.

Suggestions for Integrating Language Arts

- Use pre-reading activities such as discussion, writing, research, and journals. Use writing to tap into prior knowledge before students read; engage students in class discussions about themes, issues, and ideas explored in journals, predicting the outcome and exploring related information.
- Use prewriting activities such as reading model essays, researching, interviewing others, combining sentences and other prewriting activities. Remember that developing language proficiency is a recursive process and involves practice in reading, writing, thinking, speaking, listening and viewing.
- Create writing activities that are relevant to students by having them write and share with real audiences.
- Connect correctness - including developing skills of conventional usage, spelling, grammar, and punctuation - to the revision and editing stage of writing. Review of mechanics and punctuation can be done with mini-lessons that use sentences from student papers, sentence combining strategies, and modeling passages of skilled writers.
- Connect reading, writing, listening, speaking, and viewing by using literature read as a springboard for a variety of activities.

In middle school, the emphasis on reading instruction spans the range of comprehension skills - literal, inferential, and critical. Most instruction in grades five and six is based on the skills delineated in basal readers adopted for those grade levels. Reading instruction in grades seven through nine is usually part of the general language arts class instead of being a distinct subject in the curriculum, unless the instruction is remedial. Reading in tenth through twelfth grades is part of the literature curriculum - World, American, and British.

Reading emphasis in middle school

Reading for comprehension of factual material - content area textbooks, reference books, and newspapers - is closely related to study strategies in the middle/junior high. Organized study models, such as the SQ3R method, a technique that makes it possible and feasible to learn the content of even large amounts of text (Survey, Question, Read, Recite, and Review Studying), teach students to locate main ideas and supporting details, to recognize sequential order, to distinguish fact from opinion, and to determine cause/ effect relationships.

Strategies

1. Teacher-guided activities that require students to organize and to summarize information based on the author's explicit intent are pertinent strategies in middle grades. Evaluation techniques include oral and written responses to standardized or teacher-made worksheets.

2. Reading of fiction introduces and reinforces skills in inferring meaning from narration and description. Teaching-guided activities in the process of reading for meaning should be followed by cooperative planning of the skills to be studied and of the selection of reading resources. Many printed reading for comprehension instruments as well as individualized computer software programs exist to monitor the progress of acquiring comprehension skills.

3. Older middle-school students should be given opportunities for more student-centered activities - individual and collaborative selection of reading choices based on student interest, small group discussions of selected works, and greater written expression. Evaluation techniques include teacher monitoring and observation of discussions and written work samples.

4. Certain students may begin some fundamental critical interpretation - recognizing fallacious reasoning in news media, examining the accuracy of news reports and advertising, explaining their reasons for preferring one author's writing to another's. Development of these skills may require a more learning-centered approach in which the teacher identifies a number of objectives and suggested resources from which the student may choose his course of study. Self-evaluation through a reading diary should be stressed. Teacher and peer evaluation of creative projects resulting from such study is encouraged.

5. Reading aloud before the entire class as a formal means of teacher evaluation should be phased out in favor of one-to-one tutoring or peer-assisted reading. Occasional sharing of favored selections by both teacher and willing students is a good oral interpretation basic.

Skill 6.3   **Identify strategies for selecting and organizing a range of reading materials (e.g., fiction, nonfiction, drama, reference) at various levels of difficulty for all students**

Teachers should select a variety of texts to give students a broad experience in the reading process. Exposure to both narrative and expository texts allows them to build and expand their knowledge base, identify and distinguish genres, learn how different texts are structured, and experience a variety of authors' writing styles, ideas and language usage across eras.

Fiction: Students should read an assortment of fiction works to provide opportunity to learn about character and plot development in the various genres, the role of setting and dialog, themes and narrative story structure, as well as the ability to define and identify elements of fiction (e.g., tone, mood, foreshadowing, irony, symbolism). Types of texts to be included in the reading curriculum are folktales, myths, legends, short stories, mysteries, historical fiction, science fiction, plays and general-interest novels.

Nonfiction: Appropriate selection of nonfiction materials provides the opportunity to practice and reinforce the complex reading comprehension skills necessary to succeed across the curriculum. Topics should contain a high level of detail, covering diverse topics that encourage active discussion, questioning, synthesizing and evaluation of the information presented. Readers should be exposed to complex content structures and be required to apply critical reading skills to evaluate the quality of information. Text selection should include textbooks, autobiographies/biographies, informational books, websites, newspapers, magazines, encyclopedias, and brochures.

Materials selection should take several factors into consideration. Reading curriculum should consist of literary and non-literary texts in a variety of formats and include selections from the science, history, and social sciences areas.

Texts should be grade-level appropriate, where approximately 75% of the words are decodable, with appropriately challenging English words. Illustrations and photographs should enhance and clarify the meaning of the text, and expository materials should use graphical organizers (or provide supplemental materials that do) when content is complex. The length of text should be both grade-appropriate (i.e., manageable by students within the given time frame) and lesson-appropriate (e.g., if reading and discussing a poem in class, make sure the poem is an appropriate length to allow time for clarification, questioning, interpretation, and discussion).

COMPETENCY 7.0 UNDERSTAND READING FOR INFORMATION IN MULTIPLE SUBJECT AREAS

Skill 7.1 **Analyze recurrent ideas, messages, or themes across a variety of texts and disciplines**

It's human nature to compare objects, ideas, and even people and look for commonalities. We can't take our eyes off of someone who reminds us of a lost love, for example. This naturally occurring phenomenon can be very useful in literary analysis. For example, in *The Five People You Meet in Heaven,* Mitch Albom's theme of giving one's life to save another calls to mind the biblical teaching that the greatest love is to give up one's life for a friend. This is called a biblical allusion. The same theme can be found in newspapers as well. For example, a man in New York City risked his life to rescue a homeless man from the wheels of a train. Stories of animals that show extraordinary bravery to save their masters or mistresses are very popular.

War is a very popular theme for literature of all kinds. For example, Ernest Hemingway's novels based on his experience in the Spanish Civil War make familiar and poignant statements about the effects of war. Much poetry has been written about this theme: "Johnny, I Hardly Know Ye," an anonymous eighteenth-century Irish ballad; Wilfred Owen's World War I poem, "Dulce et Decorum Est," and Richard Lovelace's seventeenth-century "To Lucasta," for example. Comparing the treatment of such a common theme and its treatment by different writers adds depth and interest to an interpretation of a literary work. One's own experience is useful in interpreting war literature. Few of us have had the privilege of living our lives out without experiencing our country at war and of seeing its destructive effects on human beings.

In analyzing literature and in looking for ways to bring a work to life for an audience, the use of comparable themes, ideas, etc., from other pieces of literature and from one's own life experiences, including the daily newspaper, is very important and useful.

Skill 7.2 **Demonstrate the ability to use features of texts from a range of disciplines (e.g., tables, charts, graphs, maps, photographs, illustrations)**

See Skill 3.7.

Skill 7.3   Demonstrate knowledge of methods for locating, gathering, interpreting, synthesizing, and evaluating information from a variety of printed texts and electronic sources

Searching for information from printed and electronic sources is a critical literacy-related activity. Increasingly, teachers realize that it is impossible to memorize or even be exposed to the majority of basic facts in our world today. Information is produced so rapidly that knowing how to access, judge, and synthesize it will help students throughout their lives.

To understand what this standard means, let's examine it in detail. First, gathering information requires that students are competent with everything from a traditional library catalog system to web-based collections. The best way to get students to feel comfortable with these sources of information is simply to have to search for specific items with proper teacher guidance. It is usually not a good idea to set students out on a journey for information without first explaining the tools and modeling how information can be found from them.

One of the most important parts of gathering information is judging sources. One simple cause of the rapid increase in information is that it is easier now than it has ever been for anyone to provide information to the public. For example, anyone can post wikis, blogs, and websites. Print material is no safer: more journals and magazines are published today and many have very uncertain records of reliability. While even the best teacher can fall prey to bad sources of information, generally experienced adult readers will know when quality is not sufficient. A good way to teach students how to evaluate the quality of an information source is to model how decisions are made in the judging process. For example, a teacher can show students a variety of websites on a particular topic. While showing students these sites, the teacher can do a "think aloud," whereby she expresses her opinions about the ways in which the information presented demonstrates quality or a lack thereof.

Interpreting information from a variety of sources can be challenging, as well. Many students who have experienced little non-fiction will tend to view information sources in much the same way they view their textbooks: objective and straightforward. Experienced readers will note that information sources are often opinionated, embedded in other ideas or works, part of a greater dialogue, or highly slanted. Often, the sources found are not necessarily meant for extraction of ideas from students; rather, intended audiences vary incredibly for each work. Even though we may have access to quite a bit, we may not be the anticipated audience of the writer.

To teach students how to interpret non-fiction sources, have them focus on these components of the work:

- **Purpose**—the author's intended purpose in writing the piece

- **Audience**—the author's intended audience (for example, an article about a scientific phenomenon could be written for other scientists, the general public, a source of funding for an experiment, etc.)

- **Argument**—it is important for students to determine if the author has an argument and what that argument is. All the information in the piece will make better sense when this is figured out.

Finally, synthesizing information is a complex task. When multiple sources regarding the same concept are used, students can outline the main points of each source and look at how the pieces differ. Students can also trace similar ideas through each of the pieces to see how authors treat subjects differently or similarly. Graphic organizers can be very helpful in the synthesis of a variety of sources.

Skill 7.4 Recognize an author's purpose for writing and how to vary reading strategies (e.g., skimming, scanning, rereading) for different purposes and texts

When reading a piece of writing for comprehension, it's useful to determine first of all just exactly what its purpose is. Was it written to persuade the reader to a point of view or to get a reader to take some action? Was it written simply to communicate information such as a news feature on a local institution? A college catalog may include some parts that encourage students to enroll and attend; however, for the most part, college catalogs are written to inform. A piece of writing might be intended simply to communicate an experience the writer has had in such a way that the reader might also experience it, such as the destructive force of a flood. This is called descriptive writing. Another possibility is that the piece of writing is intended simply to tell a story—a this-happened, and this-happened, and this-happened sort of approach.

Persuasive writing will have a thesis, either stated or implied, so it's good to look first for that. What does this writer want me to believe or do? Once that has been determined, the supporting reasons should be isolated and examined. Are they adequate to persuade? Can this reasoning be accepted or is it flawed or fallacious? Can this writer be trusted to write objectively about this topic or is there bias? Is this writer knowledgeable enough to write reliably about this topic? These questions can only be answered reliably after carefully picking out the reasons the writer gives for your accepting his/her point of view or advice.

In understanding an informative piece of writing—one whose purpose is not to persuade but simply to give information—it's important to determine what the outline of the piece of writing is. Is the information presented spatially, chronologically, or visually? What are the steps in the information-giving process? Are they in logical order? Are they understandable enough that you could explain it to another person?

In reading descriptive writing, the questions to ask are whether you can experience what the writer is attempting to share with you. Can you see what he/she is describing, can you hear it, can you smell it, etc.? Are the descriptions complete enough for comprehension and reaction? A good example of effective and powerful descriptive writing is Wilfred Owen's poem *Dulce et Decorum Est.* Read some of the lines:

> Bent double, like old beggars under sacks,
> Knock-kneed, coughing like hags, we cursed through sludge,
> Till on the haunting flares we turned our backs
> And towards our distant rest began to trudge.
> Men marched asleep. Many had lost their boots
> But limped on, blood-shod. All went lame; all blind;
> Drunk with fatigue; deaf even to the hoots
> Of tired, outstripped Five-Nines (gas shells) that dropped behind.

Someone has said, "War is hell," but this poem lets us see and feel how bad it truly is for those who experience it firsthand, which is the purpose of descriptive language.

In reading a narrative, the questions to ask are whether the incidents lead to a resolution. What is the purpose of the story? What is the meaning? Why did the writer write it?

The question to be asked first when approaching a reading task is: What is my objective? What do I want to achieve from this reading? How will I use the information I gain from this reading? Do I only need to grasp the gist of the piece? Do I need to know the line of reasoning—not only the thesis but also the subpoints? Will I be reporting important and significant details orally or in a written document?

A written document can be expected to have a thesis—either expressed or derived. To discover the thesis, the reader needs to ask what point the writer intended to make. The writing can also be expected to be organized in some logical way and to have subpoints that support or establish that the thesis is valid. It is also reasonable to expect that there will be details or examples that will support the subpoints. Knowing this, the reader can make a decision about reading techniques required for the purpose that has already been established. If the reader only needs to know the gist of a written document, speed-reading skimming techniques may be sufficient by using the forefinger, moving the eyes down the page, picking up the important statements in each paragraph and deducing mentally that this piece is about such-and-such. If the reader needs to a little better grasp of how the writer achieved his/her purpose in the document, a quick and cursory glance — a skimming — of each paragraph will yield what the subpoints are, the topic sentences of the paragraphs, and the manner in which the thesis is developed, yielding a greater understanding of the author's purpose and method of development.

In-depth reading requires the scrutiny of each phrase and sentence with care, looking for the thesis first of all and then the topic sentences in the paragraphs that provide the development of the thesis, also looking for connections such as transitional devices that provide clues to the direction the reasoning is taking.

Sometimes rereading is necessary in order to make use of a piece of writing for an oral or written report upon a document. If this is the purpose of reading it, the first reading should provide a map for the rereading or second reading. The second time through should follow this map and those points that are going to be used in a report or analysis will be focused upon on more carefully. Some new understandings may occur in this rereading and it may become apparent that the "map" that was derived from the first reading will need to be adjusted. If this rereading is for the purpose of writing an analysis or using material for a report, either highlighting or note taking is advisable.

COMPETENCY 8.0   UNDERSTAND READING TO EXPAND CONTENT VOCABULARY AND MODES OF DISCOURSE ACROSS SUBJECT AREAS

Skill 8.1   Identify instructional strategies and activities that integrate content vocabulary from other disciplines in order to expand students' abilities to respond to new words through the use of context clues and idioms

Whenever possible, teachers should use vocabulary that is relevant to their students' lives; this includes using vocabulary from other coursework they are taking. It makes sense to increase students' knowledge of the English language by reinforcing the new vocabulary they will encounter in their classes, where they will see it applied and used in their daily school lives.

Students will learn new vocabulary words most easily when they can place them in a context. Context means placing the words in the setting in which they belong, to show the relationship of the words to surrounding elements. This helps students begin to see the connections between the words and the subject, and between similar words. This is more effective than giving students lists of random words, taken out of context, which students are unlikely to encounter in their daily activities.

Good vocabulary lists should have a theme behind them; they should be related in some way. The hardest vocabulary list to remember is one in which each word has no clear relationship to the next. Therefore, it is more helpful to have lists of words that cohere than long lists of random unrelated words.

For example, one vocabulary list could include words borrowed from another language that have made their way into common English usage; another list could include words a students is likely to encounter in science class; and a third list could include words pertaining to the study of music. Note that words that begin in one academic discipline often come to have broader meanings that can apply in general use.

If teachers use other subjects as themes for vocabulary list creation, this will help students to see how different fields share a common language or jargon. One of the first ways to acquire expertise in a subject area is to begin speaking the language—using the terminology common to the field. Also, students may begin to notice common roots in words drawn from similar fields. Teachers may need to point these out to help students recognize them. For example, many words in music class share Italian roots, whereas science words often derive from Greek or Latin roots. It is also helpful to share the etymology of the words, which is the word's origin and history.

The incorporation of subject-specific vocabulary provides teachers with the opportunity to foster interdisciplinary learning. This means learning that is carried from one course to the next. English teachers could begin by asking other subject matter teachers to share some of their textbooks and to search them for appropriate vocabulary. Also, ask other teachers which vocabulary words are difficult for students. These words may require special emphasis and reinforcement. Making this effort supports the other teachers and promotes interdisciplinary understanding while building the students' vocabularies.

A <u>foreign language</u> course may be a good source of new vocabulary lists. It will be helpful if the teacher will limit each list to one language, to avoid confusion. Many words from other languages have found their way into common spoken English; being able to recognize them in reading and using them in conversation (and understanding them when others use them) marks an individual as well-educated and worldly. Teachers will also want to explore the options for vocabulary in students' core courses of <u>science</u>, <u>math</u>, and <u>history</u>. By explicitly relating these words back to their sources, students can understand the origins of the words they are learning; this knowledge aids comprehension and memory.

English teachers will want to stay away from highly specific and technical jargon and narrow course terminology and stick with words and phrases that have found their way into common usage in the English language.

Teachers should be alert for appropriate idioms to include on vocabulary lists, as well. Idioms are groups of words that cannot be understood from the literal definitions of each of the words, and as such often cause considerable confusion. They are sometimes referred to as, "figures of speech" which gain their meaning through conventional use. Phrases like "kick the bucket" or "pull someone's leg" are idiomatic expressions.

Teachers will also want to point out to students how context clues can be used to help figure out the meanings of unfamiliar words. Context clues come from the surrounding text and other information surrounding the new word that can be used to guess at the correct meaning of the word. The number of helpful context clues will increase when vocabulary lists share a common theme or background.

Skill 8.2 **Recognize the relationships of certain words and concepts from one discipline to another and how similes, metaphors, and analogies can be used to compare ideas across disciplines**

It's easy for teachers and students to fall into the attitude that the study of literature and writing is confined to the English classroom and curriculum, but nothing could be further from the truth. When teachers in English classes work with teachers of history, sociology, psychology or even science, student skills can make leaps. To use Steinbeck's *Grapes of Wrath* as an example once again, if English teacher and social-studies teacher cooperate in helping students see that literature is real and emerges out of human experience, students will begin to write papers of a different quality. American people and politicians used many of the same themes that Steinbeck used in his book during the run up to the election in 1932 to defeat President Hoover and elect President Roosevelt. Understanding the history and geography of the Dust Bowl, states such as Oklahoma, and westward migration dating from the time of the Louisiana Purchase, is very useful in reading this piece of literature with greater depth and understanding.

Identifying similes, metaphors, and analogies in a piece of writing is made easier by relating it to other subject areas such as history and geography. The title of the novel *Grapes of Wrath* is an allusion to a popular and well-known hymn, *Battle Hymn of the Republic*, and introduces Steinbeck's theme of injustice for the downtrodden. The hymn suggests that God will rid the world of that kind of injustice:

> *Mine eyes have seen the glory of the coming of the Lord:*
> *He is trampling out the vintage where the **grapes of wrath** are stored;*
> *He hath loosed the fateful lightning of His terrible swift sword:*
> *His truth is marching on*

Teaching literary analysis, particularly taking students to the point where they can see such things as metaphors, allusions, etc., is a slow and difficult process. Using across-the-curriculum tools increases student growth in this area.

Skill 8.3   Recognize how unfamiliar messages and themes from any discipline may be explored and better understood by relating them to familiar messages and themes from prior learning or personal experience

Jean Piaget's theory of cognitive development suggests that children can be aided in learning by what he called **scaffolding,** which involves presenting new information by building upon previously acquired knowledge. This means that teachers link new information to old, familiar information to help students see connections. Students learn by connecting something new to something they already know very well. Learning is all about forming these connections.

In the beginning of a new course or school year, new information may all seem to be unrelated and unfamiliar to students. In a literature class, each new story or novel may at first seem completely new. When students are young, everything they learn in school seems separate and unrelated. As students grow and their frame of reference expands, they begin to see that many things that may have seemed new in the past are merely variations on a theme.

A **theme** is an idea or motif that recurs. For example, movies often have theme music which is replayed whenever a certain character appears. English teachers should remain alert for examples of universal themes in course literature such as "good versus evil" "betrayal," "redemption," "courage," and "boy gets girl" and point these out to students. These basic stories are played out again and again in human experience and history and throughout literature and art.

By helping students to begin to recognize these universal themes, teachers facilitate and simplify understanding. Suddenly, what seemed new becomes familiar and relatable. This recognition provides scaffolding to help students move to higher levels of recognition and understanding. This knowledge also provides a shortcut for understanding and interpreting new works. Most every experience in the human condition has been written about in literature. Students, who have a small frame of reference, may need help understanding that what they see happening around them is often similar to things that have happened before and to things that have been written about in the past.

Many common themes that occur in literature can be related to real stories and events from history or social studies, thus fostering interdisciplinary understanding. The same themes that emerge in literature also often emerge in art and music, giving expression to the familiar range of human emotion. Many famous artworks depict the themes from literary works. Even in science or mathematics, the same types of problems that have plagued earlier scientists are revisited with new generations, and old methods of problem-solving are reapplied, extending a theme.

Student learning will proceed more rapidly when they begin to recognize that not everything has to be learned completely new, from scratch; rather, many learning experiences are merely variations on a theme which is already familiar.

An example of how the study of a theme could be employed in an English class could begin with the "Cinderella" story, which has reappeared in countless forms, both in literature and in movies. Students could be prompted to discuss the many ways in which this same, basic story has been retold in different settings during different time periods, yet the central story remains the same.

Other resources with very familiar stories that have become thematic include the Bible, ancient myths and fables, and children's stories—especially fairy tales. The universality of these stories shows that humankind shares the same stories over and over again with each generation. Real events can also have themes; history is filled with stories of leaders making the same, predictable mistakes over and over again. These can be considered thematic.

Teachers can begin pointing out similarities between familiar messages and themes in different stories or disciplines and then ask students to draw comparisons between different works with similar themes. This is an excellent topic for an essay; papers or classwork can be assigned asking students to list comparisons between two similar works or historical events. Teachers may have to point out connections that are not obvious to students, depending on their age or level of experience.

COMPETENCY 9.0   UNDERSTAND READING TO DEVELOP SKILLS OF CRITICAL ANALYSIS AND EVALUATION AND TO FORM PERSONAL RESPONSES

Skill 9.1   **Evaluate the relevance, importance, and sufficiency of facts or examples provided to support an argument presented in a text**

It is important to continually assess whether or not a sentence contributes to the overall task of supporting the main idea. When a sentence is deemed irrelevant it is best to either omit it from the passage or to make it relevant by one of the following strategies:

1. Adding detail – Sometimes a sentence can seem out of place if it does not contain enough information to link it to the topic. Adding specific information can show how the sentence is related to the main idea.

2. Adding an example – This is especially important in passages in which information is being argued or compared or contrasted. Examples can support the main idea and give the document overall credibility.

3. Using diction effectively – It is important to understand connotation, avoid ambiguity, and steer clear of too much repetition when selecting words.

4. Adding transitions – Transitions are extremely helpful for making sentences relevant because they are specifically designed to connect one idea to another. They can also reduce a paragraph's choppiness.

Skill 9.2   **Asses the credibility or objectivity of information and arguments presented in a text, including distinguishing fact from opinion**

An argument is a generalization that is proven or supported with facts. If the facts are not accurate, the generalization remains unproven. Using inaccurate "facts" to support an argument is called a *fallacy* in reasoning. Some factors to consider in judging whether the facts used to support an argument are accurate are as follow:

1. Are the facts current or are they out of date? For example, if the proposition is that "birth defects in babies born to drug-using mothers are increasing," then the data must be the most recent available.
2. Another important factor to consider in judging the accuracy of a fact is its source. Where was the data obtained and is that source reliable?
3. The calculations on which the facts are based may be unreliable. It's a good idea to run one's own calculations before using a piece of derived information.

Even facts that are true and have a sharp impact on the argument may not be relevant to the case at hand.

1. Health statistics from an entire state may have little or no relevance to a particular county or zip code. Statistics from an entire country cannot be used to prove very much about a particular state or county.
2. An analogy can be useful in making a point, but the comparison must match up in all characteristics or it will not be relevant. Analogy should be used very carefully. It is often just as likely to destroy an argument as it is to strengthen it.

The importance or significance of a fact may not be sufficient to strengthen an argument. For example, given the millions of immigrants in the U.S., using a single family to support a solution to the immigration problem will not make much difference overall even though those single-example arguments are often used to support one approach or another. They may achieve a positive reaction, but they will not prove that one solution is better than another. If enough cases were cited from a variety of geographical locations, the information might be significant. How much is enough? Generally speaking, three strong supporting facts are sufficient to establish the thesis of an argument.

A writer makes choices about which facts will be used and which will be discarded in developing an argument. Those choices may exclude anything that is not supportive of the point of view the arguer is taking. It's always a good idea for the reader to do some research to spot the omissions and to ask whether they have impact on acceptance of the point of view presented in the argument. No judgment is either black or white. If the argument seems too neat or too compelling, there are probably facts that might be relevant that have not been included.

Distinguish between fact and opinion

Facts are statements that are verifiable. Opinions are statements that must be supported in order to be accepted such as beliefs, values, judgments or feelings. Facts are objective statements used to support subjective opinions. For example, "Jane is a bad girl" is an opinion. However, "Jane hit her sister with a baseball bat" is a *fact* upon which the opinion is based. Judgments are opinions—decisions or declarations based on observation or reasoning that express approval or disapproval. Facts report what has happened or exists and come from observation, measurement, or calculation. Facts can be tested and verified whereas opinions and judgments cannot. They can only be supported with facts.

Most statements cannot be so clearly distinguished. "I believe that Jane is a bad girl" is a fact. The speaker knows what he/she believes. However, it obviously includes a judgment that could be disputed by another person who might believe otherwise. Judgments are not usually so firm. They are, rather, plausible opinions that provoke thought or lead to factual development.

Joe DiMaggio, a Yankees' center-fielder, was replaced by Mickey Mantle in 1952.
This is a fact. If necessary, evidence can be produced to support it.

First-year players are more ambitious than seasoned players.
This is an opinion. There is no proof to support that everyone feels this way.

Bias is defined as an opinion, feeling or influence that strongly favors one side in an argument. A statement or passage is biased if an author attempts to convince a reader of something.

Practice Activity: Read the following statement.

1. Using a calculator cannot help a student understand the process of graphing, so its use is a waste of time.

   Is there evidence of bias in the above statement?

   (A) yes
   (B) no

2. There are teachers who feel that computer programs are quite helpful in helping students grasp certain math concepts. There are also those who disagree with this feeling. It is up to each individual math teacher to decide if computer programs benefit her particular group of students.

   Is there evidence of bias in this paragraph?
   (A) yes
   (B) no

Answers:

1. Since the author makes it perfectly clear that he does not favor the use of the calculator in graphing problem, the answer is (A). He has included his opinion in this statement.

2. (B) is the correct answer. The author seems to state both sides of the argument without favoring a particular side.

Skill 9.3   Recognize the deliberate omission of facts or examples in an argument

Effective persuasive writing usually includes fair treatment of the main points that are in opposition to the opinion the writer is promoting. This fair treatment of opposing material is known as *making concessions*. Since the purpose of persuasive writing is to change the minds of people who see things differently than the writer and not merely to preach to the choir, making concessions serves to establish the *credibility* of the writer with an initially resistant or indifferent audience. If writers ignore inconvenient facts or examples that seem to oppose their thesis, they create the impression that they either have no answers for those points or that they have not thought about the situation sufficiently thoroughly. In short, they seriously weaken their credibility. Instead of giving the thesis a fair hearing, the audience is likely to regard it as propaganda and to resort to several "yes, but's" in response to the writers' assertions.

This being so, it is important for readers of persuasive material to evaluate the concession strategies employed by the writer. If the writer simply ignores major facts or examples that would seemingly have a bearing on the discussion, readers should see those omissions as serious flaws and should resist accepting the writer's thesis.

In order to recognize these deliberate omissions, readers must themselves be conversant with the salient facts and examples pertaining to the issue under discussion, the argument. Then they should evaluate the persuasive material to see if the writer is both fair and sufficiently informed. If the writer does address fairly what seem to be the major facts and examples having a bearing on the argument, then readers should give the writer's thesis careful consideration.

Skill 9.4   Recognize fallacies in logic

On the test, the terms **valid** and **invalid** have special meaning. If an argument is valid, it is reasonable. It is objective (not biased) and can be supported by evidence. If an argument is invalid, it is not reasonable. It is not objective. In other words, one can find evidence of bias.

Practice Questions: Read the following passages and select an answer.

1.   Most dentists agree that Bright Smile Toothpaste is the best for fighting cavities. It tastes good and leaves your mouth minty fresh.

       Is this a valid or invalid argument?

       (A) valid
       (B) invalid

2.   It is difficult to decide who will make the best presidential candidate, Senator Johnson or Senator Keeley. They have both been involved in scandals and have both gone through messy divorces while in office.

       Is this argument valid or invalid?

       (A) valid
       (B) invalid

Answers:

1. It is invalid (B). It mentions that "most" dentists agree. What about those who do not agree? The author is clearly exhibiting bias in leaving those who disagree out.

2. A is the correct choice. The author appears to be listing facts. He does not seem to favor one candidate over the other.

Skill 9.5   **Analyze how the point of view, tone, and style of a text can affect the response to the text**

Tailoring language for a particular **audience** is an important skill. Writing to be read by a business associate will surely sound different from writing to be read by a younger sibling. Not only are the vocabularies different, but the formality/informality of the discourse will need to be adjusted.

Determining what the language should be for a particular audience, then, hinges on two things: **word choice** and formality/informality. The most formal language does not use contractions or slang. The most informal language will probably feature a more casual use of common sayings and anecdotes. Formal language will use longer sentences and will not sound like a conversation. The most informal language will use shorter sentences—not necessarily simple sentences—but shorter constructions and may sound like a conversation.

In both formal and informal writing there exists a **tone**, the writer's attitude toward the material and/or readers. Tone may be playful, formal, intimate, angry, serious, ironic, outraged, baffled, tender, serene, depressed, etc. The overall tone of a piece of writing is dictated by both the subject matter and the audience. Tone is also related to the actual words which make up the document, as we attach affective meanings to words, called **connotations**. Gaining this conscious control over language makes it possible to use language appropriately in various situations and to evaluate its uses in literature and other forms of communication. By evoking the proper responses from readers/listeners, we can prompt them to take action.

The following questions are an excellent way to assess the audience and tone of a given piece of writing.

1. Who is your audience? (friend, teacher, business person, someone else)
2. How much does this person know about you and/or your topic?
3. What is your purpose? (to prove an argument, to persuade, to amuse, to register a complaint, to ask for a raise, etc.)
4. What emotions do you have about the topic? (nervous, happy, confident, angry, sad, no feelings at all)
5. What emotions do you want to register with your audience? (anger, nervousness, happiness, boredom, interest)
6. What persona do you need to create in order to achieve your purpose?
7. What choice of language is best suited to achieving your purpose with your particular subject? (slang, friendly but respectful, formal)
8. What emotional quality do you want to transmit to achieve your purpose (matter of fact, informative, authoritative, inquisitive, sympathetic, angry) and to what degree do you want to express this tone?

The **tone** of a written passage is the author's attitude toward the subject matter. The tone (mood, feeling) is revealed through the qualities of the writing itself and is a direct product of such stylistic elements as language and sentence structure. The tone of the written passage is much like a speaker's voice; instead of being spoken, however, it is the product of words on a page.

Often, writers have an emotional stake in the subject and their purpose, either explicitly or implicitly, is to convey those feelings to the reader. In such cases, the writing is generally subjective—that is, it stems from opinions, judgments, values, ideas, and feelings. Both sentence structure (syntax) and word choice (diction) are instrumental tools in creating tone.

Tone may be thought of generally as positive, negative, or neutral. Below is a statement about snakes that demonstrates this.

> *Many species of snakes live in Florida. Some of those species, both poisonous and non-poisonous, have habitats that coincide with those of human residents of the state.*

The voice of the writer in this statement is neutral. The sentences are declarative (not exclamations or fragments or questions). The adjectives are few and nondescript—*many, some, poisonous* (balanced with *non -poisonous*). Nothing much in this brief paragraph would alert the reader to the feelings of the writer about snakes. The paragraph has a neutral, objective, detached, impartial tone.

Then again, if the writer's attitude toward snakes involves admiration or even affection the tone would generally be positive:

> *Florida's snakes are a tenacious bunch. When they find their habitats invaded by humans, they cling to their home territories as long as they can, as if vainly attempting to fight off the onslaught of the human hordes.*

An additional message emerges in this paragraph: The writer quite clearly favors snakes over people. The writer uses adjectives like *tenacious* to describe his/her feelings about snakes. The writer also humanizes the reptiles, making them brave, beleaguered creatures. Obviously the writer is more sympathetic to snakes than to people in this paragraph.

If the writer's attitude toward snakes involves active dislike and fear, then the tone would also reflect that attitude by being negative:

> *Countless species of snakes, some more dangerous than others, still lurk on the urban fringes of Florida's towns and cities. They will often invade domestic spaces, terrorizing people and their pets.*

Here, obviously, the snakes are the villains. They *lurk,* they *invade,* and they *terrorize.* The tone of this paragraph might be said to be distressed about snakes.

In the same manner, a writer can use language to portray characters as good or bad. A writer uses positive and negative adjectives, as seen above, to convey the manner of a character.

SUBAREA III.   WRITING PROCESSES, PURPOSES, AND CONVENTIONS

COMPETENCY 10.0   UNDERSTAND EFFECTIVE AND APPROPRIATE ORGANIZATIONAL STRUCTURE AND FOCUS IN WRITING

Skill 10.1   Demonstrate knowledge of methods for organizing writing effectively and appropriately according to purpose, genre, audience, and format requirements

See Skill 10.2.

Skill 10.2   Demonstrate knowledge of traditional structures used to convey information in writing (e.g., chronological order, cause and effect, comparison and contrast, question and answer)

The **organization** of a written work includes two factors: the order in which the writer has chosen to present the different parts of the discussion or argument, and the relationships he or she constructs between these parts.

Written ideas need to be presented in a **logical order** so that a reader can follow the information easily and quickly. There are many different ways in which to order a series of ideas but they all share one thing in common: to lead the reader along a desired path while avoiding backtracking and skipping around in order to give a clear, strong presentation of the writer's main idea. *Some* of the ways in which a paragraph may be organized:

Sequence of events – In this type of organization the details are presented in the order in which they have occurred. Paragraphs that describe a process or procedure, give directions or outline a given period of time (such as a day or a month) are often arranged chronologically.

Statement support – In this type of organization the main idea is stated and the rest of the paragraph explains or proves it. This is also referred to as relative importance. There are four ways in which this type of order is organized: most to least, least to most, most-least-most, and least-most-least.

Comparison-Contrast – In this type of organization the compare-contrast pattern is used when a paragraph describes the differences or similarities of two or more ideas, actions, events, or things. Usually the topic sentence describes the basic relationship between the ideas or items and the rest of the paragraph explains this relationship.

Classification – in this type of organization, the paragraph presents grouped information about a topic. The topic sentence usually states the general category and the rest of the sentences show how various elements of the category have a common base and also how they differ from the common base.

Cause and Effect – This pattern describes how two or more events are connected. The main sentence usually states the primary cause(s) and the primary effect(s) and how they are basically connected. The rest of the sentences explain the connection – how one event caused the next.

Spatial/Place – In this type of organization, certain descriptions are organized according to the location of items in relation to each other and to a larger context.

Skill 10.3   Demonstrate knowledge of methods for identifying and removing material in writing that is extraneous, irrelevant or inappropriate

See Skill 9.3.

The following passage has several irrelevant sentences that are highlighted in bold

The New City Planning Committee is proposing a new capitol building to represent the multicultural face of New City. **The current mayor is a Democrat.** The new capitol building will be on 10th Street across from the grocery store and next to the Recreational Center. It will be within walking distance of the subway and bus depot, as the designers want to emphasize the importance of public transportation. Aesthetically, the building will have a contemporary design featuring a brushed-steel exterior and large, floor to ceiling windows. **It is important for employees to have a connection with the outside world even when they are in their offices.** Inside the building, the walls will be moveable. This will not only facilitate a multitude of creative floor plans, but it will also create a focus on open communication and flow of information. **It sounds a bit gimmicky to me.** Finally, the capitol will feature a large outdoor courtyard full of lush greenery and serene fountains. **Work will now seem like Club Med to those who work at the New City capitol!**

Skill 10.4   Recognize the appropriate length for addressing a particular topic or telling a story

Establishing a specific length for a piece of student writing inevitably leads to meaningless fill, which is a natural tendency in student writing anyway. Microsoft Word makes it easy nowadays to establish a required word-length because it does the counting. Establishing single- or double-spaced pages with specific margins is another way to measure length. However, it's better to teach the skills for self-criticism and self-analysis than to use these means to establish assignment-fulfillment. The students should develop the ability to objectify their own creations and ask the important questions about a piece of writing that professional critics and analysts ask: Does it fulfill its stated or implied purpose? Is the point made? Is the purpose or point valuable or worthwhile (worth making)? In other words, time spent on teaching students how to truly explore ideas so they can come up with genuine answers to genuine questions and teaching them to take a stand and defend an argument will be more worthwhile than setting specific lengths for an assignment.

Skill 10.5   Recognize the appropriate structural elements (e.g., transitional words and sentences, parallelism) for ensuring clarity, coherence, and conciseness in writing

Even if the sentences that make up a given paragraph or passage are arranged in logical order, the document as a whole can still seem choppy, the various ideas disconnected. **Transitions**, words that signal relationships between ideas, can help improve the flow of a document. Transitions can help achieve clear and effective presentation of information by establishing connections between sentences, paragraphs and sections of a document. With transitions, each sentence builds on the ideas in the last, and each paragraph has clear links to the preceding one. As a result, the reader receives clear directions on how to piece together the writer's ideas in a logically coherent argument. By signaling how to organize, interpret and react to information, transitions allow a writer to effectively and elegantly explain his ideas.

Logical Relationship	Transitional Expression
Exception/Contrast	but, however, in spite of, on the one hand ... on the other hand, nevertheless, nonetheless, notwithstanding, in contrast, on the contrary, still, yet
Sequence/Order	first, second, third, ... next, then, finally
Time	after, afterward, at last, before, currently, during, earlier, immediately, later, meanwhile, now, recently, simultaneously, subsequently, then
Example	for example, for instance, namely, specifically, to illustrate
Emphasis	even, indeed, in fact, of course, truly
Place/Position	above, adjacent, below, beyond, here, in front, in back, nearby, there
Cause and Effect	accordingly, consequently, hence, so, therefore, thus
Additional Support or Evidence	additionally, again, also, and, as well, besides, equally important, further, furthermore, in addition, moreover, then, in the same way, just as, to, likewise
Conclusion/Summary	finally, in a word, in brief, in conclusion, in the end, in the final analysis, on the whole, thus, to conclude, to summarize, in sum, in summary

The following example shows good logical order and transitions

No one really knows how Valentine's Day started. There are several legends, however, which are often told. The first attributes Valentine's Day to a Christian priest who lived in Rome during the third century, under the rule of Emperor Claudius. Rome was at war and apparently Claudius felt that married men didn't fight as well as bachelors. Consequently, Claudius banned marriage for the duration of the war. But Valentinus, the priest, risked his life to secretly marry couples in violation of Claudius' law. The second legend is even more romantic. In this story, Valentinus is a prisoner, having been condemned to death for refusing to worship pagan deities. While in jail, he fell in love with his jailer's daughter, who happened to be blind. Daily he prayed for her sight to return and miraculously it did. On February 14, the day that he was condemned to die, he was allowed to write the young woman a note. In this farewell letter he promised eternal love, and signed at the bottom of the page the now famous words, "Your Valentine."

Faulty parallelism
Two or more elements stated in a single clause should be expressed with the same (or parallel) structure (e.g., all adjectives, all verb forms or all nouns).

Error: She needed to be beautiful, successful, and have fame.

Problem: The phrase "to be" is followed by two different structures: *beautiful* and *successful* are adjectives, and *have fame* is a verb phrase.

Correction: *She needed to be <u>beautiful</u>, <u>successful</u>, and <u>famous</u>.*
                    (adjective) (adjective)   (adjective)
                                OR
    She needed <u>beauty</u>, <u>success</u>, and <u>fame</u>.
             (noun)   (noun)   (noun)

Error: I plan either to sell my car during the spring or during the summer.

Problem: Paired conjunctions (also called correlative conjunctions - such as either-or, both-and , neither-nor, not only-but also) need to be followed with similar structures. In the sentence above, *either* is followed by *to sell my car during the spring*, while *or* is followed only by the phrase *during the summer*.

Correction: *I plan to sell my car during either the spring or the summer.*

Error: The President pledged to lower taxes and that he would cut spending to lower the national debt.

Problem: Since the phrase *to lower taxes* follows the verb *pledged*, a similar structure of to is needed with the phrase *cut spending*.

Correction: *The President pledged to lower taxes and to cut spending to lower the national debt.*
                              OR
    The President pledged that he would lower taxes and cut spending to lower the national debt.

Skill 10.6   Recognize the appropriate supporting elements (e.g., facts, examples, descriptions, anecdotes) for ensuring valid conclusions and credible endings in writing

Primary and secondary sources

The resources used to support a piece of writing can be divided into two major groups: primary sources and secondary sources.

Primary sources are works, records, etc. that were created during the period being studied or immediately after it. Secondary sources are works written significantly after the period being studied and based upon primary sources. Primary sources are the basic materials that provide raw data and information. Secondary sources are the works that contain the explications of, and judgments on, this primary material.

Primary sources include the following kinds of materials:

- Documents that reflect the immediate, everyday concerns of people: memoranda, bills, deeds, charters, newspaper reports, pamphlets, graffiti, popular writings, journals or diaries, records of decision-making bodies, letters, receipts, snapshots, etc.
- Theoretical writings which reflect care and consideration in composition and an attempt to convince or persuade. The topic will generally be deeper and more pervasive values than is the case with "immediate" documents. These may include newspaper or magazine editorials, sermons, political speeches, philosophical writings, etc.
- Narrative accounts of events, ideas, trends, etc. written with intentionality by someone contemporary with the events described.
- Statistical data, although statistics may be misleading.
- Literature and nonverbal materials, novels, stories, poetry and essays from the period, as well as coins, archaeological artifacts, and art produced during the period.

Questions for Analyzing Primary Sources

1. Who created the source and why? Was it created through a spur-of-the-moment act, a routine transaction, or a thoughtful, deliberate process?
2. Did the recorder have firsthand knowledge of the event? Or did the recorder report what others saw and heard?
3. Was the recorder a neutral party or did the creator have opinions or interests that might have influenced what was recorded?
4. Did the recorder produce the source for personal use, for one or more individuals, or for a large audience?
5. Was the source meant to be public or private?
6. Did the recorder wish to inform or persuade others? (Check the words in the source. The words may tell you whether the recorder was trying to be objective or persuasive.) Did the recorder have reasons to be honest or dishonest?
7. Was the information recorded during the event, immediately after the event, or after some lapse of time? How large a lapse of time?

Secondary sources include the following kinds of materials:

- Books written on the basis of primary materials about the period of time.
- Books written on the basis of primary materials about persons who played a major role in the events under consideration.
- Books and articles written on the basis of primary materials about the culture, the social norms, the language, and the values of the period.
- Quotations from primary sources.
- Statistical data on the period.
- The conclusions and inferences of other historians.
- Multiple interpretations of the ethos of the time.

Guidelines for the use of secondary sources:

1. Do not rely upon only a single secondary source.
2. Check facts and interpretations against primary sources whenever possible.
3. Do not accept the conclusions of other historians uncritically.
4. Place greatest reliance on secondary sources created by the best and most respected scholars.
5. Do not use the inferences of other scholars as if they were facts.
6. Ensure that you recognize any bias the writer brings to his/her interpretation of history.
7. Understand the primary point of the book as a basis for evaluating the value of the material presented in it to your questions.

Cross-checking or comparing sources not only helps you to test their validity, it also helps you to understand your sources in context. One observer of the 1939 invasion of Poland is good; two (or three or four) are even better. Each will contribute something new to your understanding of the event, and to your sense of how you might best represent or analyze it.

COMPETENCY 11.0   UNDERSTAND TECHNIQUES FOR EFFECTIVE NARRATIVE WRITING

Skill 11.1   **Identify techniques for engaging readers through development of plot, setting, characters, and point of view appropriate to the narrative (e.g., introducing conflict, crises, or challenges; providing thematic or causal connectedness; creating mood and atmosphere through setting; showing, not telling, characters' thoughts, words, and actions; providing periodic insights from the narrator)**

Typically, the purpose of writing narratives is to entertain and maintaining a reader's interest is often an important goal of a writer. What good is a book, a short story, or a newspaper article that doesn't get read, right?

Developing creative and unique storylines is a good way to maintain readers' interest, and this factor should be addressed in the planning/brainstorming process with students. Teachers should help students develop good plots for their narrative pieces. Stories with high levels of human interest often maintain readers' interest well. When a story relates to things that most people experience or face, the reader is more likely to remain interested.

Effective **plots** are essential to narrative writing and are the framework is outlined by the narrative's characters, settings and points of view. The best plots are driven by the characters and to develop an effective plot the writer must incorporate and balance meaningful dialogue, necessary interior thoughts, and character's reactions and actions. Suspense, adventure, mystery, love and humor are just some of the good plot elements to keep readers reading.

One way to do this is by creating interesting **characters**. Describing a **character's** physical features is just the start of character development. Physical features need to be balanced with actions, thoughts, temperament, mannerism and other traits. A character's action and motives are essential in driving the plot of the story and lead to a more well-rounded character. Characters that seem real will help the reader connect to or feel for that character. Once the reader is interested in what will happen to or with the character, their interest is usually maintained to read the story.

Students should be given opportunities to practice developing different types of characters. One activity can be for the teacher to "act out" specific traits and have the students identify them based on his or her actions. Sad, happy, and shy are easy traits to start off with, and then the teacher can encourage students to suggest more difficult traits (such as jealous, lazy, cruel, witty, etc.) to portray.

However, devising a list of possible character traits is the easy part. Bringing those traits alive through writing in the narrative is the challenging part. To help bridge this gap, writing classes often work through an exercise called "Show, Don't Tell." The objective of this exercise and style of writing is the have students describe the character's traits without coming straight out and telling the reader what the trait is.

LANGUAGE ARTS   99

For example, a student should be encouraged to revise a statement such as,

"William was shy about speaking in front of the class."

This assertion tells us little, so students should be encouraged to create a more engaging description, such as:

"William slowly walked to podium at the front of the room. He lowered his eyes to his papers as he turned to face the class. A fluttering sensation filled his stomach as he inhaled to begin his speech."

Use of more descriptive language leads to more interesting characters and a more effective plot line. In addition, such wordings help to build suspense, as well as make the experience more realistic to the reader – all elements that help maintain readers' interest in the story.

Another good element for narratives is interesting and unique **settings**. Well-developed and thoroughly researched settings make a story unique and interesting. Effective settings enhance quality narrative pieces. When authors are thorough in their descriptions of unique settings, the reader feels more connected to the story – perhaps almost as if she is there. Even the simplest setting with which many readers would be familiar (i.e., modern day suburbia) warrants clear description of the area, time of day, time of year, etc. Like with character development, "Show, Don't Tell" is an excellent exercise to create an effective setting.

For example, instead of:

Sarah walked to the park in late autumn.

The author could write:

A crisp breeze cooled Sarah's cheeks as she quickened her pace, hurrying along the path littered with golden leaves.

Again, these details help the reader feel as a part of the story.

Unique settings, however, require much more detailed descriptions. Research is often needed to depict accurate historical settings or settings in another country or region. For example, a writer might have to research traditional language or slang in a region with which they are not familiar. Science fiction and fantasy require extremely in-depth description if the reader is to visualize a world that is only known in the author's mind.

Points of View

In narrative writing, the point of view is the voice of the story. It is the related experience of the narrator of the story, not that of the author. An effective point of view encourages the reader to connect with the narrator (usually the main character), not the author, of the story. The ability to use viewpoints effectively is a mark of a good writer.

Most narrative pieces are written in the first-person or the third-person point of view. In the first person, sentences are written as though the character is speaking or telling the story.

For example, *"I woke up suddenly. Realizing I was late, I grabbed my tote bag and ran out the door."*

The benefit of writing in the first person is that all the opinions and thoughts of a single character's mind are accessible to the reader. However, the limit of this style is just the same - that this character is the only viewpoint the reader has and we are limited to what this character knows.

Stories can also be written in the third person. There are two ways this can be done – the third person "omniscient" or the third person "limited." The third-person omniscient can move among different characters' viewpoints with knowledge of everyone's thoughts, actions and experience. The third-person limited follows one character throughout the book but may be more observant of other characters' actions and thoughts than the main character.

To maintain interest and/or to create a different reading experience, some authors switch among characters as they go through chapters or sections of the book. With this method, characters can take turns being read in first-person or third-person limited, but the reader is eventually exposed to the thoughts and minds of more than one character.

Purpose

When we attempt to communicate, we are usually prompted by a purpose for our communication. We may want to:

- Express feelings
- Explore an idea
- Entertain
- Inform
- Persuade
- Argue
- Explain

For most narrative writing, the purpose is to explain or entertain. When beginning a narrative piece or brainstorming session, a writer should always ask herself, "Why am I writing?" For many students, the answer to this appears to be "I have an assignment due," or "To get a good grade." An effective teacher, however, will help students move past this response in order to realize that being cognizant of the purpose helps to focus the writing so that the main theme, point, idea or reason for the piece is clearly communicated to the reader.

Audience

The audience has a lot to do with how the author writes. It is important for a writer to be aware of the intended audience of a narrative piece before beginning since knowledge of one's audience will affect the tone, vocabulary and other choice of words, level of formality, subject, and sentence structure. For example, a story written to entertain sixth-graders will be quite different than a historical fiction piece for high school seniors.

Since a writer must anticipate a reader's questions or needs, the author must be knowledgeable of this audience in order to accurately anticipate these needs and to see the story through the readers' eyes. This is a challenging task as the author has to balance what the reader expects and needs, while also fulfilling the purpose of the writing.

Context

A writer must be aware and knowledgeable of a narrative piece's context as well. Context also provides some outline to the expectations of a narrative piece. Selection of the form of writing (a report, essay, memoir, story, etc.) helps the writer achieve the purpose in determining the style, organization and tone that is associated with the selected style and context.

Skill 11.2 Recognize effective use of details to help describe incidents, events, individuals, attitudes, and situations

Details play an important role in any narrative piece. Without details, readers would likely find the story confusing, hard to follow, tedious and flat. Keeping in mind that the purpose of most narrative pieces is to entertain, details keep the reader interested and finding enjoyment in the story.

Attention to details and use of concrete language that connect the reader to the world of the story is the foundation of excellent writing. Details can take the form of true facts (especially for historical fiction), imagery, conversations, basic descriptions and more. Effective use of details means the author includes the particulars and details that matter so that the actions, characters and plot of the story seem concrete to the reader. In addition, the details have been used appropriately and not just for the sake of adding information.

Below are two strategies to help students develop detail in their stories:

- **Peer questioning** – Have students sit with a partner and review each other's stories. Have the students ask questions such as, *"What color was his hat?"*, *"How did Jake feel after having that dream?"*, *"Why was Mary so excited about that car ride?"* The answers to these questions will add details that describe, inform, and enhance the depth of the story.
- **Observe & Record** – Watching the world around them will help students notice the sounds, character traits, physical traits, smells, scenes, conflicts (and more) of life around them they may not otherwise think much of. Have students maintain a notebook or folder of observations they may be able to use in a story later.

When the writer chooses to use details (as long as they enhance the structure of the story), those details will be the key to connecting the reader to the story and thus giving the story its life.

Skill 11.3 Demonstrate knowledge of effective use of concrete and evocative language to maximize the reader's experience of plot, setting, and characters (e.g., strong verbs; modifiers that appeal to the senses; rhythm, rhyme, alliteration, and other literary effects; varied sentence length and structure)

Authors have many techniques at their disposal to create effective narrative plots, settings and characters. Teachers should expose students to a variety of these techniques within the writing process as formal or mini-lessons so that students can begin to practice and utilize these methods in their written work.

Dialogue

Dialogue is an important aspect of most narrative pieces. Without conversations, readers can easily become bored with a story since narration can become long, tedious and uninteresting without dialogue. When used properly, dialogue can:

- Keep the pace of the story moving
- Display their character's thoughts and personalities
- Create a "hook" for the opening of the story
- Condense or replace large amounts of background
- Show, Don't Tell
- Add humor

Some elements to remember when writing dialogue are:

1. **Dialogue should read like natural speech.** For example, an elderly doctor would not use the term "awesome" just as an average tenth-grader is unlikely to use the word "succinctly."
2. **Use dialogue that serves a purpose to the plot/conversation.** Dialogue should move the story while making the characters seem real. If the dialogue doesn't accomplish this, take it out and use narration instead.
3. **Keep dialogue short.** Generally, three or fewer sentences is adequate for one character to say at a time. You don't have to say everything at once; readers will recall the details.
4. **Mix dialogue and action.** Physical details help to break up the dialogue while keeping the story going. For example, *"I can't believe it!" exclaimed Beth. She crumpled her test paper between her fists until it resembled a snowball. "I studied for three hours for that test!"*
5. **Vary taglines.** But don't overdo it! Writer do not need to consult a thesaurus for every version of "said", but should be encouraged to select a tagline that adds to the purpose of the conversation.
6. **Avoid stereotypes, profanity and slang.**
7. **Punctuate dialogue correctly.**

Mood
The mood of a narrative is an important element in keeping the structure and purpose of a piece held together without being blatantly obvious. When writing a narrative, authors automatically develop a mood with their choices of words, plot, characters and more. Moods can include satirical, determined, hopeful, confused, reflective, remorseful, light or serious. However, the mood is the essence of what the reader takes with him or her.

Foreshadowing
Foreshadowing is a literary device authors employ to provide hints for events to come in the plot (and therefore maintaining reader interest and adding dimension to the narrative piece). Foreshadowing aids the author in creating suspense/tension, providing necessary information (for a future event) and more. Foreshadowing can appear anywhere in a story, but it is exceptionally useful at the end of chapters or sections, acting as a cliffhanger to keep the reader going. When reading novels with their class, teachers should help students recognize foreshadowing so they may later utilize the same device in their own writing.

Flashbacks

Another device authors can use to add depth to their plot is a flashback. Flashbacks provide information about the past during the course of the current action of a story. Flashbacks can be very useful in providing the reader with background information, but writers need to be sure to "lead" the reader with an effective transition (and not just jump backward – that is likely to confuse and/or lose the reader). An example of a simple transition is "Heather recalled that morning at work." The author must then also link the reader back to the current action so the story can be continued.

Suspense

Suspense is the feeling of uncertainty or that something is about to happen. Authors use suspense to maintain the readers' interest, and they do so by using descriptive language, foreshadowing and other techniques to keep the reader reading. The use of suspense/tension adds another level to the plot which seduces the reader to see what the outcome will be. It is an effective technique to use in thriller, mystery, and other dramatic narrative pieces.

Transitions

Technical transitions are important element that adds to the flow of the writing. Examples of these transitions include another reason, in addition, first of all, besides that, furthermore, also, moreover, and for example. However, these transitions aid more in the flow of sentences and paragraphs than in the flow of the entire narrative.

Narrative transitions are transitions that provide logical and smooth connections between events in the story. These transitions are often used between chapters, sections of chapters, and as the character moves through various settings. Effective transitions are essential to maintaining the flow of the story so that the reader can move along with the story easily.

In medias res

Latin for "into the middle of things," in medias res is a literary technique authors use when they want to start the action in the middle of the story, rather than the typical beginning point. The authors then utilize flashbacks and dialogue to introduce the characters, setting and conflict to the reader.

Skill 11.4   **Demonstrate knowledge of effective use of literary approaches to enhance writing (e.g., suspense, figurative language, realistic dialogue, flashback, flashforward, foreshadowing)**

See Skill 11.3.

COMPETENCY 12.0   UNDERSTAND TECHNIQUES FOR EFFECTIVE ANALYTICAL AND PERSUASIVE WRITING

Skill 12.1   Demonstrate knowledge of techniques for engaging readers in analytical or persuasive writing by establishing a context, providing a purpose, and creating a voice

It's important to differentiate between "subject" and "thesis." The subject is the topic of the discourse. For example, it is not enough to decide that "democracy" is the subject or topic one is going to write about. First of all, something must be predicated of the subject. The subject must be converted into a proposition. For example, "Democracy functions best when people are educated." Now we have a thesis. Many aspects of the subject "democracy" could be developed in an essay, and many have been, but the burden is upon the writer to make a decision about the aspect he/she wants to address in this particular theme. Once that aspect has been determined, the writer must develop a thesis sentence.

A cardinal principle in writing a thesis statement is that it must be stated in a single declarative sentence, and it must be stated in a single sentence. As soon as the student writer launches into the second sentence, he/she has wandered off into development and hasn't clarified the thesis statement.

It is also important that the thesis be a *declarative* sentence. For example, a hortatory sentence like "Let us fight to preserve the integrity of our democracy" or interrogatory sentences like "Is democracy a feasible form of government?" leave the subject cloudy, uncertain, and tentative and are very difficult to develop. The thesis will be clearly and firmly stated if the predicate *asserts* or *denies* something about the subject: "The integrity of our democracy can be preserved only if we fight to maintain it"; "Democracy is (is not) a feasible form of government." Both of these statements will lend themselves to clear, supporting development.

The thesis statement forces the writer to determine at the outset just what it is that he/she wants to say about the chosen subject. It also lays the foundation for a unified, coherent discourse. Besides, it often suggests some of the supporting statements that will occur in the body.

Writing a thesis statement is facilitated by pre-writing. The writing teacher does well to require that her students pre-write, free-write ideas about the subject before attempting to write a thesis statement. Pre-writing should yield several possible thesis statements, which is useful and helpful in determining exactly which one will be developed in this persuasive essay. Remember—the beginning of all good writing is a sharply defined thesis.

Skill 12.2   **Demonstrate knowledge of techniques for justifying interpretations and supporting judgments by referring to examples and evidence in a source text**

Once a thesis is put forth, there are various ways to support it. The most obvious one is reasons. Usually a reason will answer the question why. Another technique is to give examples. A third is to give details.

The presentation of a prosecutor in a court trial is a good example of an argument that uses all of these.

The **thesis** of the prosecutor may be: John O'Hara stole construction materials from a house being built at 223 Hudson Ave. by the Jones Construction Company. As a **reason**, he might cite the following: He is building his own home on Green Street and needs materials and tools. This will answer the question why. He might give **examples**: 20 bags of concrete disappeared the night before Mr. O'Hara poured the basement for his house on Green Street. The electronic nail-setter disappeared from the building site on Hudson Ave. the day before Mr. O'Hara began to erect the frame of his house on Green Street. He might fill in the **details**: Mr. O'Hara's truck was observed by a witness on Hudson Ave. in the vicinity of the Jones Construction Company site the night the concrete disappeared. Mr. O'Hara's truck was observed again on that street by a witness the night the nail-setter disappeared.

Another example of a trial might be: **Thesis**, Adam Andrews murdered Joan Rogers in cold blood on the night of December 20. **Reason #1**: She was about to reveal their affair to his wife. **Reason #2**: Andrews' wife would inherit half of his sizeable estate in case of a divorce since there is no prenuptial agreement. **Example #1**: Rogers has demonstrated that he is capable of violence in an incident with a partner in his firm. **Example #2**: Rogers has had previous affairs in which he was accused of violence. **Detail #1**: Andrews' wife once called the police and signed a warrant. **Detail #2**: A previous lover sought police protection from Andrews.

An **opinion** is a thesis and requires support. It can also use reasons, examples, and details.

Opinion: Our borders must be protected.

Reason #1: Terrorists can get into the country undetected. **Example #1**: An Iranian national was able to cross the Mexican border and live in this country for years before being detected. **Detail**: The Iranian national came up through Central America to Mexico then followed the route that Mexican illegal immigrants regularly took. **Example #2**: A group of Middle Eastern terrorists was arrested in Oregon after crossing the Canadian border. **Detail**: There was no screening at that border.

Reason #2: Illegal aliens are an enormous drain on resources such as health care. **Example**: The states of California and Texas bear enormous burdens for health care and education for illegal immigrants. **Detail**: Legal citizens are often denied care in those states because resources are stretched so thin.

Skill 12.3   Demonstrate the ability to state a clear position or perspective and offer a logical argument and convincing evidence to support that position

The two forms of argument to choose from in supporting an argument are *inductive* or *deductive*. Inductive reason goes from the particular to the general. In other words, I observe that all the green apples I have ever tasted are sour. 1) I have tasted some from my grandfather's orchard, 2) I have tasted the Granny Smiths that my mother buys in the grocery store and makes pies from, 3) I taste the green apples in my friend's kitchen. (All particular instances or bits of evidence.) All are sour (conclusion). Then I can *generalize* that all green apples are sour. This is inductive reasoning, a very prevalent aspect of the way we think and deal with each other and essential to persuasive discourse.

Deductive reasoning, on the other hand, reverses the order by going from general to particular. The generalization drawn in the previous illustration, "All green apples are sour" can be used to make a statement about a particular apple. A new variety of green apples has appeared in the grocery store. Arguing from the generalization that all green apples are sour, I may reject this new variety because I am sure that they are going to be sour. Deductive reasoning is based on the syllogism:

> All green apples are sour.
> This apple is green.
> Therefore, this apple is sour.

When a prosecutor presents a trial in a courtroom, he usually begins by putting forth a statement of fact: On November 2 in an alley between Smith and Jones Street at the 400 block, Stacy Highsmith was brutally raped and murdered. The coroner has concluded that she was bludgeoned with a blunt instrument at or around midnight and her body was found by a shopkeeper the next morning. (There may be other "knowns" presented in the statement of fact.) Following the laying out of the facts of the case, the prosecutor will use inductive reasoning (a series of particulars) to accuse the person on trial for the crime. For example, Terry Large, the accused, 1) was seen in the neighborhood at 11:30 p.m. on November 2. 2) He was carrying a carpenter's tool kit, which was later recovered, and 3) a hammer with evidence of blood on it was found in that tool kit. 4) The blood was tested and it matched the victim's DNA. (All particulars leading to a conclusion.) Etc. Ultimately, the prosecutor will reach the generalization: Terry Large murdered Stacy Highsmith in the alley in the middle of the night on November 2.

Skill 12.4   Demonstrate knowledge of techniques for anticipating reader questions, concerns, and counterarguments and formulating effective responses

The three appeals are rational, ethical (defined as establishing credibility), and emotional, according to the original Greek rhetoricians; these have stood the tests of time. Today, even with all the multimedia tools available, there are three possibilities for persuading another person to accept a position or to take some action, the purposes for writing persuasive essays or making persuasive speeches. How do politicians persuade large groups of people to accept their points of view? How do they persuade those people to take action—usually to go to the polls and vote for them? By using these three means of persuasion.

Rational Appeal. This is logical reasoning. If the essay is to change anyone's mind, it must make sense. Once the thesis is established, asking the questions how? or why? leads to the reasons the writer can use to persuade. For example: "Building a strong fence on the border will solve the immigration crisis." Why? 1) "It will stop those crossing the border that the scattered border patrol officers have not been able to stop until now." 2) "It will give the border patrol officers the tool they need to stop those who try to come across illegally." How? "The cost of the fence can be covered by a decrease in the number of officers now guarding the border." There should be at least three supporting points.

Ethical Appeal. The rhetoricians defined this as establishing credibility. Some people will accept a speaker's point of view just because of who he/she is. A veteran border patrol officer has credibility in arguing a point of view regarding protection of the border because he knows more about the issues than others. The governor of a border state usually has credibility. When Governor Schwarzenegger of California addresses border issues, people listen. There are many ways to establish credibility. The background discussion that will begin the essay or speech is a good place to demonstrate that the writer/speaker knows the issue well enough to take a position. The credentials of the speaker/writer may persuade some that this person is credible on this issue.

Emotional Appeal. Most people like to think they make decisions on the basis of logic or reasoning, but the truth is that few change their minds or go out and take action unless they have been moved emotionally. An argument that relies too heavily on emotion, on the other hand, will destroy credibility and will turn people off. There are two major ways to move an audience emotionally. The first is to describe an experience in such way that the reader/listener is able to participate in the experience. An argument against returning illegal immigrants to Mexico will often rely on heart-rending stories of families, especially children, who will suffer if they are sent back. Descriptive language is the tool to use to make an experience available through one of the senses. For example, describing a scene of suffering children in such a way that the reader/listener can see the children in his/her mind's eye or hear them crying with his "mind's ear." The second way to move a reader/listener emotionally is by using charged words—words that carry emotional overtones themselves such as "cruel" or "callous" or "unfeeling." Others are "murderers," "liars," and "prejudice."

Skill 12.5 Demonstrate knowledge of techniques for effectively concluding or resolving analytical and persuasive writing (e.g., summarizing, using a meaningful anecdote, providing an overall reaction, suggesting a broader significance, making a determination, calling for action or further study)

Teaching students to summarize analytical or persuasive writing can lead to remarkable improvement in their own writing; for this reason, it's important to include such units in the English curriculum. In order to summarize a piece of writing effectively, the student must be able to identify the framework, which will involve determining what the thesis is in a persuasive piece and what the purpose is in an analytical piece. In a persuasive essay, the supporting points must be identified. Do subpoints also have subpoints? Before a summary can be composed, just as in persuasive writing, the frame of the piece must be identified. With analytical writing, once purpose is defined, then the steps of the analysis should be picked out. Again, once the frame is clear, a valid summary can be written.

Examples such as anecdotes are important devices for making a point clear in a persuasive essay. Seeing the point in real life not only clarifies the point but fixes it in the reader's mind. If students can learn this skill, their persuasive writing will improve immensely. They need to be taught to be careful about including anecdotes that truly exemplify the point. The same is true in analytical writing. A point that may be a little fuzzy can be brought into focus with an example.

While detailed analysis of a piece of writing is extremely useful in understanding the writing process and how a piece of writing achieves its objectives, it is also worthwhile to help students step back and think about their overall reaction when they have completed reading an essay or any piece of writing. Did it affect them? Did they get the point? Did they feel a stir of emotions? Did it change their minds? Will they do something differently as a result of the reading? However, it's important to remember that this does not replace detailed analysis, which in the long run is far more useful in improving student writing.

It's also useful to encourage students to look beyond the specific piece to the larger world, and ask questions regarding the significance of these ideas to other things that are going on. A contemporary piece, for example, can provide a good opportunity to engage in discussion of current political and social events. A historical piece can provide a good opportunity to look at what was going on at the time the piece was written and make comparisons to current events. This is also a good time to start students thinking about what was going on in the life of the writer at the time the piece was written. For example, something written in an author's early years is often very different from something written later.

It's always hoped that during the years we spend helping students to become readers that they will develop the tendency to read for enlightenment and answers. They need to understand that a piece of writing can change one's viewpoint and even lead to action. For example, if children read about the suffering of the downtrodden, they may want to start or get involved in programs whose purpose is to relieve that suffering. It's not a bad thing to suggest to students that responding emotionally to a written piece is acceptable and one of the valuable benefits of reading.

COMPETENCY 13.0 **UNDERSTAND TECHNIQUES FOR EFFECTIVE EXPOSITORY AND TECHNICAL WRITING AND WRITING THAT INVOLVES RESEARCH**

Skill 13.1 **Identify organizational patterns that are appropriate for the particular type of writing (e.g., descriptive essay, business correspondence, biographical sketch)**

The first decision a writer makes is what the purpose is for a particular writing project. If the purpose is expository—providing information about a particular topic, then the next question regards how to organize the information to communicate what the writer has in mind. Students need a toolkit for developing expository essays, and the following tools should be in that kit.

1. Citing Particulars, Instances, Examples, Illustrations. This is probably the easiest way and often the best way to clarify a general statement. For example, if the point the expository essay is making is "The houses on our block represent the worst characteristics of modern tract-house architecture," then citing examples and filling in the negative aspects with regard to particular houses is the most obvious way to develop it. Another approach would be to focus on the particular negative aspects, such as identical design and appearance and then cite examples. This is an important form of development for students to master; it will be useful for many writing situations, including writing essay answers on exams.

2. Incident and Extended Illustration. Instead of a series of instances, the writer might make the point by telling a story or describing a single illustration in some detail. Say the point of the essay is "Running for the U.S. presidency in this day and age requires extraordinary fundraising skills." The development might be an extended account of George W. Bush or Bill Clinton with a focus on how they raised the funds to finance their campaigns. This will require some research, of course. However, students might also choose a topic they are familiar with and develop it with an incident or extended illustration from their own experience.

3. Cause and Effect. We use cause and effect reasoning regularly in our daily lives and conversations. The statement that "The bee-keeping business is declining in America because the use of insecticides is killing off bees" can be developed by exploring the causes of the excessive use of insecticides and the ways in which they are killing off bees. Students need help in learning to use cause-and-effect reasoning because of the tendency to fall into the *post-hoc-ergo-propter-hoc* fallacy. Just because one event occurred after another does not necessarily mean the first caused the second. The connection between the two events must be established before the reasoning is valid.

4. Analogy. Helping students develop skills in making the unknown clear by comparing it to something familiar will be useful in all their writing exercises. Analogy is the most common tool for this. In analogy, the writer draws a parallel between the point being made and an illustration that is familiar. Victor Hugo described the Battle of Waterloo as a giant letter A. Huxley says that life is like a game of chess. The similarities must be clear or the analogy does not work.

5. Comparison and Contrast. This is similar to analogy, but in this case, the two examples would be compared example by example. For example, a proposition like "Boston is not a small New York" would call for side-by-side comparisons of the two showing ways in which they are alike and ways in which they are not. Students might compare their grade school experiences with their high-school experiences or where they live now with where they lived previously.

6. Restatement and Amplification. Sometimes an extended restatement of the topic with amplifications will make the point clear.

Skill 13.2   Identify effective controlling ideas that convey perspective on a subject

The formal outline has lost favor in recent years as a way of controlling the development of a thesis statement, but helping students develop a working sentence outline will improve their ability to write coherent themes. If the essay is conveying a particular perspective on a subject, the form will be persuasive discourse. The thesis will be arguable and will have two possible sides. For example, "The best way to control illegal immigration is to build a fence." This is only one perspective on the immigration issue. Another one might be, "The best way to control illegal immigration is to penalize companies that hire illegal immigrants." In either case, the supporting arguments should be determined ahead of time. A useful tool for students in developing this kind of essay is to ask the questions "Why?" and "How?" of the topic sentence and use the answers as topic sentences in the development of the essay. This will keep development on track.

For example, if the thesis is "The best way to control illegal immigration is to build a fence along the border." Why? 1) An adequate physical barrier will prevent the individuals and groups who are now crossing over from coming into the United States. 2) Border guards are not sufficient to stop individuals and groups. 3) Penalizing companies that hire illegal workers is too difficult and doesn't work. How? 1) Instead of spending the money on more border guards, that money can be used to pay for the fence.

It's best to develop at least three points. This will not produce a formal outline but a working outline that can be changed as each section of the essay is developed.

Skill 13.3   Recognize relevant and focused questions about a subject

In the early stages of critical reading, students will ask irrelevant and often off-the-wall questions, so teachers need to remember that this is a learned skill and improves with maturity, just as a toddler's walking ability does. Beginning these sessions with questions that are relevant and focused and demonstrating the connections to the subject are useful. Liberality in judging the questions students ask in the early stages is also recommended. Leading them will work effectively in the development of this skill. It just takes patience and practice.

Skill 13.4   Recognize appropriate contexts for providing opinions about a subject

Often students become enamored of their newly acquired opportunities to make judgments about written works and feel that they are now permitted to offer an opinion about everything. Families and friends will not appreciate this, nor is it appropriate. There are times and situations where silence is the best policy and students need to learn this maxim along with the ability and the value of analyzing and critiquing what they read. Their analytical skills will only be useful as they mature if they are acceptable and accepted.

Skill 13.5   Demonstrate the ability to state a thesis clearly

See Skill 12.1.

Skill 13.6   Demonstrate the ability to organize and display information in charts, graphs, maps, and multimedia presentations

See Skill 3.7.

Skill 13.7   Demonstrate the ability to summarize and paraphrase ideas, concepts, and quotations from primary and secondary sources, including electronic texts

The proliferation of sources for ideas and communications has not made the control of plagiary any easier in the classroom. First of all, the ethics and legalities of attribution (documentation) of sources should be firmly stressed, especially in the elementary classroom; then the acceptable ways to do so need to be taught and practiced. If students have already learned to cite sources before they get into high school, they will be equipped to tackle the research projects that will be a part of their high school experience and will have an opportunity to mature these skills.

Documenting a quotation or an idea involves citing the following: name of author; name of source (title of magazine article, book, newspaper report, etc.); place of publication; name of publisher; and date of publication. How these are arranged and how magazine articles, for example, are cited depends on the authority selected either by the school, school system, or teacher. Some examples include *MLA Style Manual* and *Chicago Manual of Style*. Some classroom textbooks include directions for the arrangement of citations. The teacher must decide which authority to teach. At some point, it's useful for students to understand that there are several accepted authorities, but that a single one should be used for a single piece of writing and that the decision about which one to use may not be theirs.

The latest wrinkle in documenting sources is the use of the Internet, the best possible source nowadays for information. Standard requirements for citing the source apply and most authorities recommend citing the URL and the accessed date. For example, "(accessed June 07, 2006)."

Students also need to understand the difference between primary and secondary sources. A primary source is a document or other source of information that was created at or near the time being studied, by an authoritative source, usually one with direct personal knowledge of the events being described. A secondary source is a work that is built up from primary sources. For example, a vaccine for polio was discovered by Jonas Salk and he reported it to the world; that report is a primary source. Many people have written works based on the discovery of Dr. Salk, referring to what he discovered, but these are secondary sources and must be treated as such. Primary sources are to be preferred, of course. A statement from the horse's mouth is much more reliable than another person's report of what was said, so the two should be balanced and the writer should always question how reliable a statement is based on the integrity and practices of the one who is reporting.

Skill 13.8   Demonstrate the ability to achieve an effective balance between researched information and original ideas in writing

Perhaps the most important accomplishment English teachers can achieve in the years when a student comes under their influence and training is the student's development of the ability and the willingness to claim responsibility for his/her own thoughts and ideas. Students need to be given the tools for critical thinking and plenty of opportunities to practice using them, but they also need to mature to the point where they are willing to say, "I believe this to be true," and defend their positions clearly, rationally, and without undue bias. At the same time, they need to learn to explore what others think and bring that into their own compositions. When they refer to sources, it may be for the purpose of refuting an idea they believe to be wrongheaded but also to refer to reliable and credible sources to support the points they are trying to make.

Skill 13.9   Identify various sources of information, including technological resources, and methods for assessing the credibility, objectivity, and reliability of a source of information

When evaluating sources, first go through this checklist to make sure the source is even worth reading:
- Title (How relevant is it to your topic?)
- Date (How current is the source?)
- Organization (What institution is this source coming from?)
- Length (How in depth does it go?)

Check for signs of bias:
- Does the author or publisher have political ties or religious views that could affect their objectivity?
- Is the author or publisher associated with any special-interest groups that might only see one side of an issue, such as Greenpeace or the National Rifle Association?
- How fairly does the author treat opposing views?
- Does the language of the piece show signs of bias?

Keep an open mind while reading, and don't let opposing viewpoints prevent you from absorbing the text. Remember that you are not judging the author's work, you are examining its assumptions, assessing its evidence and weighing its conclusions.

Before accepting as gospel anything that is printed in a newspaper or advertising or presented on radio, television, or the Internet, it is wise to first of all consider the source. Even though news reporters and editors claim to be unbiased in the presentation of news, they usually take an editorial point of view. A newspaper may avow that it is Republican or conservative and may even make recommendations at election time, but it will still claim to present the news without bias. Sometimes this is true and sometimes it is not. For example, Fox News declares itself to be conservative and to support the Republican Party. Its presentation of news often reveals that bias. When Vice-President Cheney made a statement about his shooting of a friend in a duck-hunting accident, it was only made available to Fox News.

On the other hand, CBS has tended to favor more liberal politicians although it avows that it is even-handed in its coverage. Dan Rather presented a story critical of President Bush's military service that was based on a document that could not be validated. His failure to play by the rules of certification of evidence cost him his job and his career. Even with authentication, such a story would not have gotten past the editors of a conservative-leaning news system.

Even politicians usually play by the rules of fairness in the choices they make about going public. They usually try to be even-handed. However, some channels and networks will show deference to one politician over another.

Advertising, whether in print or electronic media, is another thing. Will using a certain toothpaste improve a person's love life? Is a dish better than cable? The best recourse a reader/viewer has is to ask around and find someone who has experience that is relevant or conduct research and conduct interviews of users of both.

COMPETENCY 14.0 UNDERSTAND TECHNIQUES FOR EFFECTIVELY REVISING AND EDITING WRITING AND FOR APPROPRIATELY DOCUMENTING SOURCES USED IN WRITING

Skill 14.1 Demonstrate knowledge of techniques for planning and drafting preliminary versions of writing (e.g., outlining, freewriting, graphic organizers)

Topic Analysis

Even before you select a topic, determine what each prompt is asking you to discuss. This first decision is crucial. If you pick a topic you don't really understand or about which you have little to say, you'll have difficulty developing your essay. So take a few moments to analyze each topic carefully *before* you begin to write.

Topic A: A modern invention that can be considered a wonder of the world

In general, the topic prompts have two parts:
the *SUBJECT* of the topic and
an *ASSERTION* about the subject.

The **subject** is *a modern invention*. In this prompt, the word *modern* indicates you should discuss something invented recently, at least in this century. The word *invention* indicated you're to write about something created by humans (not natural phenomena such as mountains or volcanoes). You may discuss an invention that has potential for harm, such as chemical warfare or the atomic bomb, or you may discuss an invention that has the potential for good, such as the computer, DNA testing, television, antibiotics, and so on.

The **assertion** (a statement of point of view) is that *the invention has such powerful or amazing qualities that it should be considered a wonder of the world*. The assertion states your point of view about the subject, and it limits the range for discussion. In other words, you would discuss particular qualities or uses of the invention, not just discuss how it was invented or whether it should have been invented at all.

Note also that this particular topic encourages you to use examples to show the reader that a particular invention is a modern wonder. Some topic prompts lend themselves to essays with an argumentative edge, one in which you take a stand on a particular issue and persuasively prove your point. Here, you undoubtedly could offer examples or illustrations of the many "wonders" and uses of the particular invention you chose.

Be aware that misreading or misinterpreting the topic prompt can lead to serious problems. Papers that do not address the topic occur when one reads too quickly or only half-understands the topic. This may happen if you misread or misinterpret words. Misreading can also lead to a paper that addresses only part of the topic prompt rather than the entire topic.

To develop a complete essay, spend a few minutes planning. Jot down your ideas and quickly sketch an outline. Although you may feel under pressure to begin writing, you will write more effectively if you plan out your major points.

Prewriting

Before actually writing, you'll need to generate content and to develop a writing plan. Three prewriting techniques that can be helpful are:

Brainstorming

When brainstorming, quickly create a list of words and ideas that are connected to the topic. Let your mind roam free to generate as many relevant ideas as possible in a few minutes. For example, on the topic of computers you may write

    computer- modern invention
    types- personal computers, micro-chips in calculators and watches
    wonder - acts like an electronic brain
    uses - science, medicine, offices, homes, schools
    problems- too much reliance; the machines aren't perfect

This list could help you focus on the topic and states the points you could develop in the body paragraphs. The brainstorming list keeps you on track and is well worth the few minutes it takes to jot down the ideas. While you haven't organized the ideas, seeing them on paper is an important step.

Questioning

Questioning helps you focus as you mentally ask a series of exploratory questions about the topic. You may use the most basic questions, such as **who, what, where, when, why, and how.**

"**What** is my subject?"
    [computers]

"**What** types of computers are there?"
    [personal computers, micro-chip computers]

"**Why** have computers been a positive invention?"
    [acts like an electronic brain in machinery and equipment; helps solve complex scientific problems]

"How have computers been a positive invention?"
    [used to make improvements in:
- science (space exploration, moon landings)
- medicine (MRIs, CAT scans, surgical tools, research models)
- business (PCs, FAX, telephone equipment)
- education (computer programs for math, languages, science, social studies), and
- personal use (family budgets, tax programs, healthy diet plans)]

"How can I show that computers are good?"
    [citing numerous examples]

"What problems do I see with computers?"
    [too much reliance; not yet perfect]

"What personal experiences would help me develop examples to respond to this topic?
    [my own experiences using computers]

Of course, you may not have time to write out the questions completely. You might just write the words *who, what, where, why, how* and the major points next to each. An abbreviated list might look as follows:

What — computers/modern wonder/making life better
How — through technological improvements: lasers, calculators, CAT scans, MUs.
Where – in science and space exploration, medicine, schools, offices

In a few moments, your questions should help you to focus on the topic and to generate interesting ideas and points to make in the essay. Later in the writing process, you can look back at the list to be sure you've made the key points you intended.

Clustering

Some visual thinkers find clustering an effective prewriting method. when clustering, you draw a box in the center of your paper and write your topic within that box. Then you draw lines from the center box and connect it to small satellite boxes that contain related ideas. Note the cluster on the next page on computers:

SAMPLE CLUSTER

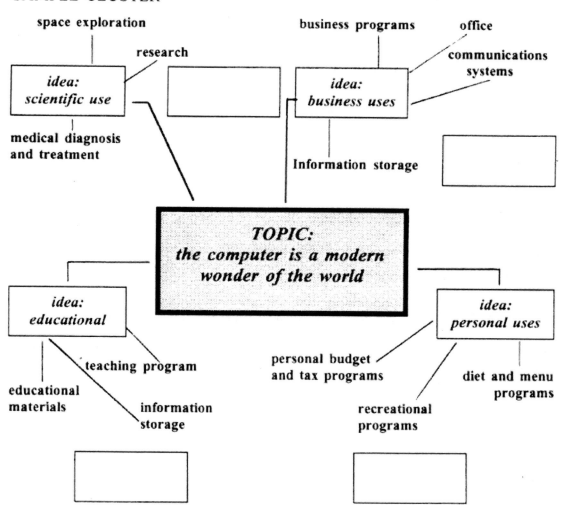

Writing the Thesis

After focusing on the topic and generating your ideas, form your thesis, the controlling idea of your essay. The thesis is your general statement to the reader that expresses your point of view and guides your essay's purpose and scope. The thesis should allow you either to explain your subject or to take an arguable position about it. A strong thesis statement is neither too narrow nor too broad.

Subject and Assertion of the Thesis

From the analysis of the general topic, you saw the topic in terms of its two parts - *subject* and *assertion*. On the exam, your thesis or viewpoint on a particular topic is stated in two important points:

1.   the *SUBJECT* of the paper
2.   the *ASSERTION* about the subject.

The **subject of the thesis** relates directly to the topic prompt but expresses the specific area you have chosen to discuss. (Remember the exam topic will be general and will allow you to choose a particular subject related to the topic.) For example, the computer is one modern invention.

The **assertion of the thesis** is your viewpoint, or opinion, about the subject. The assertion provides the motive or purpose for your essay, and it may be an arguable point or one that explains or illustrates a point of view.

For example, you may present an argument for or against a particular issue. You may contrast two people, objects, or methods to show that one is better than the other. You may analyze a situation in all aspects and make recommendations for improvement. You may assert that a law or policy should be adopted, changed or abandoned. You may also, as in the computer example, explain to your reader that a situation or condition exists; rather than argue a viewpoint, you would use examples to illustrate your assertion about the essay's subject.

Specifically, the **subject** of Topic A is *the computer*. The **assertion** is that *it is a modern wonder that has improved our lives and that we rely on*. Now you quickly have created a workable thesis in a few moments:

> *The computer is a modern wonder of the world that has improved our lives and that we have come to rely on.*

Guidelines for Writing Thesis Statements

The following guidelines are not a formula for writing thesis statements but rather are general strategies for making your thesis statement clearer and more effective.

1. State a *particular point* of *view* about the topic with both a *subject* and an *assertion*. The thesis should give the essay purpose and scope and thus provide the reader a guide. If the thesis is vague, your essay may be undeveloped because you do not have an idea to assert or a point to explain. Weak thesis statements are often framed as facts, questions or announcements:

    a. Avoid a fact statement as a thesis. While a fact statement may provide a subject, it generally does not include a point of view about the subject that provides the basis for an extended discussion. Example: *Recycling saved our community over $10,000 last year.* This fact statement provides a detail, *not* a point of view. Such a detail might be found within an essay but it does not state a point of view.

    b. Avoid framing the thesis as a vague question. In many cases, rhetorical questions do not provide a clear point of view for an extended essay. Example: *How do people recycle?* This question neither asserts a point of view nor helpfully guides the reader to understand the essay's purpose and scope.

    c. Avoid the "announcer" topic sentence that merely states the topic you will discuss.
        Example: *I will discuss ways to recycle.* This sentence states the subject but the scope of the essay is only suggested. Again, this statement does not assert a viewpoint that guides the essay's purpose. It merely announces that the writer will write about the topic.

2. Start with a workable thesis. You might revise your thesis as you begin writing and discover your own point of view.

3. If feasible and appropriate, perhaps state the thesis in multi-point form, expressing the scope of the essay. By stating the points in parallel form, you clearly lay out the essay's plan for the reader.
    Example: *To improve the environment, we can recycle our trash, elect politicians who see the environment as a priority, and support lobbying groups who work for environmental protection.*

4. Because of the exam time limit, place your thesis in the first paragraph to key the reader to the essay's main idea.

Creating a working outline

A good thesis gives structure to your essay and helps focus your thoughts. When forming your thesis, look at your prewriting strategy – clustering, questioning, or brainstorming. Then decide quickly which two or three major areas you'll discuss. Remember you must limit *the scope* of the paper because of the time factor.

The **outline** lists those main areas or points as topics for each paragraph. Looking at the prewriting cluster on computers, you might choose several areas in which computers help us, for example in science and medicine, business, and education. You might also consider people's reliance on this "wonder" and include at least one paragraph about this reliance. A formal outline for this essay might look like the one below:

I.   Introduction and thesis
II. Computers used in science and medicine
II. Computers used in business
IV. Computers used in education
V.   People's reliance on computers
VI. Conclusion

Under time pressure, however, you may use a shorter organizational plan, such as abbreviated key words in a list. For example

1. intro: wonders of the computer OR
2. science
3. med
4. schools
5. business
6. conclusion

a. intro: wonders of computers - science
b. in the space industry
c. in medical technology
d. conclusion

Developing the essay

With a working thesis and outline, you can begin writing the essay. The essay should be in three main sections:

1) The **introduction** sets up the essay and leads to the thesis statement.
2) The **body paragraphs** are developed with concrete information leading from the **topic sentences**.
3) The **conclusion** ties the essay together.

Introduction

Put your thesis statement into a clear, coherent opening paragraph. One effective device is to use a funnel approach in which you begin with a brief description of the broader issue and then move to a clearly focused, specific thesis statement.

Consider the following introductions to the essay on computers. The length of each is an obvious difference. Read each and consider the other differences.

Does each introduce the subject generally?
Does each lead to a stated thesis?
Does each relate to the topic prompt?

Introduction 1: *Computers are used every day. They have many uses. Some people who use them are workers, teachers and doctors.*

Analysis: This introduction does give the general topic—i.e., that computers used every day—but it does not explain what those uses are. This introduction does not offer a point of view in a clearly stated thesis nor does it convey the idea that computers are a modem wonder.

Introduction 2: *Computers are used just about everywhere these days. I don't think there's an office around that doesn't use computers, and we use them a lot in all kinds of jobs. Computers are great for making life easier and work better. I don't think we'd get along without the computer.*

Analysis: This introduction gives the general topic about computers and mentions one area that uses computers. The thesis states that people couldn't get along without computers, but it does not state the specific areas the essay discusses. Note, too, the meaning is not helped by vague diction such as *a lot* or *great*.

Introduction 3: *Each day we either use computers or see them being used around us. We wake to the sound of a digital alarm operated by a micro-chip. Our cars run by computerized machinery. We use computers to help us learn. We receive phone calls and letters transferred from computers across continents. Our astronauts walked on the moon, and returned safely, all because of computer technology. The computer has a wonderful electronic brain that we have come to rely on and that has changed our world through advances in science, business, and education.*

Analysis: This introduction is the most thorough and fluent because it provides interest in the general topic and offers specific information about computers as a modern wonder. It also leads to a thesis that directs the reader to the scope of the discussion--advances in science, business, and education.

Topic Sentences

Just as the essay must have an overall focus reflected in the thesis statement, each paragraph must have a central idea reflected in the topic sentence. A good topic sentence also provides transition from the previous paragraph and relates to the essay's thesis. Good topic sentences, therefore, provide unity throughout the essay.

Consider the following potential topic sentences. Be sure that each provides transition and clearly states the subject of the paragraph.

Topic Sentence 1: *Computers are used in science.*

Analysis: This sentence simply states the topic--computers used in science. It does not relate to the thesis or provide transition from the introduction. The reader still does not know how computers are used.

Topic Sentence 2: *Now I will talk about computers used in science.*

Analysis: Like the faulty "announcer" thesis statement, this "announcer" topic sentence is vague and merely names the topic.

Topic Sentence 3: *First, computers used in science have improved our lives.*

Analysis: The transition word *First* helps link the introduction and this paragraph. It adds unity to the essay. It does not, however, give specifics about the improvement computers have made in our lives.

Topic Sentence 4: *First used in scientific research and spaceflights, computers are now used extensively in the diagnosis and treatment of disease.*

Analysis: This sentence is the most thorough and fluent. It provides specific areas that will be discussed in the paragraph and offers more than an announcement of the topic. The writer gives concrete information about the content of the paragraph that will follow.

Summary Guidelines for Writing Topic Sentences
1. Specifically relate the topic to the thesis statement.
2. State clearly and concretely the subject of the paragraph
3. Provide a transition from the previous paragraph
4. Avoid topic sentences that are facts, questions, or announcers.

Supporting Details – See Skill 5.2

End your essay with a brief straightforward **concluding paragraph** that ties together the essay's content and leaves the reader with a sense of its completion. The conclusion should reinforce the main points and offer some insight into the topic, provide a sense of unity for the essay by relating it to the thesis and signal clear closure of the essay.

Skill 14.2	**Demonstrate knowledge of techniques for revising, editing, and proofreading writing to improve organization and transitions and to correct errors in spelling, punctuation, and grammar**

Techniques for revising written texts to achieve clarity and economy of expression

Enhancing Interest:

- Start out with an attention-grabbing introduction. This sets an engaging tone for the entire piece and will be more likely to pull the reader in.
- Use dynamic vocabulary and varied sentence beginnings. Keep the reader on his toes. If he can predict what you are going to say next, switch it up.
- Avoid using clichés (as cold as ice, the best thing since sliced bread, nip it in the bud). These are easy shortcuts, but they are not interesting, memorable, or convincing.

Ensuring Understanding:

- Avoid using the words, "clearly," "obviously," and "undoubtedly." Often, things that are clear or obvious to the author are not as apparent to the reader. Instead of using these words, make your point so strongly that it is clear on its own.
- Use the word that best fits the meaning you intend for, even if they are longer or a little less common. Try to find a balance, a go with a familiar yet precise word.
- When in doubt, explain further.

Revision of sentences to eliminate wordiness, ambiguity, and redundancy

Sometimes this exercise is seen by students as simply catching errors in spelling or word use. Students need to reframe their thinking about revising and editing. Some questions that need to be asked:

- Is the reasoning coherent?
- Is the point established?
- Does the introduction make the reader want to read this discourse?
- What is the thesis? Is it proven?
- What is the purpose? Is it clear? Is it useful, valuable, interesting?
- Is the style of writing so wordy that it exhausts the reader and interferes with engagement?
- Is the writing so spare that it is boring?
- Are the sentences too uniform in structure?
- Are there too many simple sentences?
- Are too many of the complex sentences the same structure?
- Are the compounds truly compounds or are they unbalanced?
- Are parallel structures truly parallel?
- If there are characters, are they believable?
- If there is dialogue, is it natural or stilted?
- Is the title appropriate?
- Does the writing show creativity or is it boring?
- Is the language appropriate? Is it too formal? Too informal? If jargon is used, is it appropriate?

Studies have clearly demonstrated that the most fertile area in teaching writing is this one. If students can learn to revise their own work effectively, they are well on their way to becoming effective, mature writers. Word processing is an important tool for teaching this stage in the writing process. Microsoft Word has tracking features that make the revision exchanges between teachers and students more effective than ever before.

Techniques to Maintain Focus

- **Focus on a main point.** The point should be clear to readers and all sentences in the paragraph should relate to it.

- **Start the paragraph with a topic sentence.** This should be a general, one-sentence summary of the paragraph's main point, relating both back towards the thesis and toward the content of the paragraph. (A topic sentence is sometimes unnecessary if the paragraph continues a developing idea clearly introduced in a preceding paragraph or if the paragraph appears in a narrative of events where generalizations might interrupt the flow of the story.)

- **Stick to the point.** Eliminate sentences that do not support the topic sentence.

- **Be flexible.** If there is not enough evidence to support the claim your topic sentence is making, do not fall into the trap of wandering or introducing new ideas within the paragraph. Either find more evidence, or adjust the topic sentence to collaborate with the evidence that is available.

Skill 14.3   Demonstrate knowledge of appropriate methods for documenting sources used in writing (e.g., footnotes, endnotes, bibliography) in order to avoid plagiarism

This skill pertains to recognizing that stealing intellectual property is an academic and, in some cases, a legal crime; because it is so, students need to learn how to give credit where credit is due.

Students need to be aware of the rules as they apply to borrowing ideas from various sources. Increasingly, consequences for violations of these rules (plagiarism) are becoming more severe and students are expected to be aware of how to avoid such problems. Pleading ignorance is less and less of a defense. Such consequences include failing a particular assignment, losing credit for an entire course, expulsion from a learning environment, and civil penalties. Software exists that enables teachers and other interested individuals to determine quickly whether or not a given paper includes plagiarized material. As members of society in the information age, students are expected to recognize the basic justice of intellectual honesty and to conform to the systems meant to ensure it.

There are several style guides for documenting sources. Each guide has its own particular ways of signaling that information has been directly borrowed or paraphrased and familiarity with at least where to find the relevant details of the major style guides is an essential for students. Many libraries publish overviews of the major style guides for students to consult, most bookstores will carry full guides for the major systems, and relevant information is readily available on the web, as well.

Documentation of sources takes two main forms. The first form applies to citing sources in the text of the document or as footnotes or endnotes. In-text documentation is sometimes called parenthetical documentation and requires specific information within parentheses placed immediately after borrowed material. Footnotes or endnotes are placed either at the bottom of relevant pages or at the end of the document.

Beyond citing sources in the text, style guides also require a bibliography, a references section, or a works cited section at the end of the document. Sources for any borrowed material are to be listed according to the rules of the particular guide. In some cases, it may be required to include a works consulted listing even though no material is directly cited or paraphrased to the extent that an in-text citation would be required.

The major style guides to be familiar with include the <u>Modern Language Association Handbook</u> (MLA), the <u>Manual of the American Psychological Association</u> (APA), the <u>Chicago Manual of Style</u>, Turabian, and <u>Scientific Style and Format: the CBE Manual</u>.
Documentation of sources from the internet is particularly involved and continues to evolve at a pace often requiring visiting the latest online update available for a particular style guide.

Example:

In-Text Citation-
According to Steve Mandel, "our average conversational rate of speech is about 125 words per minute" (78).

Works Cited Entry-
Mandel, Steve. *Effective Presentation Skills*. Menlo Park, California: Crisp
　　　Publications, 1993.

COMPETENCY 15.0   UNDERSTAND THE RULES AND CONVENTIONS OF STANDARD AMERICAN ENGLISH GRAMMAR AND USAGE

Skill 15.1   Identify various noun forms (e.g., common, proper, abstract, collective, plural, possessive)

The multiplicity and complexity of spelling rules based on phonics, letter doubling, and exceptions to rules, if not mastered by adulthood, should be replaced by a good dictionary. As spelling mastery is also difficult for adolescents, our recommendation is the same. Learning the use of a dictionary and thesaurus will be a more rewarding use of time.

Most **plurals** of nouns that end in hard consonants or hard consonant sounds followed by a silent *e* are made by adding *s*. Some words ending in vowels only add *s*.

> fingers, numerals, banks, bugs, riots, homes, gates, radios, bananas

Nouns that end in soft consonant sounds *s, j, x, z, ch,* and *sh,* add *es*. Some nouns ending in *o* add es.

> dresses, waxes, churches, brushes, tomatoes

Nouns ending in *y* preceded by a vowel just add *s*.

> boys, alleys

Nouns ending in *y* preceded by a consonant change the *y* to *i* and add *es*.

> babies, corollaries, frugalities, poppies

Some nouns' plurals are formed irregularly or remain the same.
> sheep, deer, children, leaves, oxen

Some nouns derived from foreign words, especially Latin, may make their plurals in two different ways - one of them Anglicized. Sometimes, the meanings are the same; other times, the two plurals are used in slightly different contexts. It is always wise to consult the dictionary.

> appendices, appendixes   criterion, criteria
> indexes, indices   crisis, crises

Make the plurals of closed (solid) compound words in the usual way except for words ending in *ful* which make their plurals on the root word.

> timelines, hairpins

Make the plurals of open or hyphenated compounds by adding the change in inflection to the word that change in number.

> fathers-in-law, courts-martial, masters of art, doctors of medicine

Make the plurals of letters, numbers, and abbreviations by adding *s*.

> fives and tens, IBMs, 1990s, *p*s and *q*s (Note that letters are italicized.)

Possessive nouns

Make the possessives of singular nouns by adding an apostrophe followed by the letter *s* (*'s*).

> baby's bottle, father's job, elephant's eye, teacher's desk, sympathizer's protests, week's postponement

Make the possessive of singular nouns ending in *s* by adding either an apostrophe or an (*'s*) depending upon common usage or sound. When making the possessive causes difficulty, use a prepositional phrase instead. Even with the sibilant ending, with a few exceptions, it is advisable to use the (*'s*) construction.

> dress's color, species' characteristics or characteristics of the species, James' hat or James's hat, Delores's shirt. Make the possessive of plural nouns ending in *s* by adding the apostrophe after the *s*. horses' coats, jockeys' times, four days' time

Make possessives of plural nouns that do not end in *s* the same as singular nouns by adding *'s*.

> children's shoes, deer's antlers, cattle's horns

Make possessives of compound nouns by adding the inflection at the end of the word or phrase.

> the mayor of Los Angeles' campaign, the mailman's new truck, the mailmen's new trucks, my father-in-law's first wife, the keepsakes' values, several daughters-in-law's husbands

Skill 15.2 **Identify types, characteristics, and uses of pronouns (e.g., personal, possessive, interrogative, demonstrative, reflexive, indefinite) and recognize how to decline pronouns by gender and case and use them correctly in a sentence**

Agreements between pronoun and antecedent

A pronoun must correspond to its antecedent in number (singular or plural), person (first, second or third person) and gender (male, female or neutral). A pronoun must refer clearly to a single word, not to a complete idea.

A **pronoun shift** is a grammatical error in which the author starts a sentence, paragraph, or section of a paper using one particular type of pronoun and then suddenly shifts to another. This often confuses the reader.

Error: A teacher should treat all their students fairly.

Problem: Since *A teacher* is singular, the pronoun referring to it must also be singular. Otherwise, the noun has to be made plural.

Correction: *Teachers should treat all their students fairly.*

Error: When an actor is rehearsing for a play, it often helps if you can memorize the lines in advance.

Problem: *Actor* is a third-person word; that is, the writer is talking about the subject. The pronoun *you* is in the second person, which means the writer is talking to the subject.

Correction: *When actors are rehearsing for plays, it helps if they can memorize the lines in advance.*

Error: The workers in the factory were upset when his or her paychecks didn't arrive on time.

Problem: *Workers* is a plural form, while *his or her* refers to one person.

Correction: *The workers in the factory were upset when their paychecks didn't arrive on time.*

Error: The charity auction was highly successful, which pleased everyone.

Problem: In this sentence the pronoun *which* refers to the idea of the auction's success. In fact, *which* has no antecedent in the sentence; the word success is not stated.

Correction: *Everyone was pleased at the success of the auction.*

Error: Lana told Melanie that she would like aerobics.
Problem: The person that she refers to is unclear; it could be either Lana or Melanie.

Correction: *Lana said that Melanie would like aerobics.*

OR

Lana told Melanie that she, Melanie, would like aerobics.

Error: I dislike accounting, even though my brother is one.

Problem: A person's occupation is not the same as a field, and the pronoun *one* is thus incorrect. Note that the word *accountant* is not used in the sentence, so *one* has no antecedent.

Correction: *I dislike accounting, even though my brother is an accountant.*

Rules for clearly identifying pronoun reference

Make sure that the antecedent reference is clear and cannot refer to something else

A "distant relative" is a relative pronoun or a relative clause that has been placed too far away from the antecedent to which it refers. It is a common error to place a verb between the relative pronoun and its antecedent.

Error: Return the books to the library that are overdue.
Problem: The relative clause "that are overdue" refers to the "books" and should be placed immediately after the antecedent.
Correction: Return the books that are overdue to the library.
              or
              Return the overdue books to the library.

A pronoun should not refer to adjectives or possessive nouns

Adjectives, nouns or possessive pronouns should not be used as antecedents. This will create ambiguity in sentences.

Error: In Todd's letter he told his mom he'd broken the priceless vase.
Problem: In this sentence the pronoun "he" seems to refer to the noun phrase "Todd's letter" though it was probably meant to refer to the possessive noun "Todd's."
Correction: In his letter, Todd told his mom that he had broken the priceless vase.

A pronoun should not refer to an implied idea

A pronoun must refer to a specific antecedent rather than an implied antecedent. When an antecedent is not stated specifically, the reader has to guess or assume the meaning of a sentence. Pronouns that do not have antecedents are called expletives. "It" and "there" are the most common expletives, though other pronouns can also become expletives as well. In informal conversation, expletives allow for casual presentation of ideas without supporting evidence. However, in more formal writing, it is best to be more precise.

Error: She said that it is important to floss every day.
Problem: The pronoun "it" refers to an implied idea.
Correction: She said that flossing every day is important.

Error: They returned the book because there were missing pages.
Problem: The pronouns "they" and "there" do not refer to the antecedent.
Correction: The customer returned the book with missing pages.

Using Who, That and Which

Who, whom and **whose** refer to human beings and can either introduce essential or nonessential clauses. **That** refers to things other than humans and is used to introduce essential clauses. **Which** refers to things other than humans and is used to introduce nonessential clauses.

Error: The doctor that performed the surgery said the man would be fully recovered.
Problem: Since the relative pronoun is referring to a human, "who" should be used.
Correction: The doctor who performed the surgery said the man would be fully recovered.

Error: That ice cream cone that you just ate looked really delicious.
Problem: That has already been used so you must use *which* to introduce the next clause, whether it is essential or nonessential.
Correction: That ice cream cone, which you just ate, looked really delicious.

Proper case forms

Pronouns, unlike nouns, change case forms. Pronouns must be in the subjective, objective, or possessive form according to their function in the sentence.

Personal Pronouns

Subjective (Nominative)		Possessive		Objective	
	Singular	Plural	Singular	Plural	Singular	Plural
1st person	I	We	My	Our	Me	Us
2nd person	You	You	Your	Your	You	You
3rd person	He She It	They	His Her Its	Their	Him Her It	them

Relative Pronouns
Who	Subjective/Nominative
Whom	Objective
Whose	Possessive

Error: Tom and me have reserved seats for next week's baseball game.

Problem: The pronoun *me* is the subject of the verb *have reserved* and should be in the subjective form.

Correction: *Tom and I have reserved seats for next week's baseball game.*

Error: Mr. Green showed all of we students how to make paper hats.

Problem: The pronoun *we* is the object of the preposition *of*. It should be in the objective form, us.

Correction: *Mr. Green showed all of us students how to make paper hats.*

Error: Who's coat is this?

Problem: The interrogative possessive pronoun is whose; *who's* is the contraction for who is.

Correction: *Whose coat is this?*

Error: The voters will choose the candidate whom has the best qualifications for the job.

Problem: The case of the relative pronoun who or whom is determined by the pronoun's function in the clause in which it appears. The word who is in the subjective case and whom is in the objective. Analyze how the pronoun is being used within the sentence.

Correction: *The voters will choose the candidate who has the best qualifications for the job.*

Skill 15.3   Demonstrate knowledge of various types of verbs and verb phrases (e.g., action, transitive, intransitive, linking, helping)

Past tense and past participles
Both regular and irregular verbs must appear in their standard forms for each tense. Note: the ed or d ending is added to regular verbs in the past tense and for past participles.

Infinitive	Past Tense	Past Participle
Bake	Baked	Baked

Irregular Verb Forms

Infinitive	Past Tense	Past Participle
Be	Was, were	Been
Become	Became	Become
Break	Broke	Broken
Bring	Brought	Brought
Choose	Chose	Chosen
Come	Came	Come
Do	Did	Done
Draw	Drew	Drawn
Eat	Ate	Eaten
Fall	Fell	Fallen
Forget	Forgot	Forgotten
Freeze	Froze	Frozen
Give	Gave	Given
Go	Went	Gone
Grow	Grew	Grown
Have/has	Had	Had
Hide	Hid	Hidden
Know	Knew	Known
Lay	Laid	Laid
Lie	Lay	Lain
Ride	Rode	Ridden
Rise	Rose	Risen
Run	Ran	Run
See	Saw	Seen
Steal	Stole	Stolen
Take	Took	Taken
Tell	Told	Told
Throw	Threw	Thrown
Wear	Wore	Worn
Write	Wrote	Written

Error: She should have went to her doctor's appointment at the scheduled time.

Problem: The past participle of the verb *to go* is *gone*. *Went* expresses the simple past tense.

Correction: *She should have gone to her doctor's appointment at the scheduled time.*

Error: My train is suppose to arrive before two o'clock.

Problem: The verb following *train* is a present tense passive construction which requires the present tense verb *to be* and the past participle.

Correction: *My train is supposed to arrive before two o'clock.*

Error: Linda should of known that the car wouldn't start after leaving it out in the cold all night.

Problem: *Should of* is a nonstandard expression. *Of is* not a verb.

Correction: *Linda should have known that the car wouldn't start after leaving it out in the cold all night.*

Inappropriate shifts in verb tense

Verb tenses must refer to the same time period consistently, unless a change in time is required.

Error: Despite the increased amount of students in the school this year, overall attendance is higher last year at the sporting events.

Problem: The verb *is* represents an inconsistent shift to the present tense when the action refers to a past occurrence.

Correction: *Despite the increased amount of students in the school this year, overall attendance was higher last year at sporting events.*

Error: My friend Lou, who just competed in the marathon, ran since he was twelve years old.

Problem: Because Lou continues to run, the present perfect tense is needed.

Correction: *My friend Lou, who just competed in the marathon, has ran since he was twelve years old.*

Error: The Mayor congratulated Wallace Mangham, who renovates the city hall last year.

Problem: Although the speaker is talking in the present, the action of renovating the city hall was in the past.

Correction: *The Mayor congratulated Wallace Mangham, who renovated the city hall last year.*

Agreement between subject and verb

A verb must correspond in the singular or plural form with the simple subject; it is not affected by any interfering elements. Note: A simple subject is never found in a prepositional phrase (a phrase beginning with a word such as of, by, over, through, until).

Present Tense Verb Form

	Singular	Plural
1st person (talking about oneself)	I do	We do
2nd person (talking to another)	You do	You do
3rd person (talking about someone or something)	He She does It	They do

Error: Sally, as well as her sister, plan to go into nursing.

Problem: The subject in the sentence is *Sally* alone, not the word *sister*. Therefore, the verb must be singular.

Correction: *Sally, as well as her sister, plans to go into nursing.*

Error: There has been many car accidents lately on that street.

Problem: The subject accidents in this sentence is plural; the verb must be plural also --even though it comes before the subject.

Correction: *There have been many car accidents lately on that street.*

Error: Everyone of us have a reason to attend the school musical.

Problem: The simple subject is the word *everyone*, not the *us* in the prepositional phrase. Therefore, the verb must be singular also.

Correction: *Everyone of us has a reason to attend the school musical.*

Error: Either the police captain or his officers is going to the convention.

Problem: In either/or and neither/nor constructions, the verb agrees with the subject closer to it.

Correction: *Either the police captain or his officers are going to the convention.*

Skill 15.4 Differentiate between adverbs and adjectives

Adjectives are words that modify or describe nouns or pronouns. Adjectives usually precede the words they modify, but not always; for example, an adjective occurs after a linking verb.

Adverbs are words that modify verbs, adjectives, or other adverbs. They cannot modify nouns. Adverbs answer such questions as how, why, when, where, how much, or how often something is done. Many adverbs are formed by adding "ly."

Error: The birthday cake tasted sweetly.

Problem: *Tasted* is a linking verb; the modifier that follows should be an adjective, not an adverb.

Correction: *The birthday cake tasted sweet.*

Error: You have done good with this project.

Problem: *Good* is an adjective and cannot be used to modify a verb phrase such as "have done."

Correction: *You have done well with this project.*

Error: The coach was positive happy about the team's chance of winning.

Problem: The adjective *positive* cannot be used to modify another adjective, *happy*. An adverb is needed instead.

Correction: *The coach was positively happy about the team's chance of winning.*

Error: The fireman acted quick and brave to save the child from the burning building.

Problem: *Quick and brave* are adjectives and cannot be used to describe a verb. Adverbs are needed instead.

Correction: *The fireman acted quickly and bravely to save the child from the burning building.*

Skill 15.5   **Identify characteristics and uses of conjunctions, prepositions, and prepositional phrases**

Conjunctions are used to join various grammatical units. There are three main types of conjunctions.

Coordinating conjunctions join equal grammatical units and include the words *and, but, or, so, nor, yet* (meaning 'but'), and *for* (meaning something close to "because").
And and *or* very often join words or phrases. Examples:

John **and** Mary ate **and** slept. Joe must do it in the beginning **or** at the end.

All the coordinating conjunctions can be used to join independent clauses to form compound sentences. When so used, the coordinating conjunction must be preceded by a comma. Examples:

John took a seat**, but** Mary remained standing. Mary slept**, and** John went for a walk.

Subordinating conjunctions join dependent clauses (clauses that cannot stand alone as complete sentences) to independent clauses to create complex sentences. Subordinating conjunctions include *after, although, as, as if, as long as, as much as, as though, because, before, even if, even though, how, if, inasmuch, in order that, lest, now that, provided that, since, so that, that, though, till ('til), unless, until, when, whenever, where, wherever,* and *while.*

If the subordinate (dependent) clause comes before the independent clause, it is called an introductory subordinate clause, and you must use a comma between it and the independent clause. If the dependent clause comes after the independent clause, do not use a comma. Examples:

Although John is very intelligent, he has trouble with spelling.

John has trouble spelling **although he is very intelligent**.

Correlative conjunctions join various sentence elements that are to be considered as equals or related. They include *both/and, not only/but also, not/but, either/or, neither/nor, whether/or,* and *as/so.* Examples:

Not only smoking cigarettes yourself, *but also* inhaling secondhand smoke, can be lethal.

Neither screaming *nor* weeping, John faced the verdict with stoic determination.

Prepositions occur only in phrases and these phrases function as modifiers indicating a relationship between the preposition's object and some other sentence element. **Prepositional phrases** can be adverbial or adjectival. Examples:

The man *under the bridge* is a criminal. This prepositional phrase modifies *man* and is adjectival.

The man slept *under the bridge.* This prepositional phrase modifies *slept* and is adverbial.

In both examples, the word *under* is the actual preposition and the word *bridge* is the object of the preposition.

The following is a list of words that are prepositions when governing objects in phrases: *about, above, across, after, against, along, among, around, at, before, behind, below, beneath, beside, between, beyond, but for, by, despite, down, during, except, for, from, in, inside, into, like, near, of, off, on, onto, out, outside, over, past, since, through, throughout, till, to toward, under, underneath, until, up, upon, with, within,* and *without.*

Skill 15.6 **Recognize parts of sentences (e.g., subject, verb, clause, phrase, direct and indirect objects, subject and object complements) and identify simple, compound, and complex sentences**

Sentence structure

Recognize simple, compound, complex, and compound-complex sentences. Use dependent (subordinate) and independent clauses correctly to create these sentence structures.

Simple – Consists of one independent clause
>> Joyce wrote a letter.

Compound – Consists of two or more independent clauses. The two clauses are usually connected by a coordinating conjunction (and, but, or, nor, for, so, yet). Compound sentences are sometimes connected by semicolons.
>> Joyce wrote a letter and Dot drew a picture.

Complex- Consists of an independent clause plus one or more dependent clauses. The dependent clause may precede the independent clause or follow it.
>> While Joyce wrote a letter, Dot drew a picture.

Compound/Complex – Consists of one or more dependent clauses plus two or more independent clauses.
>> When Mother asked the girls to demonstrate their new-found skills, Joyce wrote a letter and Dot drew a picture.

Note: Do **not** confuse compound sentence elements with compound sentences.

> Simple sentence with compound subject
>> <u>Joyce</u> and <u>Dot</u> wrote letters.
>> The <u>girl</u> in row three and the <u>boy</u> next to her were passing notes across the aisle.

> Simple sentence with compound predicate
>> Joyce <u>wrote letters</u> and <u>drew pictures</u>.
>> The captain of the high school debate team <u>graduated with honors</u> and <u>studied broadcast journalism in college</u>.

> Simple sentence with compound object of preposition
>> Colleen graded the students' essays for <u>style</u> and <u>mechanical accuracy</u>.

Types of Clauses

Clauses are connected word groups that are composed of *at least* one subject and one verb. (A subject is the doer of an action or the element that is being joined. A verb conveys either the action or the link.)

Students are waiting for the start of the assembly.
Subject   Verb

At the end of the play, students wait for the curtain to come down.
               Subject   Verb

Clauses can be independent or dependent.

Independent clauses can stand alone or can be joined to other clauses.

Independent clause	for and nor	
Independent clause,	but or yet so	Independent clause
Independent clause	;	Independent clause
Dependent clause	,	Independent clause
Independent clause		Dependent clause

Dependent clauses, by definition, contain at least one subject and one verb. However, they cannot stand alone as a complete sentence. They are structurally dependent on the main clause.

There are two types of dependent clauses: (1) those with a subordinating conjunction and (2) those with a relative pronoun

Sample coordinating conjunctions:
Although
When
If
Unless
Because

Unless a cure is discovered, many more people will die of the disease.
    Dependent clause   +   Independent clause

Sample relative pronouns:
Who
Whom
Which
That

The White House has an official website, which contains press releases, news updates, and biographies of the President and Vice-President.
(Independent clause + relative pronoun + relative dependent clause)

Skill 15.7   Recognize fragments, run-on sentences, and dangling modifiers and demonstrate the ability to correct them

Fragments occur (1) if word groups standing alone are missing either a subject or a verb, and (2) if word groups containing a subject and verb and standing alone are actually made dependent because of the use of subordinating conjunctions or relative pronouns.

Error: The teacher waiting for the class to complete the assignment.

Problem: This sentence is not complete because an ing word alone does not function as a verb. When a helping verb is added (for example, was waiting), it will become a sentence.

Correction: *The teacher was waiting for the class to complete the assignment.*

Error: Until the last toy was removed from the floor.

Problem: Words such as until, because, although, when, and if make a clause dependent and thus incapable of standing alone. An independent clause must be added to make the sentence complete.

Correction: *Until the last toy was removed from the floor, the kids could not go outside to play.*

Error: The city will close the public library. Because of a shortage of funds.

Problem: The problem is the same as above. The dependent clause must be joined to the independent clause.

Correction: *The city will close the public library because of a shortage of funds.*

Error: Anyone planning to go on the trip should bring the necessary items. Such as a backpack, boots, a canteen, and bug spray.

Problem: The second word group is a phrase and cannot stand alone because there is neither a subject nor a verb. The fragment can be corrected by adding the phrase to the sentence.

Correction: *Anyone planning to go on the trip should bring the necessary items, such as a backpack, boots, a canteen, and bug spray.*

Run-on sentences and comma splices

Comma splices appear when two sentences are joined by only a comma. Fused sentences appear when two sentences are run together with no punctuation at all.

Error: Dr. Sanders is a brilliant scientist, his research on genetic disorders won him a Nobel Prize.

Problem: A comma alone cannot join two independent clauses (complete sentences). The two clauses can be joined by a semicolon or they can be separated by a period.

Correction: *Dr. Sanders is a brilliant scientist; his research on genetic disorders won him a Nobel Prize.*
OR
Dr. Sanders is a brilliant scientist. His research on genetic disorders won him a Nobel Prize.

Error: Florida is noted for its beaches they are long, sandy, and beautiful.

Problem: The first sentence ends with the word beaches and the second sentence cannot be joined with the first. The fused sentence error can be corrected in several ways: (1) one clause may be made dependent on another with a subordinating conjunction or a relative pronoun; (2) a semicolon may be used to combine two equally important ideas; (3) the two independent clauses may be separated by a period.

Correction: *Florida is noted for its beaches, which are long, sandy, and beautiful.*

OR

Florida is noted for its beaches; they are long, sandy, and beautiful.

OR

Florida is noted for its beaches. They are long, sandy, and beautiful.

Error: The number of hotels has increased, however, the number of visitors has grown also.

Problem: The first sentence ends with the word increased, and a comma is not strong enough to connect it to the second sentence. The adverbial transition "however" does not function the same way as a coordinating conjunction and cannot be used with commas to link two sentences. Several different corrections are available.

Correction: *The number of hotels has increased; however, the number of visitors has grown also.*
[Two separate but closely related sentences are created with the use of the semicolon.]

OR

The number of hotels has increased. However, the number of visitors has grown also.
[Two separate sentences are created.]

OR

Although the number of hotels have increased, the number of visitors has grown also.
[One idea is made subordinate to the other and separated with a comma.]

OR

The number of hotels has increased, but the number of visitors has grown also.
[The comma before the coordinating conjunction *but* is appropriate. The adverbial transition "however" does not function the same way as the coordinating conjunction but does.]

Skill 15.8   Demonstrate the ability to use punctuation and capitalization correctly

Commas

Commas indicate a brief pause. They are used to set off dependent clauses and long introductory word groups, to separate words in a series, to set off unimportant material that interrupts the flow of the sentence, and to separate independent clauses joined by conjunctions.

Error: After I finish my master's thesis I plan to work in Chicago.

Problem: A comma is needed after an introductory dependent word-group containing a subject and verb.

Correction: *After I finish my master's thesis, I plan to work in Chicago.*

Error: I washed waxed and vacuumed my car today.

Problem: Nouns, phrases, or clauses in a list, as well as two or more coordinate adjectives that modify one word should be separated by commas. Although the word *and* is sometimes considered optional, it is often necessary to clarify the meaning.

Correction: *I washed, waxed, and vacuumed my car today.*

Error: She was a talented dancer but she is mostly remembered for her singing ability.

Problem: A comma is needed before a conjunction that joins two independent clauses (complete sentences).

Correction: *She was a talented dancer, but she is mostly remembered for her singing ability.*

Semicolons and colons

Semicolons are needed to separate two or more closely related independent clauses when the second clause is introduced by a transitional adverb. (These clauses may also be written as separate sentences, preferably by placing the adverb within the second sentence). **Colons** are used to introduce lists and to emphasize what follows.

Error:	I climbed to the top of the mountain, it took me three hours.
Problem:	A comma alone cannot separate two independent clauses. Instead a semicolon is needed to separate two related sentences.
Correction:	*I climbed to the top of the mountain; it took me three hours.*
Error:	In the movie, asteroids destroyed Dallas, Texas, Kansas City, Missouri, and Boston, Massachusetts.
Problem:	Semicolons are needed to separate items in a series that already contains internal punctuation.
Correction:	*In the movie, asteroids destroyed Dallas, Texas; Kansas City, Missouri; and Boston, Massachusetts.*
Error:	Essays will receive the following grades, A for excellent, B for good, C for average, and D for unsatisfactory.
Problem:	A colon is needed to emphasize the information or list that follows.
Correction:	*Essays will receive the following grades: A for excellent, B for good, C for average, and D for unsatisfactory.*
Error:	The school carnival included: amusement rides, clowns, food booths, and a variety of games.
Problem:	The material preceding the colon and the list that follows is not a complete sentence. Do not separate a verb (or preposition) from the object.
Correction:	*The school carnival included amusement rides, clowns, food booths, and a variety of games.*

Apostrophes

Apostrophes are used to show either contractions or possession.

Error: She shouldnt be permitted to smoke cigarettes in the building.

Problem: An apostrophe is needed in a contraction in place of the missing letter.

Correction: *She shouldn't be permitted to smoke cigarettes in the building.*

Error: My cousins motorcycle was stolen from his driveway.

Problem: An apostrophe is needed to show possession.

Correction: *My cousin's motorcycle was stolen from his driveway.* (Note: The use of the apostrophe before the letter "s" means that there is just one cousin. The plural form would read the following way: My cousins' motorcycle was stolen from their driveway.)

Error: The childrens new kindergarten teacher was also a singer.

Problem: An apostrophe is needed to show possession.

Correction: *The childrens' new kindergarten teacher was also a singer.* (Note: The apostrophe after the "s" indicates that there is more than one child.)

Error: Children screams could be heard for miles.

Problem: An apostrophe and the letter s are needed in the sentence to show whose screams it is.

Correction: *Children's screams could he heard for miles.*

Quotation marks

In a quoted statement that is either declarative or imperative, place the period inside the closing quotation marks.

> "The airplane crashed on the runway during takeoff."

If the quotation is followed by other words in the sentence, place a comma inside the closing quotations marks and a period at the end of the sentence.

> "The airplane crashed on the runway during takeoff," said the announcer.

In most instances in which a quoted title or expression occurs at the end of a sentence, the period is placed before either the single or double quotation marks.

> "The middle school readers were unprepared to understand Bryant's poem 'Thanatopsis.'"

> Early book-length adventure stories like *Don Quixote* and *The Three Musketeers* were known as "picaresque novels."

There is an instance in which the final quotation mark would precede the period—if the content of the sentence were about a speech or quote so that the understanding of the meaning would be confused by the placement of the period.

> The first thing out of his mouth was "Hi, I'm home."
> *but*
> The first line of his speech began "I arrived home to an empty house".

In sentences that are interrogatory or exclamatory, the question mark or exclamation point should be positioned outside the closing quotation marks if the quote itself is a statement or command or cited title.

> Who decided to lead us in the recitation of the "Pledge of Allegiance"?

> Why was Tillie shaking as she began her recitation, "Once upon a midnight dreary..."?

> I was embarrassed when Mrs. White said, "Your slip is showing"!

In sentences that are declarative but the quotation is a question or an exclamation, place the question mark or exclamation point inside the quotation marks.

The hall monitor yelled, "Fire! Fire!"

"Fire! Fire!" yelled the hall monitor.

Cory shrieked, "Is there a mouse in the room?" (In this instance, the question supersedes the exclamation.)

Quotations - whether words, phrases, or clauses - should be punctuated according to the rules of the grammatical function they serve in the sentence.

The works of Shakespeare, "the bard of Avon," have been contested as originating with other authors.

"You'll get my money," the old man warned, "when 'Hell freezes over'."

Sheila cited the passage that began "Four score and seven years ago...." (Note the ellipsis followed by an enclosed period.)

"Old Ironsides" inspired the preservation of the U.S.S. Constitution.
Use quotation marks to enclose the titles of shorter works: songs, short poems, short stories, essays, and chapters of books. (See "Using Italics" for punctuating longer titles.)

"The Tell-Tale Heart"   "Casey at the Bat"   "America the Beautiful"

Dashes and Italics

Place **dashes** to denote sudden breaks in thought.

>   Some periods in literature - the Romantic Age, for example -
>   spanned different time periods in different countries.

Use dashes instead of commas if commas are already used elsewhere in the
sentence for amplification or explanation.

>   The Fireside Poets included three Brahmans - James Russell
>   Lowell, Henry David Wadsworth, Oliver Wendell Holmes -
>   and John Greenleaf Whittier.

Use **italics** to punctuate the titles of long works of literature, names of
periodical publications, musical scores, works of art and motion picture
television, and radio programs. (When unable to write in italics, students
should be instructed to underline in their own writing where italics would
be appropriate.)

The Idylls of the King	*Hiawatha*	*The Sound and the Fury*
Mary Poppins	*Newsweek*	*The Nutcracker Suite*

Capitalization

Capitalize all proper names of persons (including specific organizations or
agencies of government); places (countries, states, cities, parks, and specific
geographical areas); and things (political parties, structures, historical and
cultural terms, and calendar and time designations); and religious terms (any
deity, revered person or group, sacred writings).

>   Percy Bysshe Shelley, Argentina, Mount Rainier National Park,
>   Grand Canyon, League of Nations, the Sears Tower, Birmingham,
>   Lyric Theater, Americans, Midwesterners, Democrats, Renaissance,
>   Boy Scouts of America, Easter, God, Bible, Dead Sea Scrolls, Koran

Capitalize proper adjectives and titles used with proper names.

California gold rush, President John Adams, French fries, Homeric epic,
Romanesque architecture, Senator John Glenn

Note: Some words that represent titles and offices are not capitalized unless used with a proper name.

<u>Capitalized</u>	<u>Not Capitalized</u>
Congressman McKay	the congressman from Florida
Commander Alger	commander of the Pacific Fleet
Queen Elizabeth	the queen of England

Capitalize all main words in titles of works of literature, art, and music.

Error: Emma went to Dr. Peters for treatment since her own Doctor was on vacation.

Problem: The use of capital letters with Emma and Dr. Peters is correct since they are specific (proper) names; the title Dr. is also capitalized. However, the word doctor is not a specific name and should not be capitalized.

Correction: *Emma went to Dr. Peters for treatment since her own doctor was on vacation.*

Error: Our Winter Break does not start until next wednesday.

Problem: Days of the week are capitalized, but seasons are not capitalized.

Correction: *Our winter break does not start until next Wednesday.*

Error: The exchange student from israel who came to study biochemistry spoke spanish very well.

Problem: Languages and the names of countries are always capitalized. Courses are also capitalized when they refer to a specific course; they are not capitalized when they refer to courses in general.

Correction: *The exchange student from Israel who came to study Biochemistry spoke Spanish very well.*

COMPETENCY 16.0   UNDERSTAND LISTENING AND SPEAKING SKILLS THAT ARE EFFECTIVE AND APPROPRIATE FOR COMMUNICATION IN A CLASSROOM SETTING

Skill 16.1   Demonstrate the ability to clarify, illustrate, or expand on an idea or topic of discussion (e.g., paraphrasing, asking open-ended questions)

A successful speech requires three stages of preparation and/or adaptation: pre-speech, during the speech, and post-speech.

Pre-speech Preparation

- Know the audience. In order to generate positive feedback, one must know to whom it is that he or she will be speaking. Factors such as the audience's size, background/s, relationship to the speaker, and the audience's knowledge of the speech's topic must be considered when preparing the presentation.
- If the speaker has the opportunity to discuss the topic with an audience member or members prior to the speech, do so in order to learn about their backgrounds, experiences, expectations, and knowledge of the subject.
- If the audience addressed is primarily homogenous, try to incorporate material and references relevant to that group into the speech. Doing so can help to persuade people and establish rapport with them. But take care to not say anything that might exclude or demean any member of the audience.
- If the speaker is unfamiliar with the audience that he or she will be addressing, ask the relevant person—the boss, one's contact person, the event organizer, etc.—for information about the audience.
- When preparing the speech topic, keep in mind just what the speech's goal is and how it might best be achieved.
- Anticipate disagreement. If one is promoting a particular product, course of action, or viewpoint, think beforehand about any possible objections that might be raised in response to the speech. Then prepare clear and appropriate answers.

During the Speech

When delivering a speech before a live audience one must be aware of non-verbal feedback that may be given by the listeners: eye contact or no eye contact, nodding or shaking of the head, facial expressions indicating engagement or boredom, and raised hands indicating the desire to make comments or ask questions. In order to reciprocate and respond to these types of feedback, the speaker should:

- Make clear at the beginning of the speech if questions will be fielded during or after the speech, or both.
- Make sustained eye contact with all audience members or, if speaking to a large group, with all parts of the room, hall, etc.
- Decide whether or not the speech will be given from a fixed point—from behind a podium, for instance—or if one is going to work the audience by moving about the room, up and down aisles, etc. Doing the latter can enhance the audience's sense of closeness to the speaker.
- If using Power Point or a blackboard during the speech, be careful to not spend too much time facing away from the audience.
- Make sure that the speech doesn't conclude abruptly. Otherwise the audience may be surprised or left with the impression that the speaker was overly eager to be done speaking.
- When concluding a speech make clear to the audience that questions or comments are welcome.

Post-speech

- Answer any audience member's questions or comments forthrightly. If a speaker doesn't know the answer to a question, he or she should tell the questioner that an answer would be quickly provided. Get the questioner's contact information, then respond accordingly.
- If relevant, speakers should provide audience members with contact information in case further questions or comments arise.
- As the question-and-answer session comes to a close, be sure to thank the audience for their time and attention.

An excellent guide to all facets of speech preparation and performance is *The St. Martin's Guide to Public Speaking* by Joseph S. Tuman and Douglas M. Fraleigh.

Skill 16.2   Analyze strategies for organizing, delivering, and sharing information

The content in material to be presented orally plays a big role in how it is organized and delivered. For example, a literary analysis or a book report will be organized inductively, laying out the details and then presenting a conclusion, which will usually be what the author's purpose, message, and intent are. If the analysis is focusing on multiple layers in a story, it will probably follow the preliminary conclusion. On the other hand, keeping in mind that the speaker will want to keep the audience's attention, if the content has to do with difficult-to-follow facts and statistics, slides (or PowerPoint) may be used as a guide to the presentation, and the speaker will intersperse interesting anecdotes, jokes, or humor from time to time so the listeners don't fall asleep. Preparing to speak on a topic should be seen as a process that has stages:

Discovery: There are many possible sources for the information that will be used to create an oral presentation. The first step in the discovery process is to settle on a topic or subject. Answer the question, What is the speech going to be about? For example, the topic or subject could be immigration. In the discovery stage, one's own knowledge, experience, and beliefs should be the first source, and notes should be taken as the speaker probes this source. The second source can very well be interviews with friends and possibly experts. The third source will be research: what has been written or said publicly on this topic. This stage can get out of hand very quickly, so a plan for the collecting of source information should be well-organized with time limits set for each part.

Organization: At this point, several decisions need to be made. The first is what the *purpose* of the speech is. Does the speaker want to persuade the audience to believe something or to act on something, or does the speaker simply want to present information that the audience might not have? Once that decision is made, a thesis should be developed. What point does the speaker want to make? And what are the points that will support that point? And in what order will those points be arranged? Introductions and conclusions should be written last. The purpose of the introduction is to draw the audience into the topic. The purpose of the conclusion is to polish off the speech, making sure the thesis is clear, reinforcing the thesis, or summarizing the points that have been made.

Editing: This is the most important stage in preparing a speech. Once decisions have been made in the discovery and organization stages, it's good to allow time to let the speech rest for awhile and to go back to it with fresh eyes. Objectivity is extremely important and the speaker should be willing to make drastic changes if they are needed. It's difficult to let go of one's own composition, but good speechmakers are able to do that. On the other hand, this can also get out of hand, and it should be limited. The speaker must recognize that at some point, the decisions must be made, the die must be cast, and commitment to the speech as it stands must be made if the speaker is to deliver the message with conviction.

The concept of recursiveness is very useful to one who writes speeches. That is, everything must be written at the outset with full knowledge that it can be changed and the willingness to go backward, even to the discovery stage, is what makes a good speechwriter.

Skill 16.3   Evaluate the effectiveness and appropriateness of details and examples given to support an opinion or explain a point of view

The more information a speaker has about an audience, the more likely he/she is to communicate effectively with them. Several factors figure into the speaker/audience equation: age, ethnic background, educational level, knowledge of the subject, and interest in the subject.

Speaking about computers to senior citizens who have, at best, rudimentary knowledge about the way computers work must take that into account. Perhaps handing out a glossary would be useful for this audience. Speaking to first-graders about computers presents its own challenges. On the other hand, the average high-school student has more experience with computers than most adults and that should be taken into account. Speaking to a room full of computer systems engineers requires a rather thorough understanding of the jargon related to the field.

In considering the age of the audience, it's best not to make assumptions. The gathering of senior citizens might include retired systems engineers or people who have made their livings using computers, so research about the audience is important. It might not be wise to assume that high-school students have a certain level of understanding, either.

With an audience that is primarily Hispanic with varying levels of competence in English, the speaker is obligated to adjust the presentation to fit that audience. The same would be true when the audience is composed of people who may have been in the country for a long time but whose families speak their first language at home. Black English presents its own peculiarities, and if the audience is composed primarily of African-Americans whose contacts in the larger community are not great, some efforts need to be made to acquaint oneself with the specific peculiarities of the community those listeners come from.

It's unwise to talk down to an audience; they will almost certainly be insulted. On the other hand, speaking to an audience of college graduates will require different skills than speaking to an audience of people who have never attended college.

Finally, has the audience come because of an interest in the topic or because they have been influenced or forced to come to the presentation? If the audience comes with an interest in the subject already, efforts to motivate or draw them into the discussion might not be needed. On the other hand, if the speaker knows the audience does not have a high level of interest in the topic, it would be wise to use devices to draw them into it, to motivate them to listen.

Skill 16.4 Analyze the role of critical thinking skills (e.g., selecting and evaluating supporting data, evaluating a speaker's point of view) in effective listening and speaking

More and more, teachers are encouraged to develop critical thinking skills in their students rather than only filling their heads with facts and information, as important as that is. If students are not able to use their knowledge to gain understanding and to think independently, they will not be truly educated. Critical thinking depends on the principles of classical rhetoric. Even though they were originally devised by the Greek orators, they have evolved and are still pertinent in the twenty-first century.

Types of Appeal

- Ethos—Refers to the credibility of the speaker. It utilizes the credentials of the speaker as a reliable and trustworthy authority.
- Pathos—Refers to the emotional appeal made by the speaker to the listeners. It emphasizes the fact that the audience responds to ideas with emotion. For example, when the government is trying to persuade citizens to go to war for the sake of "the fatherland," it is using the appeal to *pathos* to target their love of their country.
- Logos—Refers to the logic of the speaker's argument. It utilizes the idea that facts, statistics and other forms of evidence can convince an audience to accept a speaker's argument. Remember that information can be just as, if not more than, persuasive than appeal tactics.

Types of Persuasive Speech

1. Fact: Similar to an informative speech, a persuasive speech on a question of fact seeks to find an answer where there isn't a clear one. The speaker evaluates evidence and attempts to convince the audience that his/her conclusion is correct. The challenge is to accept a certain carefully crafted view of the facts presented.

2. Value: This kind of persuasion tries to convince the audience that a certain thing is good or bad, moral or immoral, valuable or worthless. It focuses less on knowledge and more on beliefs and values.

3. Policy: This speech is a call to action, arguing that something should be done, improved or changed. Its goal is action from the audience, but it also seeks passive agreement with the proposition proposed. It appeals to both reason and emotion, and tells listeners what they can do and how to do it.

Logical Fallacies

A fallacy is essentially an error in reasoning. In persuasive speech, logical fallacies are instances of reasoning flaws that make an argument invalid. For example, a premature generalization occurs when you form a general rule based on only one or a few specific cases, which do not represent all possible cases. An illustration of this is the statement, "Bob Marley was a Rastafarian singer. Therefore, all Rastafarians sing."

Skill 16.5   Demonstrate knowledge of effective group communication techniques (e.g., brainstorming)

Research shows that students that work together in groups or teams develop their skills in organizing, leadership, research, communication, and problem solving. Working in teams can help students to overcome anxiety in distance learning courses and contribute a sense of community and belonging for the students.

What is Cooperative/Collaborative Learning?

When students work together in small groups, research shows that students tend to learn more material being taught and retain the information longer than when the same information is taught using different methods.

The process in both cooperative and collaborative learning is that students work in groups or teams to reach a goal. Cooperative and collaborative discussions actively encourage the student to interact with faculty, other students, and the material in meaningful ways. Providing opportunities for students to communicate with each other what they are learning in an online environment is one highly effective way to engage students in the active learning process. Some collaborative or cooperative learning strategies include:

- **Panel discussion** - A panel/group of students is given a set of questions from which they prepare a group response.
- **Case study** - A group of students is given a narrative description of a problematic situation and then asked to identify and/or solve the problem.
- **Action maze** - A group of students is given a description of an incident that requires analysis and action. They provide a brief response and then forward it to another group. The group that received that response must determine the consequences of the first group's response and either agree or come up with a better response. This process can go on through as many levels as the instructor feels is meaningful.
- **Role-playing** - A team of students is asked to take on the parts of characters in a dramatic representation of a real situation or organizational unit. Role-playing can take place in a chat room or via bulletin board response to questions. Students respond as their character would respond throughout the planned dialog.
- **Students as teachers** - A group of students develops the presentation of a course topic for the rest of the class, perhaps posing one or more interesting questions for class discussion.
- **Formal debate** - Students are divided into teams to present opposing viewpoints; some students may act as respondents or judges.
- **Writing groups** - Students present drafts of written assignments to one another for critique and then revise their drafts based on other student comments.

Group Interactions

Assign a student in each group a specific role they will take on for the source of the activity:

- Leader—the leader directs the action for the day once the teacher has given the instructions.
- Recorder—this group member does the writing for the entire group; he or she uses one sheet, which saves paper.
- Encourager—the encourager gives compliments related to how the group is working, such as "That was a great answer!"
- Checker—this member checks and hands in the work for the group.

Collaboration

- Students decide on goals and the means to accomplish those goals.
- Students decide which roles to play to reach goals.
- Students practice negotiation and social skills and evaluate both their own contributions and those of the other group members.
- Students learn to collaborate and reinforce one another's strengths and observe that people with different strengths may accomplish goals differently or more efficiently.

A good activity to enforce the importance of collaboration breaks the students into groups of four. They use a problem-solving plan and work together during class time as well as outside of class. A recent problem: Would it be cheaper to get to New York City from Long Island by car, bus, or plane? The students show their plans and all their work for each mode of transportation so there are no questions about their answers. The groups may have a little trouble getting started and getting all parties involved, but the final outcome will ensure improved cooperation skills as well as real world training.

Skill 16.6   Demonstrate knowledge of problem-solving sequences (i.e., defining a problem and identifying possible solutions, selecting the optimal solution, and implementing and evaluating the solution)

Effective problem solving involves several sequential steps. First of all, students must carefully articulate a problem to be solved. Vague generalizations will not do and the effort and attention devoted to stating the problem in specific and manageable terms will be amply rewarded by the efficiency with which the succeeding steps unfold.

After stating the problem, students brainstorm for possible solutions. During this stage, they try to come up with several viable options and to be innovative.

Once they have generated these options, students evaluate them in order to identify which one seems the most promising for solving the problem. This involves devising and employing a rubric delineating evaluative criteria.

Having chosen a possible solution, the students next test it on the problem. During this phase, they pay strict attention to the actual results even if those results suggest that the possible solution is not working as they had hoped.

After analyzing the results of their experiment, students either congratulate themselves on having devised an altogether perfect solution, revise the solution to address relatively minor drawbacks, or scrap it entirely and select another approach.

All phases of the problem-solving sequence require students to employ principles of effective speaking and listening. They need to be on task; open to, and supportive of, each other's ideas; willing to contribute their insights; and capable of devising, and sticking to, democratic processing routines.

COMPETENCY 17.0 UNDERSTAND LISTENING AND SPEAKING SKILLS THAT ARE EFFECTIVE AND APPROPRIATE FOR INTERACTING SOCIALLY IN A VARIETY OF FORMAL AND INFORMAL SITUATIONS

Skill 17.1 Distinguish among styles of language (e.g., formal, informal, technical, regional) appropriate for various purposes, content, audiences, and occasions

It's important to take the consistency of the audience into account when organizing a presentation. If the audience can be counted on to have a high level of interest in what is being presented, little would need to be done in the way of organizing and presenting to hold interest. On the other hand, if many of those in the audience are there because they have to be, or if the level of interest can be counted on not to be very high, something like a PowerPoint presentation can be very helpful. Also, the lead-in and introduction need to be structured not only to be entertaining and interest-grabbing, but also to create an interest in the topic. If the audience is senior citizens, it's important to keep the presentation lively and to be careful not to talk down to them. Carefully written introductions aimed specifically at this audience will go a long way to attract their interest in the topic.

No speaker should stand up to make a presentation if the purpose has not been carefully determined ahead of time. If the speaker is not focused on the purpose, the audience will quickly lose interest. As to organizing for a particular purpose, some of the decisions to be made are where it will occur in the presentation—beginning, middle, or end—and whether displaying the purpose on a chart, PowerPoint or banner will enhance the presentation. The purpose might be the lead-in for a presentation if it can be counted on to grab the interest of the listeners, in which case the organization will be deductive. If it seems better to save the purpose until the end, the organization will then be inductive.

The occasion, of course, plays an important role in the development and delivery of a presentation. A celebration speech when the company has achieved an important accomplishment will be organized around congratulating those who were most responsible for the accomplishment and giving some details about how it was achieved and probably something about the competition for the achievement. The presentation will be upbeat and not too long. On the other hand, if bad news is being presented, it will probably be the CEO who is making the presentation and the bad-news announcement will come first followed with details about the news itself and how it came about, and probably end with a pep talk and encouragement to do better the next time.

Skill 17.2 **Demonstrate knowledge of effective techniques for listening and speaking in conversation (e.g., using appropriate language, providing verbal and nonverbal responses to the speaker, responding to and initiating new topics of discussion, soliciting comments, asserting opinions without dominating discussions)**

The successful conversationalist is a person who keeps up with what's going on in the world both far and near and ponders the meanings of events and developments. That person also usually reads about the topics that are of the most interest to him, both in printed materials and online. In addition, the effective conversationalist has certain areas that are of particular interest that have been probed in some depth. An interest in human behavior is usually one of this person's most particular interests. Why do people behave as they do? Why do some succeed and some fail? This person will also be interested in and concerned about social issues, particularly in the immediate community but also on a wider scale and will have ideas for solving some of those problems.

With all of this, the most important thing a good conversationalist can do is to *listen*, not just to wait until the other person quits speaking so he or she can take the floor again but actually listening to learn what the other person has to say and also to learn more about that other person. Following a gathering, the best thing a person can think about another is that a person was interested enough to listen to the one's ideas and opinions, and that is the person who will be remembered the longest and with the most regard.

It's acceptable to be passionate about one's convictions in polite conversation; it is not acceptable to be overbearing or unwilling to hear and consider another's point of view. It's important to keep one's emotions under control in these circumstances even if the other person does not.

Skill 17.3 **Demonstrate knowledge of effective techniques for listening and speaking in small and large-group situations (e.g., monitoring reactions by interpreting nonverbal cues, displaying appropriate turn-taking behavior)**

Different from the basic writing forms of discourse is the art of debating, discussion, and conversation. The ability to use language and logic to convince the audience to accept your reasoning and to side with you is an art. This form of writing/speaking is extremely confined or structured, is logically sequenced, and includes supporting reasons and evidence. At its best, it is the highest form of propaganda. A position statement, evidence, reason, evaluation and refutation are integral parts of this writing schema.

Interviewing provides opportunities for students to apply expository and informative communication. It teaches them how to structure questions to evoke fact-filled responses. Compiling the information from an interview into a biographical essay or speech helps students to list, sort, and arrange details in an orderly fashion.

Speeches that encourage them to describe persons, places, or events in their own lives or oral interpretations of literature help them sense the creativity and effort used by professional writers.

Listening

Communication skills are crucial in a collaborative society. In particular, a person can not be a successful communicator without being an active listener.

Focus on what others say, rather than planning on what to say next. By listening to everything another person is saying, you may pick up on natural cues that lead to the next conversation move without so much added effort.

Facilitating

It is quite acceptable to use standard opening lines to facilitate a conversation. Don't agonize over trying to come up with witty one-liners, as the main obstacle in initiating conversation is just getting the first statement over with. After that, the real substance begins. A useful technique may be to make a comment or ask a question about a shared situation. This may be anything from the weather, to the food you are eating, to a new policy at work. Use an opener you are comfortable with, because most likely, your partner in conversation will be comfortable with it as well.

Stimulating Higher Level Critical Thinking Through Inquiry

Many people rely on questions to communicate with others. However, most fall back on simple clarifying questions rather than open-ended inquiries. Try to ask open-ended, deeper-level questions, since those tend to have the greatest reward and lead to a greater understanding. In answering those questions, more complex connections are made and more significant realizations are achieved.

Political correctness is a concept bandied about frequently in the twenty-first century. It has always existed, of course. The successful speaker of the nineteenth century understood and was sensitive to audiences. However, that person was typically a man and the only audience that was important was a male audience; more often than not, the only important audience was a white one.

Many things have changed in discourse since the nineteenth century just as the society the speaker lives in and addresses has changed and the speaker who disregards the existing conventions for political correctness usually finds himself in trouble. Rap music makes a point of ignoring those conventions, particularly with regard to gender, and is often the target of very hostile attacks.

TEACHER CERTIFICATION STUDY GUIDE

On the other hand, rap performers often intend to be revolutionary and have developed their own audiences and have become outrageously wealthy by exploiting those newly-developed audiences based primarily on thumbing their noses at establishment conventions.

Even so, the successful speaker must understand and be sensitive to what is current in political correctness. The "n word" is a case in point. There was a time when that term was deployed at will by politicians and other public speakers, but no more. Nothing could spell the end of a politician's career more certainly than using that term in his campaign or public addresses.

These terms are called "pejorative"—a word or phrase that expresses contempt or disapproval. Such terms as _redneck_, _queer_, or _cripple_ may only be considered pejorative if used by a non-member of the group they apply to. For example, the "n word," which became very inflammatory in the 1960s, is now being used sometimes by African-American artists to refer to themselves, especially in their music, with the intention of underscoring their protest of the establishment.

References to gender became particularly sensitive in the twenty-first century as a result of the women's rights movement and the speaker who disregards these sensitivities does so at his/her peril. The generic "he" is no longer acceptable and this requires a strategy to deal with pronominal references without repetitive he/she, his/her, etc. There are several ways to approach this: switch to a passive construction that does not require a subject; switch back and forth, using the male pronoun in one reference and the female pronoun in another one, being sure to sprinkle them reasonably evenly; or switch to the plural. The last alternative is the one most often chosen. This requires some care and the speaker should spend time developing these skills before stepping in front of an audience.

Debates and panel discussions fall under the umbrella of formal speaking and the rules for formal speaking should apply here, although lapsing into conversational language is acceptable. Swear words should be avoided in these situations.

LANGUAGE ARTS 169

A debate presents two sides of a debatable thesis—pro and con. Each side will posit a hypothesis, prove it, and defend it. A formal debate is a sort of formal dance with each side following a strictly defined format. However, within those guidelines, debaters are free to develop their arguments and rebuttals as they choose. The successful debater prepares by developing very thoroughly both sides of the thesis: "Mexico's border with the United States must be closed" and "Mexico's border with the United States must remain open." Debaters must be thoroughly prepared to argue their own side, but they must also have a strategy for rebutting the opposing side's arguments. All aspects of critical thinking and logical argument are employed, and the successful debaters will use ethical appeal (their own credibility) and emotional appeal to persuade the judges who will determine who wins—that is, the side that best establishes its thesis, proves it logically, but also *persuades* the audience to come over to its position.

A panel is typically composed of *experts* who explain and defend a particular topic. Often, panels will include representatives from more than one field of study and more than one position on the topic. Typically, each will have a limited amount of time to make an opening statement either presenting explanatory material or arguing a point of view. Then the meeting will be opened up to the audience for questions. A moderator will keep order and will control the time limits on the opening statements and responses and will sometimes intervene and ask a panel member that was not the target of a particular question from the audience to elaborate or rebut the answer of the panel member who was questioned. Panels are usually limited to four or five people although in special cases, they may be much larger.

COMPETENCY 18.0   UNDERSTAND VIEWING, LISTENING, AND
                  SPEAKING SKILLS THAT ARE EFFECTIVE FOR
                  RESPONDING TO AND DELIVERING VARIOUS
                  FORMS OF MEDIA PRESENTATIONS

Skill 18.1   Recognize the characteristics and uses of various media (e.g.,
             television, radio, film, computer graphics, the Internet)

Still visual media includes pictures, drawings, photographs, tables, charts, maps,
and diagrams. Techniques employed by still visual media include choosing colors
appropriate to the purpose, placing important information in strategic locations
within the still, sequencing stills (stages, overlays), sizing stills for optimum effect,
placing stills in understandable contexts, and providing sufficient key or legend
information.

Moving visual media includes movies and videos. Techniques employed by
visual media include most of those applicable to the still media plus determining
a storyline or presentation rationale. In other words, the moving presentation
needs to have an understandable beginning, development, and conclusion.
Obviously, choosing effective transitions between scenes and installing a
reasonable pace of image movement figure importantly in visual media. If the
presentation is in slow motion or going by at warp speed for no discernable
reason, that is going to detract from the intended impact.

Oral media includes songs, chants, speeches, and readings of stories, poems
and articles. It can be stored on records, tapes, CDs, and an ever-evolving array
of computer-like implements. Techniques employed by oral media include
choosing an appropriate volume, applying principles of prosody (pace, pitch,
inflection, voice modulation, accents, etc.), employing rhythm and rhyme, and
enhancing the impact through musical instruments or sound effects.

Skill 18.2   Analyze ways in which visual images communicate
             information, influence attitudes, and change opinions and
             impressions

Posters. The power of the political poster in the twenty-first century seems trivial
considering the barrage of electronic campaigning, mudslinging, and reporting
that seem to take over the video and audio media in election season. Even so,
the political poster is a powerful propaganda tool, and it has been around for a
long time. For example, in the first century AD, a poster that calls for the election
of a Satrius as quinquennial has survived to this day. Nowhere have political
posters been used more powerfully or effectively than in Russia in the 1920s in
the campaign to promote communism. Many of the greatest Russian writers of
that era were the poster writers. Those posters would not be understood at all
except in the light of what was going on in the country at the time.

However, today we see them primarily at rallies and protests where they are usually hand-lettered and hand-drawn. The message is rarely subtle. Understanding the messages of posters requires little thought as a rule. However, they are usually meaningless unless the context is clearly understood. For example, a poster reading "Camp Democracy" can only be understood in the context of the protests of the Iraq War near President Bush's home near Crawford, Texas. "Impeach" posters are understood in 2006 to be directed at President Bush, not a local mayor or representative.

Cartoons. The political cartoon (aka editorial) presents a message or point of view concerning people, events, or situations using caricature and symbolism to convey the cartoonist's ideas, sometimes subtly, sometimes brashly, but always quickly. A good political cartoon will have wit and humor, which is usually obtained by exaggeration that is slick and not used merely for comic effect. It will also have a foundation in truth; that is, the characters must be recognizable to the viewer and the point of the drawing must have some basis in fact even if it has a philosophical bias. The third requirement is a moral purpose.

Using political cartoons as a teaching tool enlivens lectures, prompts classroom discussion, promotes critical thinking, develops multiple talents and learning styles, and helps prepare students for standardized tests. It also provides humor. However, it may be the most difficult form of literature to teach. Many teachers who choose to include them in their social studies curricula caution that, while students may enjoy them, it's doubtful whether they are actually getting the cartoonists' messages.

The best strategy for teaching such a unit is through a subskills approach that leads students step-by-step to higher orders of critical thinking. For example, the teacher can introduce caricature and use cartoons to illustrate the principles. Students are able to identify and interpret symbols if they are given the principles for doing so and get plenty of practice, and cartoons are excellent for this. It can cut down the time it takes for students to develop these skills, and many of the students who might lose the struggle to learn to identify symbols may overcome the roadblocks through the analysis of political cartoons. Many political cartoons exist for the teacher to use in the classroom and they are more readily available than ever before.

A popular example of an editorial cartoon that provides a way to analyze current events in politics is the popular comic strip "Doonesbury" by Gary Trudeau. For example, in the time period prior to the 2004 presidential election, Alex, the media-savvy teenager, does her best to participate in the political process. In January she rallies her middle school classmates to the phones for a Deanathon and by August she is luring Ralph Nader supporters into discussions on Internet chat rooms. Knowledgeable about government, active in the political process, and willing to enlist others, Alex has many traits that educators intend to develop.

Skill 18.3   **Analyze oral presentations by identifying a speaker's purpose and paraphrasing a speaker's point of view**

Questions: Ask students what strategies the spoken message uses, how well those strategies respond to the requirements of the situation, and how well the speaker responded to spontaneous occurrences, questions, or problems.

Perception Checking: This is a feedback technique. It refers to the effort to understand the feelings behind the words.

Ask students to describe their impressions of the speaker's feelings. They should not relay any feelings of approval or disapproval.

Paraphrasing: When students paraphrase, it is significant to stress that the resulting summary reflects what the spoken message meant to the student, not what it actually meant or was intended to mean. Have students practice different types of paraphrasing, such as restating the original statement in more specific terms, using an example, or restating it in more general terms.

Skill 18.4   **Identify effective methods for using media to express a point of view and inform and persuade others**

Visual graphics include a spectrum of artifacts. Pictures, graphs, charts, tables, and drawings are all useful to a greater or lesser degree in a wide variety of educational communications. There are several principles to keep in mind regarding these graphic communications. One principle addresses aesthetics; effective graphics should be pleasing to look at. This is especially true if the graphic is some type of picture. It should be strategically placed, its colors should be well-chosen, and the size of the graphic should be suited to its intended purpose. Within the graphic itself, design features should enhance the intended communication. At the very least, it needs to be large enough to easily view. Legends associated with a given graphic should be clear and thorough. The graphic, to be most effective, should be presented in a context that allows students to understand its function and importance.

Audiovisual communications include films and film strips, and the principles that apply singly to graphic and oral communications respectively both apply to audiovisual communications. In a classroom context, it is important to present audiovisual resources in ways that ensure student engagement. Thus, rather than simply inserting a video and playing it for the whole period, it is better to pause the video at least a few times during the period and lead the class through some type of processing routines. This will build in some accountability and some engagement for the students. Technologies that incorporate interactive dimensions of audiovisual material are especially effective in communicating information and ensuring adequate student focus, especially in the absence of dynamic, teacher-directed processing.

A common classroom assignment that applies to this skill is to view the movie version of a book studied by a particular class, to compare and contrast the two media, and to argue which did the better job of conveying the intended message(s).

It is difficult to convey the same message across different media due to the dynamics specific to those media. The degree of difficulty increases as the complexity of the message does. Nonetheless, certain general observations inform the discussion.

A print message has two kinds of unique features. Some seem to be positive. For instance, print messages have longevity; they are also easily portable. Print messages appeal almost exclusively to the mind, and allow students to recursively read sections that warrant more thought. Other features of print seem potentially negative. For instance, a print message requires an active reader; without such a reader, print messages are not very effective. Print messages are not accessible to non-readers.

A graphic message in the hands of an artistic genius can produce images that seem to be Jungian archetypes. More commonly, a graphic message gives a quick overview of some quantifiable situation. Some learners find that graphic information works for them better than print, and many struggling readers find graphic messages more helpful, too. However, compared to print, graphic messages convey a much shorter range of information. If the particular graphic is inspiring, the inspirations it conveys are subject to the descriptions of the various 'readers' who view it. With print, the inspired scripts are already there for the reader, provided the reader is applying active reading skills.

An audio message allows for messages delivered with attention to prosody. Students who can't read can access the material. Audio messages invite the "reader" to form mental images consistent with the topic of the audio. Audio messages allow the learners to close their eyes for better mental focus. Listening to an audio message is a more passive modality than reading a print message. As a rule, people read faster than normal speech patterns, so print conveys more information in a given time span.

An audiovisual message offers the easiest accessibility for learners. It has the advantages of each, the graphic and the audio, medium. Learners' eyes and ears are engaged. Non-readers get significant access to content. On the other hand, viewing an audiovisual presentation is an even more passive activity than listening to an audio message because information is coming to learners effortlessly through two senses. Activities to foster a critical perspective on an audiovisual presentation serve as valuable safeguards against any overall and unwelcome passivity.

Skill 18.5 **Demonstrate knowledge of techniques for making effective dramatic presentations or interpretations, including appropriate changes in delivery (e.g., gestures, expression, tone, pace, visuals)**

Delivery Techniques

Posture: Maintain a straight, but not stiff posture. Instead of shifting weight from hip to hip, point your feet directly at the audience and distribute your weight evenly. Keep shoulders orientated towards the audience. If you have to turn your body to use a visual aid, turn 45 degrees and continue speaking towards the audience.

Movement: Instead of staying glued to one spot or pacing back and forth, stay within four to eight feet of the front row of your audience, and take maybe a step or half-step to the side every once in a while. If you are using a lectern, feel free to move to the front or side of it to engage your audience more. Avoid distancing yourself from the audience, you want them to feel involved and connected.

Gestures: Gestures are a great way to keep a natural atmosphere when speaking publicly. Use them just as you would when speaking to a friend. They shouldn't be exaggerated, but they should be utilized for added emphasis. Avoid keeping your hands in your pockets or locked behind your back, wringing your hands and fidgeting nervously, or keeping your arms crossed.

Eye Contact: Many people are intimidated by using eye contact when speaking to large groups. Interestingly, eye contact usually *helps* the speaker overcome speech anxiety by connecting with their attentive audience and easing feelings of isolation. Instead of looking at a spot on the back wall or at your notes, scan the room and make eye contact for one to three seconds per person.

Voice: Many people fall into one of two traps when speaking: using a monotone, or talking too fast. These are both caused by anxiety. A monotone restricts your natural inflection, but can be remedied by releasing tension in upper and lower body muscles. Subtle movement will keep you loose and natural. Talking too fast on the other hand, is not necessarily a bad thing if the speaker is exceptionally articulate. If not though, or if the speaker is talking about very technical things, it becomes far too easy for the audience to become lost. When you talk too fast and begin tripping over your words, consciously pause after every sentence you say. Don't be afraid of brief silences. The audience needs time to absorb what you are saying.

Volume: Problems with volume, whether too soft or too loud, can usually be combated with practice. If you tend to speak too softly, have someone stand in the back of the room and give you a signal when your volume is strong enough. If possible, have someone in the front of the room as well to make sure you're not overcompensating with excessive volume. Conversely, if you have a problem with speaking too loud, have the person in the front of the room signal you when your voice is soft enough and check with the person in the back to make sure it is still loud enough to be heard. In both cases, note your volume level for future reference. Don't be shy about asking your audience, "Can you hear me in the back?" Suitable volume is beneficial for both you and the audience.

Pitch: Pitch refers to the length, tension and thickness of a person's vocal bnds. As your voice gets higher, the pitch gets higher. In oral performance, pitch reflects upon the emotional arousal level. More variation in pitch typically corresponds to more emotional arousal, but can also be used to convey sarcasm or highlight specific words.

Skill 18.6 Demonstrate the ability to organize information and use multimedia tools to present information for various purposes and audiences

More money is spent each year on advertising towards children than educating them. Thus, the media's strategies are considerably well thought out and effective. They employ large, clear letters, bold colors, simple line drawings, and popular symbols to announce upcoming events, push ideas and advertise products. By using attractive photographs, brightly colored cartoon characters or instructive messages, they increase sales, win votes or stimulate learning. The graphics are designed to communicate messages clearly, precisely, and efficiently. Some even target subconscious yearnings for sex and status.

Because so much effort is being spent on influencing students through media tactics, just as much effort should be devoted to educating those students about media awareness. A teacher should explain that artists and the aspect they choose to portray, as well as the ways in which they portray them, reflect their attitude and understanding of those aspects. The artistic choices they make are not entirely based on creative license—they also reflect an imbedded meaning the artist wants to represent. Colors, shapes, and positions are meant to arouse basic instincts for food, sex, and status, and are often used to sell cars, clothing, or liquor.

To stimulate analysis of media strategies, ask students such questions as:

- Where/when do you think this picture was taken/film was shot/piece was written?
- Would you like to have lived at this time in history, or in this place?
- What objects are present?
- What do the people presented look like? Are they happy or sad?
- Who is being targeted?
- What can you learn from this piece of media?
- Is it telling you something is good or bad?
- What message is being broadcasted?

Advertising Techniques

Beauty Appeal: Beauty attracts us; we are drawn to beautiful people, places, and things.

Celebrity Endorsement: Associates product use with a well-known person. By purchasing this product we are led to believe that we will attain characteristics similar to the celebrity.

Compliment the Consumer: Advertisers flatter the consumer who is willing to purchase their product. By purchasing the product the consumer is recognized by the advertisers for making a good decision with their selection.

Escape: Getting away from it all is very appealing; you can imagine adventures you cannot have; the idea of escape is pleasurable.

Independence/Individuality: Associates product with people who can think and act for themselves. Products are linked to individual decision making.

Intelligence: Associates product with smart people who can't be fooled.

Lifestyle: Associates product with a particular style of living/way of doing things.

Nurture: Every time you see an animal or a child, the appeal is to your paternal or maternal instincts. Associates products with taking care of someone.

Peer Approval: Associates product use with friendship/acceptance. Advertisers can also use this negatively, to make you worry that you'll lose friends if you don't use a certain product.

Rebel: Associates products with behaviors or lifestyles that oppose society's norms.

Rhetorical Question: This technique poses a question to the consumer that demands a response. A question is asked and the consumer is supposed to answer in such a way that affirms the product's goodness.

Scientific/Statistical Claim: Provides some sort of scientific proof or experiment, very specific numbers, or an impressive-sounding mystery ingredient.

Unfinished Comparison/Claim: Use of phrases such as "Works better in poor driving conditions!" Works better than what?

Skill 18.7 **Recognize appropriate ways to respond to oral communications through questions, challenges, or affirmations**

It has been reported that Socrates, the Great Questioner, said "No one can teach, if by teaching we mean the transmission of knowledge, in any mechanical fashion, from one person to another. The most that can be done is that one person who is more knowledgeable than another can, by asking a series of questions, stimulate the other to think, and so cause him to learn for himself."

Socrates was able to forcefully defeat his opponents simply by asking them a series of questions that would reveal inconsistencies in their arguments. He prized intellectual independence very highly and only considered that when his students had overcome habit and prejudice had they learned anything. Modern teachers, if they wish to succeed in turning out students who are willing and capable of thinking for themselves critically and responsibly, must learn to be effective questioners.

Before using this teaching tool, the teacher should ask herself what *purpose* is served by the questioning. Questioning can be a very effective way to check for understanding at various levels of cognition.

Convergent questions (direct or closed questions) should be used for assessing lower levels of cognition. Divergent questions (indirect or open questions) are useful for assessing higher levels of cognition.

Questions can be used to promote critical thinking and can help the teacher determine whether students understand organizational and managerial directions. Questioning facilitates the pacing of instructional content.

The teacher should assure that each student's success rate when answering questions is increasing, that every student is provided an equal opportunity to answer questions, and the maximum number of students will be involved in the questioning activity.

The teacher should allow time for students to think about a question at least three seconds. After a three-second pause, the teacher should call on a student to answer. If a student has answered during that wait-time, the teacher should use a "stop" hand signal to prevent students from responding before the "wait" is over. After three seconds, it's wise to repeat the question, and then call on a student to answer. Teachers should specify how students are to answer when called upon and should train students to abide by this procedure until they become used to it. It's best to ignore students who do not abide by the rules established for answering.

To increase students' opportunities to respond, the teacher should follow these steps:

    1) Ask specific questions requiring short answers.
    2) redirect questions to other students.
    3) solicit unison responses from students.

In order to enable all students to have an equal opportunity to answer questions, the teacher must

    4) prompt students how to answer,
    5) wait 3-5 seconds after asking a question,
    6) ignore or correct inappropriate answering behaviors, and
    7) praise appropriate answering behavior.

To improve student success when answering questions, the teacher should

    8) use a wait time for thinking and
    9) provide hints to unsuccessful or inhibited students.

Sample Test

Essay Question

Read the passage below from *The Diary of Anne Frank* (1947); then complete the exercise that follows.

Written on July 15, 1944, three weeks before the Frank family was arrested by the Nazis, Anne's diary entry explains her world view and future hopes.

"It's difficult in times like these: ideals, dreams and cherished hopes rise within us, only to be crushed by grim reality. It's a wonder I haven't abandoned all my ideals, they seem so absurd and impractical. Yet I cling to them because I still believe, in spite of everything, that people are truly good at heart.

"It's utterly impossible for me to build my life on a foundation of chaos, suffering and death. I see the world being slowly transformed into a wilderness, I hear the approaching thunder that, one day, will destroy us too, I feel the suffering of millions, And yet, when I look up at the sky, I somehow feel that everything will change for the better, that this cruelty too shall end, that peace and tranquility will return once more. In the meantime, I must hold on to my ideals. Perhaps the day will come when I will be able to realize them!"

Using your knowledge of literature, write a response in which you:

- Compare and contrast Anne's ideals with her awareness of the conditions in which she lives; and
- Discuss how the structure of Anne's writing—her sentences and paragraphs—emphasize the above contrast.

Sample Weak Response

Anne Frank's ideals in this writing make readers clear on the point that she was strongly against Hitler and the Nazis. You can tell that she knows the Nazis are very dangerous and violent people who cause "the suffering of millions." Otherwise, why would she have written this? This fact of Nazis causing the suffering of millions of people, and killing them, is a large contrast to how much she believes "that people are truly good at heart." Anne Frank is right about her ideals. And that is why her whole book is such a large contrast to the conditions in which she lived in WWII, when everything was going wrong in the world. You can also tell from this passage that she is a lot smarter than Hitler was. That is another big contrast in the book.

Anne's sentences and paragraphs emphasize the above contrast. They are not fiction; they are her own real thoughts, and these thoughts don't cause "a grim reality" of "cruelty" or the "absurd and impractical" things that she talks about as the war's fault. No, Anne's words cause us to see what is true and real in her art and in her heart. She makes us see that love is not the fiction. Hitler and the Nazis are the ones who make the fiction. We can read this in between the lines, which sometimes has to be done.

Back when Anne Frank wrote her words down on paper, everything was going wrong around her but she knew what to do, and she did it. She wrote a world classic story about her life. This story is a big contrast to what the Germans were doing.

Sample Strong Response

This excerpt from *The Diary of Anne Frank* reveals the inner strength of a young girl who refuses, despite the wartime violence and danger surrounding her, to let her idealism be overcome by hatred and mass killing. This idealism is reflected, in part, by her emphases on universal human hopes such as peace, tranquility, and goodwill. But Anne Frank is no dreamy Pollyanna. Reflecting on her idealism in the context of the war raging around her, she matter-of-factly writes: "my dreams, they seem so absurd and impractical."

This indicates Anne Frank's awareness of not only her own predicament but of human miseries that extend beyond the immediate circumstances of her life. For elsewhere she writes in a similar vein, "In times like these... I see the world being slowly transformed into a wilderness"; despite her own suffering she can "feel the suffering of millions."

And yet Anne Frank believes, "in spite of everything, that people are truly good at heart." This statement epitomizes the stark existential contrast of her worldview with the wartime reality that ultimately claimed her life.

The statement also exemplifies how Anne's literary form—her syntax and diction—mirror thematic content and contrasts. "In spite of everything," she still believes in people. She can "hear the approaching thunder...yet, when I look up at the sky, I somehow feel that everything will change for the better." At numerous points in this diary entry, first-hand knowledge of violent tragedy stands side-by-side with belief in humanity and human progress.

"I must hold on to my ideals," Anne concludes. "Perhaps the day will come when I'll be able to realize them!" In her diary she has done so, and more.

Multiple-Choice Questions

Choose the best answer for each of the questions.

1. Children's literature became established in the (Rigorous)(Skill 1.0)
   A. seventeenth century
   B. eighteenth century
   C. nineteenth century
   D. twentieth century

2. The first African American to receive the Pulitzer Prize for Poetry was (Rigorous)(Skill 1.3)
   A. Gwendolyn Brooks
   B. Harriet E. Wilson
   C. Richard Wright
   D. James Edwin Campbell

3. The Old English period refers to (Rigorous)(Skill 1.3)
   A. The Fourth Century
   B. The Third through the Eighth Century
   C. The Fifth through the Tenth Century
   D. The Fifth through the Eighth Century

4. The principal writer of *The Declaration of Independence* was(Rigorous)(Skill 1.3)

   A. Patrick Henry
   B. Thomas Jefferson
   C. Ben Franklin
   D. George Washington

5.. Pearl appears as an important character in(Rigorous)(Skill 1.3)
   A. *The Scarlet Letter*
   B. *Moby Dick*
   C. *The House of the Seven Gables*
   D. "The Cask of Amontillado"

6. Which of the following would be the most significant factor in teaching Homer's *Iliad* and *Odyssey* to any particular group of students? (Average)(Skill 1.3)
   A. Identifying a translation on the appropriate reading level
   B. Determining the student's interest level
   C. Selecting an appropriate evaluative technique
   D. Determining the scope and delivery methods of background study

7. Which of the following is not a theme of Native American writing? (Rigorous)(Skill1.4)
   A. Emphasis on the hardiness of the human body and soul
   B. The strength of multi-cultural assimilation
   C. Indignation about the genocide of native peoples
   D. Remorse for the loss of the Indian way of life

8. The appearance of a Yankee from Connecticut in the Court of King Arthur is an example of a/an (Average)(Skill 2.8)
   A. rhetoric.
   B. parody.
   C. paradox.
   D. anachronism.

9. Which of the following terms does *not* denote a figure of speech (figurative language)? (Average)(Skill2.8)
   A. Simile
   B. Euphemism
   C. Onomatopoeia
   D. Allusion

10. A conversation between two or more people is called a/an (Rigorous)(Skill 2.8)
    A. parody.
    B. dialogue.
    C. monologue.
    D. analogy.

11. This statement, "I'll die if I don't pass this course," exemplifies a/an (Easy)(Skill2.8)
    A. barbarism.
    B. oxymoron.
    C. hyperbole.
    D. antithesis.

12. The substitution of "went to his rest" for "died" exemplifies a/an (Easy)(Skill2.8)
    A. bowdlerism.
    B. jargon.
    C. euphemism.
    D. malapropism.

13. The literary device of personification is used in which example below? (Easy)(Skill2.8)
    A. "Beg me no beggary by soul or parents, whining dog!"
    B. "Happiness sped through the halls cajoling as it went."
    C. "O wind thy horn, thou proud fellow."
    D. "And that one talent which is death to hide."

14. "Clean as a whistle" and "easy as falling off a log" exemplify (Easy)(Skill2.8)
    A. semantics.
    B. parody.
    C. irony.
    D. clichés.

15. Which of the following responses to literature typically give middle school students the most problems? (Rigorous)(Skill3.1)
    A. Interpretive
    B. Evaluative
    C. Critical
    D. Emotional

16. Which of the four underlined sections of the following sentence contains an error that a word processing spellchecker probably <u>wouldn't</u> catch?(Easy)(Skill 4.1)

He <u>tuc</u> the <u>hors</u> by the <u>rains</u> and pulled it back to the <u>stabel</u>.

A. tuc
B. hors
C. rains
D. stabel

17. Use the table below to answer the question that follows it.

	Math Usage	General Usage
bi (two)	bilinear bimodal <u>binomial</u>	bicycle biplane <u>bifocals</u>
cent (100)	centimeter centigram <u>percent</u>	century centigrade <u>centipede</u>
circum (around)	circumference circumradius circumcenter	circumnavigate circumstance Circumspect

Which vocabulary strategy does the table above exemplify? (Rigorous)(Skill 4.1)

A. Frayer method
B. morphemic analysis
C. semantic mapping
D. word mapping

18. Which aspect of language is innate?(Average)(Skill 4.1)
A. Biological capability to articulate sounds understood by other humans
B. Cognitive ability to create syntactical structures
C. Capacity for using semantics to convey meaning in a social environment
D. Ability to vary inflections and accents

19. A teacher should refer all of the following concerns to the appropriate expert <u>except for</u> (Rigorous)(Skill 4.4)
A. Auditory trauma.
B. Ear infection.
C. Vision problems.
D. Underdeveloped vocabulary.

20. What factor below introduced Modern English?(Rigorous)(Skill 4.5)
A. The Great Vowel Shift
B. The printing press
C. The invasion of the Normans
D. Phonetic spelling

21. Which of the following bits of information best describes the structure of English?(Rigorous)(Skill 4.5)
A. Syntax based on word order.
B. Inflected.
C. Romantic.
D. Orthography is phonetic.

22. **Which of the following is not true about English?(Easy)(Skill 4.5)**
    A. English is the easiest language to learn.
    B. English is the least inflected language.
    C. English has the most extensive vocabulary of any language.
    D. English originated as a Germanic tongue.

23. **Middle-School students bring little, if any, initial experience in** (Rigorous)(Skill 5.1)
    A. Phonics.
    B. Phonemics.
    C. Textbook reading assignments.
    D. Stories read by the teacher.

24. **Before reading a passage, a teacher gives her students an anticipation guide with a list of statements related to the topic they are about to cover in the reading material. She asks the students to indicate their agreement or disagreement with each statement on the guide. This activity is intended to** (Average)(Skill 5.1)
    A. elicit students' prior knowledge of the topic and set a purpose for reading
    B. help students to identify the main ideas and supporting details in the text
    C. help students to synthesize information from the text
    D. help students to visualize the concepts and terms in the text

25. **To enhance reading comprehension, experts recommend all of these techniques <u>except for</u> (Rigorous)(Skill 5.4)**
    A. Read material through only once, but read slowly and carefully.
    B. Read material through more than once according to a plan.
    C. Create a map for the next reading.
    D. Highlight or take notes during reading.

26. **Students are fluent readers if they (Rigorous)(Skill5.4)**
    A. read texts fast enough and with appropriate expression, or prosody.
    B. read word-to-word and haltingly.
    C. must intentionally decode a majority of the words.
    D. write disorganized sentences

27. **Regularly requiring students to practice reading short, instructional-level texts at least three times to a peer and to give and receive peer feedback about these readings mainly addresses which reading skill?(Rigorous)(Skill5.4)**
    A. Comprehension
    B. fluency
    C. evaluation
    D. word-solving

28. Which of the following approaches is *not* useful in assessing slower or immature readers? (Rigorous)(Skill 6.1)
    A. Repeated readings.
    B. Echo reading.
    C. Wide reading.
    D. Reading content that is more difficult than their skill levels in order to "stretch" their abilities.

29. Computer-assisted instruction (CAI) accommodates all of the following factors in reading instruction *except for* (Rigorous)(Skill 6.1)
    A. free-form responses to comprehension questions
    B. increased motivation
    C. the addition of speech with computer-presented text
    D. the use of computers for word processing, and the integration of writing instruction with reading

30. Overcrowded classes prevent the individual attention needed to facilitate language development. This drawback can be best overcome by(Rigorous)(Skill6.1)
    A. dividing the class into independent study groups.
    B. assigning more study time at home.
    C. using more drill practice in class.
    D. team teaching.

31. Which item below is not a research-based strategy that supports reading? (Averge)(Skill 6.1)
    A. reading more
    B. reading along with a more proficient reader
    C. reading a passage no more than twice
    D. self-monitoring progress

32. What is the best course of action when a child refuses to complete an assignment on the ground that is morally objectionable?(Rigorous)(Skil l 6.2)
    A. Speak with the parents and explain the necessity of studying this work.
    B. Encourage the child to sample some of the text before making a judgment.
    C. Place the child in another teacher's class where students are studying an acceptable work.
    D. Provide the student with alternative material that serves the same curricular purpose.

33. Written on the sixth grade reading level, most of S. E. Hinton's novels (for instance, *The Outsiders*) have the greatest reader appeal with (Rigorous)(Skill6.2)
    A. sixth graders.
    B. ninth graders.
    C. twelfth graders.
    D. adults.

34. **Varying the complexity of a graphic organizer exemplifies differentiating which aspect of a lesson?(Rigorous)(Skill6.3)**
    A. its content/topic
    B. its environment
    C. its process
    D. its product

35. **Among junior-high school students of low-to-average readability levels, which work would most likely stir reading interest?(Rigorous)(skill 6.3)**
    A. *Elmer Gantry*, Sinclair Lewis
    B. *Smiley's People*, John Le Carre
    C. *The Outsiders*, S.E. Hinton
    D. *And Then There Were None*, Agatha Christie.

36. **A teacher has taught his students to self-monitor their reading by locating where in the passage they are having difficulty, by identifying the specific problem there, and by restating the difficult sentence or passage in their own words. These strategies are examples of (Rigorous)(Skill 6.3)**
    A. graphic and semantic organizers
    B. metacognition
    C. recognizing story structure
    D. summarizing

37. **The students in Mrs. Cline's seventh grade language arts class were invited to attend a performance of *Romeo and Juliet* presented by the drama class at the high school. To best prepare, they should (Easy)(Skill 6.3)**
    A. read the play as a homework exercise.
    B. read a synopsis of the plot and a biographical sketch of the author.
    C. examine a few main selections from the play to become familiar with the language and style of the author.
    D. read a condensed version of the story and practice attentive listening skills.

38. **For students with poor vocabularies, the teacher should recommend first that (Rigorous)(Skill 8.1)**
    A. they enroll in a Latin class.
    B. they read newspapers, magazines and books on a regular basis.
    C. they write the words repetitively after looking them up in the dictionary.
    D. they use a thesaurus to locate and incorporate the synonyms found there into their vocabularies.

39. **If a student uses slang and expletives, what is the best course of action to take in order to improve the student's formal communication skills?(Average)(Skill 10.1)**
   A. ask the student to rephrase their writing; that is, translate it into language appropriate for the school principal to read.
   B. refuse to read the student's papers until he conforms to a more literate style.
   C. ask the student to read his work aloud to the class for peer evaluation.
   D. rewrite the flagrant passages to show the student the right form of expression.

40. **The arrangement and relationship of words in sentences or sentence structures best describes (Average)(Skill 10.1)**
   A. style.
   B. discourse.
   C. thesis.
   D. syntax.

41. **A paper explaining the relationship between food and weight gain contains the signal words "because," "consequently," "this is how," and "due to." These words suggest that the paper has which text structure?(Average)(Skill 10.2)**
   A. cause and effect structure
   B. compare and contrast structure
   C. descriptive structure
   D. sequential structure

42. **Modeling is a practice that requires students to (Easy)(Skill 11.1)**
   A. create a style unique to their own language capabilities.
   B. emulate the writing of professionals.
   C. paraphrase passages from good literature.
   D. peer evaluate the writings of other students.

43. **A paper written in first person and having characters, a setting, a plot, some dialogue, and events sequenced chronologically with some flashbacks exemplifies which genre?(Average)(Skill 13.1)**
   A. exposition
   B. narration
   C. persuasion
   D. speculation

44. *Diction* is best defined as(Average)(Skill 13.1)
   A. The specific word choices an author makes in order to create a particular mood or feeling in the reader.
   B. Writing that explains something thoroughly.
   C. The background, or exposition, for a short story or drama.
   D. Word choices that help teach a truth or moral.

45. To explain or to inform belongs in the category of (Average)(skill 13.1)
   A. exposition.
   B. narration.
   C. persuasion.
   D. description.

46. What type of comprehension do questions beginnings with "who," "what," "where," or "how" assess?(Average)(Skill 14.1)
   A. evaluative
   B. inferential
   C. literal
   D. narrative

47. In a timed essay test of an hour's duration, how much time should be devoted to prewriting.(Average)(Skill 14.1)
   A. five
   B. ten
   C. fifteen
   D. twenty

48. In 'inverted triangle' introductory paragraphs, the thesis sentence occurs (Average)(Skill 14.1)
   A. at the beginning of the paragraph.
   B. in the middle of the paragraph.
   C. at the end of the paragraph.
   D. in the second paragraph.

49. Which of the following should not be included in the opening paragraph of an informative essay? (Average)(Skill 14.1)
   A. Thesis sentence
   B. Details and examples supporting the main idea
   C. broad general introduction to the topic
   D. A style and tone that grabs the reader's attention

50. Writing ideas quickly without interruption of the flow of thoughts or attention to conventions is called (Easy)(Skill 14.1)
   A. brainstorming.
   B. mapping.
   C. listing.
   D. Free writing.

51. Which of the following is not a technique of prewriting? (Easy)(Skill 14.1)
   A. Clustering
   B. Listing
   C. Brainstorming
   D. Proofreading

52. **Which of the following is the least effective procedure for promoting consciousness of audience? (Rigorous)(Skill 14.1)**
   A. Pairing students during the writing process
   B. Reading all rough drafts before the students write the final copies
   C. Having students compose stories or articles for publication in school literary magazines or newspapers
   D. Writing letters to friends or relatives

53. **A student informative composition should consist of a minimum of how many paragraphs?(Easy)(Skill 14.1)**
   A. three
   B. four
   C. five
   D. six

54. **Which of the following sentences contains an error in agreement? (Average)(Skill 15.2)**
   A. Jennifer is one of the women who writes for the magazine.
   B. Each one of their sons plays a different sport.
   C. This band has performed at the Odeum many times.
   D. The data are available online at the listed website.

55. **Which of the following is not true about English?(Rigorous)(Skill 15.2)**
   A. English is the easiest language to learn
   B. English is the least inflected language
   C. English has the most extensive vocabulary of any language
   D. English originated as a Germanic tongue

56. **Consider the following sentence:**

   Mr. Brown is a school volunteer with a reputation and twenty years service.

   Which phrase below best represents the logical intent of the underlined phrase above? (Choice E is identical to the underlined phrase) (Average)(Skill 15.6)
   A. with a reputation for twenty years' service
   B. with a reputation for twenty year's service
   C. who has served twenty years
   D. with a service reputation of twenty years

57. Consider the following sentence: (Average)(Skill 15.6)

   Joe *didn't hardly know his cousin Fred,* who'd had a rhinoplasty.

   Which word group below best conveys the intended meaning of the underlined section above?
   A. hardly did know his cousin Fred
   B. didn't know his cousin Fred hardly
   C. hardly knew his cousin Fred
   D. didn't know his cousin Fred

58. Which group of words is not a sentence?(Average)(Skill 15.7)
   A. In keeping with the graduation tradition, the students, in spite of the rain, standing in the cafeteria tossing their mortarboards.
   B. Rosa Parks, who refused to give up her seat on the bus, will be forever remembered for her courage.
   C. Taking advantage of the goalie's being out of the net, we scored our last and winning goal.
   D. When it began to rain, we gathered our possessions and ran for the pavilion.

59. Identify the sentence that has an error in parallel structure.(Easy)(Skill 15.7)
   A. In order to help your favorite cause, you should contribute time or money, raise awareness, and write congressmen.
   B. Many people envision scientists working alone in a laboratory and discovering scientific breakthroughs.
   C. Some students prefer watching videos to textbooks because they are used to visual presentation.
   D. Tom Hanks, who has won two Academy Awards, is celebrated as an actor, director, and producer.

60. A punctuation mark indicating omission, interrupted thought, or an incomplete statement is a/an(Easy)(Skill 15.8)
   A. ellipsis.
   B. anachronism.
   C. colloquy.
   D. idiom.

61. Which of the following sentences is unambiguously properly punctuated? (Average)(Skill 15.8)
   A. The more you eat; the more you want.
   B. The authors—John Steinbeck, Ernest Hemingway, and William Faulkner—are staples of modern writing in American literature textbooks.
   C. Handling a wild horse, takes a great deal of skill and patience
   D. The man, who replaced our teacher, is a comedian.

62. Which of the following contains an error in possessive punctuation? (Rigorous)(Skill 15.8)
   A. Doris's shawl
   B. mother's-in-law frown
   C. children's lunches
   D. ambassador's briefcase

63. Read the following passage:

   "It would have been hard to find a passer-by more wretched in appearance. He was a man of middle height, stout and hardy, in the strength of maturity; he might have been forty-six or seven. A slouched leather cap hid half his face, bronzed by the sun and wind, and dripping with sweat."

   What is its main form of discourse?(Average)(Skill 18.3)
   A. Description
   B. Narration
   C. Exposition
   D. Persuasion

64. Oral debate is most closely associated with which form of discourse? (Easy)(18.3)
   A. Description
   B. Exposition
   C. Narration
   D. Persuasion

Answer Key

1. A	38. B
2. A	39. A
3. C	40. D
4. B	41. A
5. A	42. B
6. A	43. B
7. B	44. A
8. D	45. A
9. D	46. C
10. B	47. B
11. C	48. C
12. C	49. B
13. B	50. D
14. D	51. D
15. B	52. B
16. C	53. C
17. B	54. A
18. A	55. A
19. D	56. D
20. A	57. C
21. A	58. A
22. A	59. C
23. C	60. A
24. A	61. B
25. A	62. B
26. A	63. A
27. B	64. D
28. D	
29. A	
30. A	
31. C	
32. D	
33. B	
34. C	
35. C	
36. C	
37. D	

Rigor Table

	Easy %20	Average Rigor %40	Rigorous %40
Question #	11, 12, 13, 14, 16, 22, 37, 42, 50, 51, 53, 59, 60, 63, 64	4, 6, 8, 9, 18, 24, 31, 32, 39, 40, 41, 43, 44, 45, 46, 47, 48, 49, 54, 56, 57, 58	1, 2, 3, 7, 10, 15, 19, 23, 25, 27, 29, 30, 33, 52, 55, 5, 36, 62, 21, 38, 17

Multiple-Choice Questions with Rationales

1. **Children's literature became established in the (Rigorous)(Skill 1.0)**
   A. seventeenth century
   B. eighteenth century
   C. nineteenth century
   D. twentieth century

The answer is A. In the seventeenth century, Jean de la Fontaine's *Fables*, Pierre Perreault's *Tales*, Mme. d'Aulnoye's novels based on old folktales, and Mme. de Beaumont's *Beauty and the Beast* created a children's literature genre. In England, Perreault was translated, and a work allegedly written by Oliver Smith, *The Renowned History of Little Goody Two Shoes,* helped to establish children's literature in England, too.

2. **The first African American to receive the Pulitzer Prize for Poetry was (Rigorous)(Skill 1.3)**
   A. Gwendolyn Brooks
   B. Harriet E. Wilson
   C. Richard Wright
   D. James Edwin Campbell

The correct answer is A. Gwendolyn Brooks was the first African American to receive the Pulitzer Prize for Poetry. Harriett E. Wilson, who died in 1900, was the first female African American novelist. Richard Wright was a novelist and black activist. James Edwin Campbell was a 19th century African American poet, editor, writer, and educator.

3. **The Old English period refers to (Rigorous)(Skill 1.3)**
   A. The Fourth Century
   B. The Third through the Eighth Century
   C. The Fifth through the Tenth Century
   D. The Fifth through the Eighth Century

The correct answer is C. The Old English period begins with the settlement of the British Isles in the fifth and sixth centuries by Germanic tribes and continues until the time of Chaucer.

4. **The principal writer of *The Declaration of Independence* was(Rigorous)(Skill 1.3)**
   A. Patrick Henry
   B. Thomas Jefferson
   C. Ben Franklin
   D. George Washington

The correct answer is B. Thomas Jefferson. Although Benjamin Franklin was responsible for editing it and making it the prime example of neoclassical writing that it is, *The Declaration of Independence* came directly from the mind and pen of Jefferson. Patrick Henry was a great orator, and his speeches played an important role in precipitating the revolution. Although George Washington's *Farewell to the Army of the Potomac* is an important piece of writing from that era, he was not the principal writer of the declaration.

5.. **Pearl appears as an important character in(Rigorous)(Skill 1.3)**
   A. *The Scarlet Letter*
   B. *Moby Dick*
   C. *The House of the Seven Gables*
   D. "The Cask of Amontillado"

The correct answer is A. Pearl is the illegitimate daughter of Hester Prynne in Nathaniel Hawthorne's *The Scarlet Letter*.   *Moby Dick* is Herman Melville's great opus about the pursuit of a great white whale. *The House of the Seven Gables*, like *The Scarlet Letter,* is about a society that promulgates loneliness and suspicion. "The Cask of Amontillado" is one of Poe's horror stories.

6. **Which of the following would be the most significant factor in teaching Homer's *Iliad* and *Odyssey* to any particular group of students? (Average)(Skill 1.3)**
   A. Identifying a translation on the appropriate reading level
   B. Determining the student's interest level
   C. Selecting an appropriate evaluative technique
   D. Determining the scope and delivery methods of background study

The answer is A. Students will appreciate these two works if the translation reflects both the vocabulary they know and their reading level. Choice B is moot because most students aren't initially interested in Homer. Choice C skips to later matters.   Choice D is tempting and significant, but not as crucial as having an accessible text.

7. **Which of the following is not a theme of Native American writing? (Rigorous)(Skill1.4)**
    A. Emphasis on the hardiness of the human body and soul
    B. The strength of multi-cultural assimilation
    C. Indignation about the genocide of native peoples
    D. Remorse for the loss of the Indian way of life

The answer is B. Originating in a vast body of oral traditions from as early as before the fifteenth century, Native American literature themes include "nature as sacred," "the interconnectedness of life," "the hardiness of body and soul," "indignation about the destruction of the Native American way of life," and "the genocide of many tribes by the encroaching settlements of European Americans." These themes are still present in today's Native American literature, such as in the works of Duane Niatum, Gunn Allen, Louise Erdrich and N. Scott Momaday.

8. **The appearance of a Yankee from Connecticut in the Court of King Arthur is an example of a/an (Average)(Skill 2.8)**
    A. rhetoric.
    B. parody.
    C. paradox.
    D. anachronism.

The answer is D. Anachronism is the placing of characters, persons, events or things into time frames incongruent with their actual dates. Parody is poking fun at something. Paradox is a seeming contradiction. Anachronism is something out of time frame.

9. **Which of the following terms does *not* denote a figure of speech (figurative language)? (Average)(Skill2.8)**
    A. Simile
    B. Euphemism
    C. Onomatopoeia
    D. Allusion

The answer is D. An allusion is an implied reference to a famous person, event, thing, or a part of another text. A simile is a direct comparison between two things. A euphemism is the substitution of an agreeable or inoffensive term for one that might offend. Onomatopoeia is vocal imitation to convey meaning— "bark" or "meow."

10. **A conversation between two or more people is called a/an (Rigorous)(Skill 2.8)**
    A. parody.
    B. dialogue.
    C. monologue.
    D. analogy.

The answer is B. Dialogues are the conversations virtually indispensable to dramatic work, and they often appear in narrative and poetry, as well. A parody is a work that adopts the subject and structure of another work in order to ridicule it. A monologue is a work or part of a work written in the first person. An analogy illustrates an idea by means of a more familiar one that is similar or parallel to it.

11. **This statement, "I'll die if I don't pass this course," exemplifies a/an (Easy)(Skill2.8)**
    A. barbarism.
    B. oxymoron.
    C. hyperbole.
    D. antithesis.

The answer is C. A hyperbole is an exaggeration for the sake of emphasis. It is a figure of speech not meant to be taken literally. A barbarism is the use of incorrect or unacceptable language. An oxymoron is a term comprised of opposite or incongruous elements, such as peace fighter.

12. **The substitution of "went to his rest" for "died" exemplifies a/an (Easy)(Skill2.8)**
    A. bowdlerism.
    B. jargon.
    C. euphemism.
    D. malapropism.

The answer is C. A euphemism alludes to a distasteful topic in a pleasant manner in order to obscure or soften the disturbing impact of the original. A bowdlerism is a prudish version of something. Jargon is language specific to some occupation or activity. A Malapropism is the improper use of a word that sounds like the word that would fit the context. The result is most often ludicrous.

13. **The literary device of personification is used in which example below?**
(Easy)(Skill2.8)
   A. "Beg me no beggary by soul or parents, whining dog!"
   B. "Happiness sped through the halls cajoling as it went."
   C. "O wind thy horn, thou proud fellow."
   D. "And that one talent which is death to hide."

The correct answer is B. Personification is defined as giving human characteristics to inanimate objects or concepts. It can be thought of as a sub-category of metaphor. Happiness, an abstract concept, is "speeding through the halls" and "cajoling," both of which are human behaviors, so Happiness is being compared to a human being. Choice A is figurative and metaphorical, but not a personification. Choice C is, again, figurative and metaphorical, but not a personification. The speaker is, perhaps, telling someone that they are bragging, or "blowing their own horn." Choice D is also figurative and metaphorical, but not personification. Hiding a particular talent is being compared to risking death.

14. **"Clean as a whistle" and "easy as falling off a log" exemplify**
(Easy)(Skill2.8)
   A. semantics.
   B. parody.
   C. irony.
   D. clichés.

The answer is D. A cliché is a phrase or expression that has become dull due to overuse. Semantics is a field of language study. Parody is poking fun at something. Irony is using language to create an unexpected or opposite meaning of the literal words being used.

15. Which of the following responses to literature typically give middle school students the most problems? (Rigorous)(Skill3.1)
A. Interpretive
B. Evaluative
C. Critical
D. Emotional

The answer is B. Middle school readers will exhibit both emotional and interpretive responses. In middle/junior high school, organized study models enable students to identify main ideas and supporting details, to recognize sequential order, to distinguish fact from opinion, and to determine cause/effect relationships. Middle school students can provide reasons to support their assertions that a particular book was boring or a particular poem made him or her feel sad, and this is to provide a critical reaction on a fundamental level. Evaluative responses, however, require students to address how the piece represents its genre, how well it reflects the social and ethical mores of a given society, or how well the author has employed a fresh approach to the subject. Evaluative responses are more sophisticated than critical responses, and they are appropriate for advanced high school students.

16. Which of the four underlined sections of the following sentence contains an error that a word processing spellchecker probably wouldn't catch?(Easy)(Skill 4.1)

He tuc the hors by the rains and pulled it back to the stabel.

A. tuc
B. hors
C. rains
D. stabel

The correct answer is C. Spellcheckers only catch errors in conventional modern English spelling. They cannot catch errors involving incorrect homophone usage. "Rains" is the only one of the four words to conform to conventional English spelling, but it clearly is not the word called for by the context.

17. Use the table below to answer the question that follows it.

	Math Usage	General Usage
bi (two)	bilinear	bicycle
	bimodal	biplane
	binomial	bifocals
cent	centimeter	century
(100)	centigram	centigrade
	percent	centipede
circum	circumference	circumnavigate
(around)	circumradius	circumstance
	circumcenter	Circumspect

Which vocabulary strategy does the table above exemplify? (Rigorous)(Skill 4.1)

A. Frayer method
B. morphemic analysis
C. semantic mapping
D. word mapping

The answer is B. Morphemes are the smallest units of language that have an associated meaning. The purpose of morphemic analysis is to apply morphemic awareness to the task of learning new words. The Frayer method involves having students use their own words to define new words and to link those definitions to personal experiences. Semantic mapping incorporates graphical clues to concepts and is a subset of graphic organizers. Word mapping is another subset of graphic organizers and consists of displaying such information as the various forms a word may take as it transforms through the parts of speech.

18. Which aspect of language is innate?(Average)(Skill 4.1)
    A. Biological capability to articulate sounds understood by other humans
    B. Cognitive ability to create syntactical structures
    C. Capacity for using semantics to convey meaning in a social environment
    D. Ability to vary inflections and accents

The answer is A. The biological capability to articulate sounds understood by other humans is innate; and, later, children learn semantics and syntactical structures through trial and error. Linguists agree that language is first a vocal system of word symbols that enable a human to communicate his or her feelings, thoughts, and desires to other human beings.

19. **A teacher should refer all of the following concerns to the appropriate expert <u>except for</u> (Rigorous)(Skill 4.4)**

    A. Auditory trauma.
    B. Ear infection.
    C. Vision problems.
    D. Underdeveloped vocabulary.

The answer is D. The teacher is the expert in vocabulary development. The other choices require a medical professional.

20. **What factor below introduced Modern English?(Rigorous)(Skill 4.5)**
    A. The Great Vowel Shift
    B. The printing press
    C. The invasion of the Normans
    D. Phonetic spelling

The correct answer is A. The Great Vowel Shift created guidelines for spelling and pronunciation in the wake of the invention of the printing press. Other answer choices, though related to the question, do not answer it as specifically

21. **Which of the following bits of information best describes the structure of English?(Rigorous)(Skill 4.5)**
    A. Syntax based on word order.
    B. Inflected.
    C. Romantic.
    D. Orthography is phonetic.

The correct answer is A. The syntax of English, reflective of its Germanic origins, relies on word order rather than inflection. Because of this and the many influences of other languages (particularly with regard to vocabulary), the orthography is not phonetic, which complicates the teaching of standardized spelling.

22. **Which of the following is not true about English?(Easy)(Skill 4.5)**
    A. English is the easiest language to learn.
    B. English is the least inflected language.
    C. English has the most extensive vocabulary of any language.
    D. English originated as a Germanic tongue.

The answer is A. English has its own inherent quirks which make it difficult to learn, plus it has incorporated words, ands even structures, from many disparate language groups in its lexicon and syntax. Languages with lexicons limited to words governed by a consistent set of relatively simple rules exist, so English is certainly not the easiest language to learn.

23. **Middle-School students bring little, if any, initial experience in**
(Rigorous)(Skill 5.1)
   A. Phonics.
   B. Phonemics.
   C. Textbook reading assignments.
   D. Stories read by the teacher.

The correct answer is C. In middle school, probably for the first time, the student will be expected to read textbook assignments and come to class prepared to discuss the content. Students get phonics (the systematic study of decoding) in the early grades, and they normally get phonemics (familiarity with the syllable sounds of English) even earlier. They will have almost certainly had stories read to them by a teacher by the time they get to middle school.

24. **Before reading a passage, a teacher gives her students an anticipation guide with a list of statements related to the topic they are about to cover in the reading material. She asks the students to indicate their agreement or disagreement with each statement on the guide. This activity is intended to**
(Average)(Skill 5.1)
   A. elicit students' prior knowledge of the topic and set a purpose for reading
   B. help students to identify the main ideas and supporting details in the text
   C. help students to synthesize information from the text
   D. help students to visualize the concepts and terms in the text

The correct answer is A. Establishing a purpose for reading, the foundation for a reading unit or activity, is intimately connected to activating the students' prior knowledge in strategic ways. When the reason for reading is developed in the context of the students' experiences, they are far better prepared to succeed because they can make connections from a base they thoroughly understand. This influences motivation, and with proper motivation, students are more enthused and put forward more effort to understand the text. The other choices are only indirectly supported by this activity and are more specific in focus.

25. **To enhance reading comprehension, experts recommend all of these techniques <u>except for</u>** (Rigorous)(Skill 5.4)
   A. Read material through only once, but read slowly and carefully.
   B. Read material through more than once according to a plan.
   C. Create a map for the next reading.
   D. Highlight or take notes during reading.

The correct answer is A. While reading at a rate that assures accuracy is desirable, there is no evidence to support a recommendation to avoid rereading something. Choice B is advisable because it proposes a purpose for the rereadings. Choice C is advisable because it also addresses purpose. Choice D is advisable because it helps students maintain focus as they read.

26. **Students are fluent readers if they (Rigorous)(Skill5.4)**
    A. read texts fast enough and with appropriate expression, or prosody.
    B. read word-to-word and haltingly.
    C. must intentionally decode a majority of the words.
    D. write disorganized sentences

The correct answer is A. A fluent reader reads words accurately, at target speeds, and with appropriate expression. It is a positive term. The other choices describe negative outcomes.

27. **Regularly requiring students to practice reading short, instructional-level texts at least three times to a peer and to give and receive peer feedback about these readings mainly addresses which reading skill?(Rigorous)(Skill5.4)**
    A. Comprehension
    B. fluency
    C. evaluation
    D. word-solving

The correct answer is B. Fluency is the ability to read text quickly with accuracy, phrasing, and expression. Fluency develops over time and requires substantial reading practice. This activity provides just this sort of practice. The peer feedback portion does address comprehension, evaluation, and some word-solving; but the main thrust is on fluency development.

28. **Which of the following approaches is *not* useful in assessing slower or immature readers? (Rigorous)(Skill 6.1)**
    A. Repeated readings.
    B. Echo reading.
    C. Wide reading.
    D. Reading content that is more difficult than their skill levels in order to "stretch" their abilities.

The correct answer is D. Reading content for such students should be at a level where they can read and understand the word nuances, not at a level beyond such understanding and competence. Repeated readings of appropriate material builds this foundation. So does echo reading, or listening to a skilled reader and then trying to imitate his or her delivery. Wide reading is an approach intended to motivate students to read for pleasure and information from a variety of sources and involving socially-motivating processing routines.

29. **Computer-assisted instruction (CAI) accommodates all of the following factors in reading instruction _except for_ (Rigorous)(Skill 6.1)**
   A. free-form responses to comprehension questions
   B. increased motivation
   C. the addition of speech with computer-presented text
   D. the use of computers for word processing, and the integration of writing instruction with reading

The correct answer is A. CAI does not accommodate free-form responses to comprehension questions, and relies heavily on drill-and-practice and multiple-choice formats. This is a limitation of CAI.

30. **Overcrowded classes prevent the individual attention needed to facilitate language development. This drawback can be best overcome by(Rigorous)(Skill6.1)**
   A. dividing the class into independent study groups.
   B. assigning more study time at home.
   C. using more drill practice in class.
   D. team teaching.

The correct answer is A. Dividing a class into small groups maximizes opportunities for engagement. Assigning more study time at home is passing the responsibilities on to the parents/caregivers. Using more drill practice in class is likely to bore most students to tears. Team teaching begs the question; if you can get another teacher, then your class should no longer be overcrowded.

31. **Which item below is not a research-based strategy that supports reading?**
   (Averge)(Skill 6.1)
   A. reading more
   B. reading along with a more proficient reader
   C. reading a passage no more than twice
   D. self-monitoring progress

The correct answer is C. Actually, research shows that reading a passage several times improves fluency, and, depending on the complexity of the material, improves comprehension, too. The more complex the material, the more comprehension value in repeated readings.

32. **What is the best course of action when a child refuses to complete an assignment on the ground that is morally objectionable?(Rigorous)(Skill 6.2)**
    A. Speak with the parents and explain the necessity of studying this work.
    B. Encourage the child to sample some of the text before making a judgment.
    C. Place the child in another teacher's class where students are studying an acceptable work.
    D. Provide the student with alternative material that serves the same curricular purpose.

The answer is D. This approach is the most time efficient and flexible. Choice A requires conversations involving value systems that aren't going to change. Choice B risks being open to the charge of exposing children to controversial material despite parental input. Choice C is a disproportionate disruption to the student's schedule and the school routine.

33. **Written on the sixth grade reading level, most of S. E. Hinton's novels (for instance, *The Outsiders*) have the greatest reader appeal with (Rigorous)(Skill6.2)**
    A. sixth graders.
    B. ninth graders.
    C. twelfth graders.
    D. adults.

The answer is B. Adolescents are concerned with their changing bodies, their relationships with each other and adults, and their place in society. Reading *The Outsiders* helps them confront different problems that they are only now beginning to experience as teenagers, such as gangs and social identity. The book is universal in its appeal to adolescents.

34. **Varying the complexity of a graphic organizer exemplifies differentiating which aspect of a lesson?(Rigorous)(Skill6.3)**
    A. its content/topic
    B. its environment
    C. its process
    D. its product

The correct answer is C. Differentiating the process means offering a variety of learning activities or strategies to students as they manipulate the ideas embedded within the lesson concept. For example, students may use graphic organizers, maps, diagrams, or charts to display their comprehension of concepts covered. Varying the complexity of a graphic organizer can very effectively accommodate differing levels of cognitive processing so that students of differing ability are appropriately engaged. Lesson topic and content remain the same, the lesson is still taking place in the same environment, and, in most lessons, the graphic organizer is not the product of the lesson.

35. **Among junior-high school students of low-to-average readability levels, which work would most likely stir reading interest?(Rigorous)(skill 6.3)**
    A. *Elmer Gantry*, Sinclair Lewis
    B. *Smiley's People*, John Le Carre
    C. *The Outsiders*, S.E. Hinton
    D. *And Then There Were None*, Agatha Christie.

The answer is C. The students can easily identify with the characters, the social issues, the vocabulary, and the themes in the book. The book deals with teenage concerns such as fitting-in, cliques, and appearance in ways that have proven very engaging for young readers.

36. **A teacher has taught his students to self-monitor their reading by locating where in the passage they are having difficulty, by identifying the specific problem there, and by restating the difficult sentence or passage in their own words. These strategies are examples of (Rigorous)(Skill 6.3)**
    A. graphic and semantic organizers
    B. metacognition
    C. recognizing story structure
    D. summarizing

The correct answer is C. Good readers use metacognitive strategies (various ways of thinking about thinking) to improve their reading. Before reading, they clarify their purpose for reading and preview the text. During reading, they monitor their understanding, adjusting their reading speed to fit the difficulty of the text and fixing any comprehension problems they have. After reading, they check their understanding of what they read.

37. **The students in Mrs. Cline's seventh grade language arts class were invited to attend a performance of** *Romeo and Juliet* **presented by the drama class at the high school. To best prepare, they should (Easy)(Skill 6.3)**
    A. read the play as a homework exercise.
    B. read a synopsis of the plot and a biographical sketch of the author.
    C. examine a few main selections from the play to become familiar with the language and style of the author.
    D. read a condensed version of the story and practice attentive listening skills.

The answer is D. By reading a condensed version of the play, students will know the plot and therefore be better able to follow the play on stage. They will also practice being attentive. Choice A is far less dynamic and few will do it. Choice B is likewise dull. Choice C is not thorough enough.

38. **For students with poor vocabularies, the teacher should recommend first that (Average)(Skill 8.1)**
    A. they enroll in a Latin class.
    B. they read newspapers, magazines and books on a regular basis.
    C. they write the words repetitively after looking them up in the dictionary.
    D. they use a thesaurus to locate and incorporate the synonyms found there into their vocabularies.

The answer is B. Regularly reading a wide variety of materials for pleasure and information is the best way to develop a stronger vocabulary. The other suggestions have limited application and do not serve to reinforce an enthusiasm for reading.

39. **If a student uses slang and expletives, what is the best course of action to take in order to improve the student's formal communication skills?(Average)(Skill 10.1)**
    A. ask the student to rephrase their writing; that is, translate it into language appropriate for the school principal to read.
    B. refuse to read the student's papers until he conforms to a more literate style.
    C. ask the student to read his work aloud to the class for peer evaluation.
    D. rewrite the flagrant passages to show the student the right form of expression.

The answer is A. Asking the student to write to the principal, a respected authority figure, will alert the student to the need to use formal language. Simply refusing to read the paper is not only negative, it also sets up a power struggle. Asking the student to read slang and expletives aloud to the class for peer evaluation is to risk unproductive classroom chaos and to support the class clowns. Rewriting the flagrant passages for the student to model formal expression does not immerse the student in the writing process.

40. **The arrangement and relationship of words in sentences or sentence structures best describes (Average)(Skill 10.1)**
    A. style.
    B. discourse.
    C. thesis.
    D. syntax.

The answer is D. Syntax is the grammatical structure of sentences. Style is not limited to considerations of syntax only, but includes vocabulary, voice, genre, and other language features. Discourse refers to investigating some idea. A thesis is a statement of opinion.

41. **A paper explaining the relationship between food and weight gain contains the signal words "because," "consequently," "this is how," and "due to." These words suggest that the paper has which text structure?(Average)(Skill 10.2)**
    A. cause and effect structure
    B. compare and contrast structure
    C. descriptive structure
    D. sequential structure

The answer is A. These signal words connect events in a causal chain, creating an explanation of some process or event. Compare and contrast structure presents similarities and differences. Descriptive structure presents a sensory impression of something or someone. Sequential structure references what comes first, next, last, and so on.

42. **Modeling is a practice that requires students to (Easy)(Skill 11.1)**
    A. create a style unique to their own language capabilities.
    B. emulate the writing of professionals.
    C. paraphrase passages from good literature.
    D. peer evaluate the writings of other students.

The answer is B. Modeling engages students in analyzing the writing of professional writers and in imitating the syntactical, grammatical and stylistic mastery of that writer. Choice A is an issue of voice. Choice C is a less rigorous form of the correct answer. Choice D is only very indirectly related to modeling.

43. **A paper written in first person and having characters, a setting, a plot, some dialogue, and events sequenced chronologically with some flashbacks exemplifies which genre?(Average)(Skill 13.1)**
    A. exposition
    B. narration
    C. persuasion
    D. speculation

The correct answer is B. Narrative writing tells a story, and all the listed elements pertain to stories. Expository writing explains or informs. Persuasive writing states an opinion and attempts to persuade an audience to accept the opinion or to take some specified action. Speculative writing explores possible developments from given circumstances.

44. *Diction* **is best defined as(Average)(Skill 13.1)**
    A. The specific word choices an author makes in order to create a particular mood or feeling in the reader.
    B. Writing that explains something thoroughly.
    C. The background, or exposition, for a short story or drama.
    D. Word choices that help teach a truth or moral.

The answer is A. Diction refers to an author's choice of words, expressions and style to convey his/her meaning. The other choices are only marginally related to this meaning, so the choice is a clear one.

45. **To explain or to inform belongs in the category of (Average)(skill 13.1)**
    A. exposition.
    B. narration.
    C. persuasion.
    D. description.

The answer is A. Exposition sets forth a systematic explanation of any subject and informs the audience about various topics. It can also introduce the characters of a story and their situations as the story begins. Narration tells a story. Persuasion seeks to influence an audience so that they will adopt some new point of view or take some action. Description provides sensory details and addresses spatial relationships of objects.

46. **What type of comprehension do questions beginnings with "who," "what," "where," or "how" assess?(Average)(Skill 14.1)**
    A. evaluative
    B. inferential
    C. literal
    D. narrative

The correct answer is C. Literal questions ask for facts from the reading. The student can put his finger right on the answer and prove that he is correct. These questions are sometimes referred to as "right there" questions. Evaluative questions require a judgment of some sort. Inferential questions ask students to make an educated guess. Narrative questions involve aspects of a story beyond literal considerations.

47. **In a timed essay test of an hour's duration, how much time should be devoted to prewriting.(Average)(Skill 14.1)**
    A. five
    B. ten
    C. fifteen
    D. twenty

The answer is B. Ten minutes of careful planning still allows sufficient time for the other stages of the writing process. Five minutes would result more dead-ends and backtracking. Fifteen and twenty minutes would result in rushing drafting, revising, and editing.

48. In 'inverted triangle' introductory paragraphs, the thesis sentence occurs
(Average)(Skill 14.1)
A. at the beginning of the paragraph.
B. in the middle of the paragraph.
C. at the end of the paragraph.
D. in the second paragraph.

The answer is C. The beginning of the paragraph should establish interest, the middle of the paragraph should establish a general context, and the paragraph should end with the thesis that the rest of the paper will develop. Delaying the thesis until the second paragraph would be 'outside the triangle.'

49. Which of the following should not be included in the opening paragraph of an informative essay? (Average)(Skill 14.1)
A. Thesis sentence
B. Details and examples supporting the main idea
C. broad general introduction to the topic
D. A style and tone that grabs the reader's attention

The answer is B. The introductory paragraph should introduce the topic, capture the reader's interest, state the thesis and prepare the reader for the main points in the essay. Details and examples, however, belong in the second part of the essay, the body paragraphs.

50. Writing ideas quickly without interruption of the flow of thoughts or attention to conventions is called (Easy)(Skill 14.1)
A. brainstorming.
B. mapping.
C. listing.
D. Free writing.

The answer is D. Free writing is a particular type of brainstorming (techniques to generate ideas). Mapping is another type and results in products resembling flow charts. Listing is another brainstorming technique that differs from free writing in that free writing is more open-ended and looks more like sentences.

51. **Which of the following is not a technique of prewriting?**
    (Easy)(Skill 14.1)
    A. Clustering
    B. Listing
    C. Brainstorming
    D. Proofreading

The answer is D. You cannot proofread something that you have not yet written. While it is true that prewriting involves written techniques, prewriting is not concerned with punctuation, capitalization, and spelling (proofreading). Brainstorming is a general term denoting generating ideas, and clustering and listing are specific methods of brainstorming.

52. **Which of the following is the least effective procedure for promoting**
    consciousness of audience? (Rigorous)(Skill 14.1)
    A. Pairing students during the writing process
    B. Reading all rough drafts before the students write the final copies
    C. Having students compose stories or articles for publication in school
       literary magazines or newspapers
    D. Writing letters to friends or relatives

The answer is B. Reading all rough drafts will do the least to promote consciousness of audience; they are very used to turning papers into the teacher, and most don't think much about impressing the teacher. Pairing students will ensure a small, constant audience about whom they care; and having them compose stories for literary magazines will encourage them to put their best efforts forward because their work will be read by an actual audience in an impressive format. Writing letters also engages students in thinking about how best to communicate with a particular audience.

53. **A student informative composition should consist of a minimum of**
    how many paragraphs?(Easy)(Skill 14.1)
    A. three
    B. four
    C. five
    D. six

The answer is C. This composition would consist of an introductory paragraph, three body paragraphs, and a concluding paragraph. A three or four paragraph composition could include all three types of paragraphs, but would not require the students to elaborate at sufficient length in the body of the paper. A six paragraph minimum is slightly excessive, more or less by tradition.

54. **Which of the following sentences contains an error in agreement? (Average)(Skill 15.2)**
  A. Jennifer is one of the women who writes for the magazine.
  B. Each one of their sons plays a different sport.
  C. This band has performed at the Odeum many times.
  D. The data are available online at the listed website.

The correct answer is A. "Women" is the plural antecedent of the relative pronoun "who," which is functioning as the subject in its clause; so "who" is plural and requires the 3rd person plural form for the verb: "write."

55. **Which of the following is not true about English?(Rigorous)(Skill 15.2)**
  A. English is the easiest language to learn
  B. English is the least inflected language
  C. English has the most extensive vocabulary of any language
  D. English originated as a Germanic tongue

The correct answer is A. English has its own inherent quirks which make it difficult to learn, plus it has incorporated words, and even structures, from many disparate language groups in its lexicon and syntax. Languages with lexicons limited to words governed by a consistent set of relatively simple rules exist, so English is certainly not the easiest language to learn.

56. Consider the following sentence:

  Mr. Brown is a school volunteer <u>with a reputation and twenty years service</u>.

  Which phrase below best represents the logical intent of the underlined phrase above? (Choice E is identical to the underlined phrase) (Average)(Skill 15.6)
  A. with a reputation for twenty years' service
  B. with a reputation for twenty year's service
  C. who has served twenty years
  D. with a service reputation of twenty years

The correct answer is D. His reputation pertains to his service performance, not its duration. Choice A implies that it was for its duration. Choice B has Choice A's problem plus an incorrectly punctuated possessive. Choice C ignores his service reputation. Choice E is extremely vague.

57. Consider the following sentence: (Average)(Skill 15.6)

Joe __didn't hardly know his cousin Fred__, who'd had a rhinoplasty.

Which word group below best conveys the intended meaning of the underlined section above?
A. hardly did know his cousin Fred
B. didn't know his cousin Fred hardly
C. hardly knew his cousin Fred
D. didn't know his cousin Fred

The correct answer is C. It contains a correctly-phrased negative expressed in the appropriate tense. Choice A has tense and awkwardness problems. Choice B has tense and double-negative problems. Choice D ignores the fact that he knew Fred a little. Choice E has tense and double-negative problems.

58. **Which group of words is not a sentence?(Average)(Skill 15.7)**
A. In keeping with the graduation tradition, the students, in spite of the rain, standing in the cafeteria tossing their mortarboards.
B. Rosa Parks, who refused to give up her seat on the bus, will be forever remembered for her courage.
C. Taking advantage of the goalie's being out of the net, we scored our last and winning goal.
D. When it began to rain, we gathered our possessions and ran for the pavilion.

The correct answer is A. This is a sentence fragment because sentences require a subject and a verb and there is no verb. Changing "the students, in spite of the rain, standing" to "the students, in spite of the rain, were standing" corrects the problem.

59. **Identify the sentence that has an error in parallel structure.(Easy)(Skill 15.7)**
    A. In order to help your favorite cause, you should contribute time or money, raise awareness, and write congressmen.
    B. Many people envision scientists working alone in a laboratory and discovering scientific breakthroughs.
    C. Some students prefer watching videos to textbooks because they are used to visual presentation.
    D. Tom Hanks, who has won two Academy Awards, is celebrated as an actor, director, and producer.

The answer is C. Parallel structure means that certain sentence structures in key positions match-up grammatically. In choice C, "watching videos" is a gerund phrase functioning as the direct object of the verb, and, because the verb implies a comparison, parallel construction requires that "textbooks" (functioning as the object of a currently-missing gerund) be preceded by an appropriate gerund--in this case, "reading." In order for the structure to be parallel, the sentence should read "Some students prefer <u>watching videos</u> to <u>*reading* textbooks</u> because they are used to visual presentation." They prefer something to something else. The other sentences conform to parallel structure. Recognizing parallel structure requires a sophisticated understanding of grammar.

60. **A punctuation mark indicating omission, interrupted thought, or an incomplete statement is a/an(Easy)(Skill 15.8)**
    A. ellipsis.
    B. anachronism.
    C. colloquy.
    D. idiom.

The answer is A. In an ellipsis, a word or words that would clarify the sentence's message are missing, yet it is still possible to understand them from the context. An anachronism is something out of its proper time frame. A colloquy is a formal conversation or dialogue. An idiom is a saying peculiar to some language group.

61. Which of the following sentences is unambiguously properly punctuated?
(Average)(Skill 15.8)
A. The more you eat; the more you want.
B. The authors—John Steinbeck, Ernest Hemingway, and William Faulkner—are staples of modern writing in American literature textbooks.
C. Handling a wild horse, takes a great deal of skill and patience
D. The man, who replaced our teacher, is a comedian.

The answer is B. Dashes should be used instead of commas when commas are used elsewhere in the sentence for amplification or explanation—here within the dashes. Choice A has a semicolon where there should be a comma. Choice C has a comma that shouldn't be there at all. Choice D could be correct in a non-restrictive context, and so whether or not it is correct is ambiguous.

62. Which of the following contains an error in possessive punctuation?
(Rigorous)(Skill 15.8)
A. Doris's shawl
B. mother's-in-law frown
C. children's lunches
D. ambassador's briefcase

The answer is B. Mother-in-law is a compound common noun, and the apostrophe should come at the end of the word, according to convention. The other choices are correctly punctuated.

63. Read the following passage:

"It would have been hard to find a passer-by more wretched in appearance. He was a man of middle height, stout and hardy, in the strength of maturity; he might have been forty-six or seven. A slouched leather cap hid half his face, bronzed by the sun and wind, and dripping with sweat."

What is its main form of discourse?(Average)(Skill 18.3)
A. Description
B. Narration
C. Exposition
D. Persuasion

The answer is A. The passage describes the appearance of a person in detail. Narration tells a story. Exposition explains or informs. Persuasion promotes a point of view or course of action.

64. **Oral debate is most closely associated with which form of discourse? (Easy)(18.3)**
   A. Description
   B. Exposition
   C. Narration
   D. Persuasion

The answer is D. The purpose of a debate is to convince some audience or set of judges about something, which is very much the same as persuading some audience or set of judges about something.

XAMonline, INC. 21 Orient Ave. Melrose, MA 02176
Toll Free number 800-509-4128
TO ORDER Fax 781-662-9268 OR www.XAMonline.com
GEORGIA ASSESSMENTS FOR THE CERTIFICATION OF EDUCATORS -GACE - 2008

PO#   Store/School:

Address 1:

Address 2 (Ship to other):

City, State Zip

Credit card number_____-_____-_____-_____   expiration_____

EMAIL _____

PHONE   **FAX**

13# ISBN 2007	TITLE	Qty	Retail	Total
978-1-58197-257-3	Basic Skills 200, 201, 202			
978-1-58197-528-4	Biology 026, 027			
978-1-58197-529-1	Science 024, 025			
978-1-58197-341-9	English 020, 021			
978-1-58197-569-7	Physics 030, 031			
978-1-58197-531-4	Art Education Sample Test 109, 110			
978-1-58197-545-1	History 034, 035			
978-1-58197-527-7	Health and Physical Education 115, 116			
978-1-58197-540-6	Chemistry 028, 029			
978-1-58197-534-5	Reading 117, 118			
978-1-58197-547-5	Media Specialist 101, 102			
978-1-58197-535-2	Middle Grades Reading 012			
978-1-58197-545-1	Middle Grades Science 014			
978-1-58197-345-7	Middle Grades Mathematics 013			
978-1-58197-686-1	Middle Grades Social Science 015			
978-158-197-598-7	Middle Grades Language Arts 011			
978-1-58197-346-4	Mathematics 022, 023			
978-1-58197-549-9	Political Science 032, 033			
978-1-58197-544-4	Paraprofessional Assessment 177			
978-1-58197-542-0	Professional Pedagogy Assessment 171, 172			
978-1-58197-259-7	Early Childhood Education 001, 002			
978-1-58197-548-2	School Counseling 103, 104			
978-1-58197-541-3	Spanish 141, 142			
978-1-58197-610-6	Special Education General Curriculum 081, 082			
978-1-58197-530-7	French Sample Test 143, 144			
			SUBTOTAL	
	FOR PRODUCT PRICES GO TO WWW.XAMONLINE.COM		Ship	$8.25
			TOTAL	

CPSIA information can be obtained at www.ICGtesting.com
Printed in the USA
BVOW051609060612

291960BV00003B/42/P